WENGLISH

WENGLISH

The Dialect of the South Wales Valleys

ROBERT LEWIS

First impression: 2008
© Robert Lewis and Y Lolfa Cyf., 2008
This book is subject to copyright
and may not be reproduced by any means
except for review purposes
without the prior written consent of the publishers.

Published with the financial support of the Welsh Books Council

Cover design: Sion Ilar

ISBN: 9781847710307

Printed on acid-free and partly recycled paper
and published and bound in Wales by
Y Lolfa Cyf., Talybont, Ceredigion SY24 5AP
e-mail ylolfa@ylolfa.com
website www.ylolfa.com
tel 01970 832 304
fax 832 782

Contents

PART TWO
WENGLISH IN ACTION

PART THREE
ALPHABETICAL GLOSSARY OF WENGLISH WORDS AND EXPRESSIONS

PART FOUR
THE GRAMMAR OF WENGLISH

PART ONE

AN INTRODUCTION TO WENGLISH

1.1 WHAT IS WENGLISH?

Wenglish is the name adopted by John Edwards in the 1980s when he first published his now famous **Talk Tidy** books and recordings, to denote the distinctive dialect form of English spoken in the South Wales Valleys.

Wenglish combines the intonation and accent of the Welsh language with the speech rhythms of spoken English. It originated and developed in the 'melting pot' of the Valleys during the nineteenth century as workers flocked to the area from other parts of Wales, other parts of the British Isles, and indeed further afield, in search of employment in the rapidly expanding industries, especially coal mining. It is a fusion of the intonation of South Wales Welsh (*Gwenhwyseg*) with the forms of English spoken by the incoming workers, with some influence too from Standard English. It has borrowed many words and expressions directly from Welsh, together with some grammatical structures and aspects of syntax.

Wenglish is spoken by well over a million people – about double the number of Welsh speakers in Wales. For this reason alone, it deserves far greater attention than it has received up to now. In fact, until fairly recently, the predominant attitude towards Wenglish has been rather negative and dismissive.

Wenglish developed among ordinary working people and as such possesses a directness, a warmth and humour – sometimes intentional, sometimes otherwise – which cannot be matched precisely in Standard English.

It is a spoken medium of great vitality and an excellent vehicle for the discussion of topics relating to all aspects of everyday things that matter, such as the home, family, relationships, work, sport and leisure.

Wenglish is not 'just bad English spoken with a strong Welsh accent'. As we shall discover in this book, Wenglish possesses a grammar and vocabulary of its own. As such it has its own distinctive value and identity: its warmth of expression, vitality and force often lie in those things which are different from Standard English. This book is, effectively, a celebration of those differences, of which Valleys communities should be rightly proud.

1.2 THE PURPOSE OF THIS BOOK

The purpose of this book is **to stimulate a keener interest in and a better appreciation of Wenglish** among native speakers, among South Wales residents, among 'exiles' for whom it may be a language of childhood and grandparents, and among those with an interest in the speech forms of Wales, and in dialects generally. My aims in doing so have been to place Wenglish in its historical and social context; to extend the Wenglish vocabulary already identified, and to present an accessible grammar of Wenglish, with exercises. The book thus sets Wenglish in its rightful place as an authentic regional dialect, alongside Brummie, Yorkshire, Geordie, Scouse and other more well-known dialect forms of English. It will enable the reader to gain a good understanding of and 'feel' for Wenglish as a living speech form.

The book is divided into four parts:

Part One: An Introduction to Wenglish, briefly covers the history and development of Wenglish, its internal variations, its relationship with other South Wales speech forms and with Standard English. It culminates with a section on the very important matter of pronunciation.

Part Two: Wenglish in Action consists of a variety of dialogues and texts.

Part Three: An Alphabetical Glossary of Wenglish Words and Expressions. This is the largest and most complete listing in existence.

Part Four: The Grammar of Wenglish, is aimed at the more serious student, and covers the grammar of Wenglish systematically and in some detail. After each point of grammar, there are exercises to help readers test their knowledge of Wenglish. The answers are provided at the end of the book.

This book is intended as a practical guide to Wenglish: it is not an academic paper on sociolinguistics or dialectology. However, the issues raised in **Part One**, and the material covered in **Parts Two, Three** and **Four**, certainly merit the attention of the relevant departments at our schools, colleges and universities.

While the use of some technical linguistic and grammatical terms is unavoidable, these are explained as they are encountered. Use of phonetic script to cover the sounds of Wenglish has been avoided, as its introduction presupposes some knowledge of this type of representation, which can be particularly confusing for the general reader. Rather, the sound system of

Wenglish is described and explained in terms of how the sounds occur in familiar words.

It is assumed that the reader will already have a good knowledge of Standard English and/or of Wenglish.

1.3 WHERE IS WENGLISH SPOKEN?

Some people use the term to cover all dialect forms of English spoken in Wales. However, the term is generally understood to refer to the dialect form of English spoken in the South Wales Valleys. In **Talk Tidy**, first published in 1985, John Edwards rightly describes Wenglish as:

'a unique blend of residual Welsh and the distinctive patterns of spoken English.'

He goes on to say that:

'It is the authentic voice of Anglo-Welshness in large areas of Gwent, Mid and West Glamorgan, and needs to be seen as the oral badge of identity for many who live in these areas and as a vital element in their social heritage.'

The names of the counties may have changed since **Talk Tidy** was first published, but John Edwards' description remains both apt and accurate.

Wenglish is perhaps the most well-known and distinctive of the forms of English spoken in South Wales. All the spoken forms of English in South Wales have certain features in common, and the Wenglish core area, because of its central geographical position, shares features to varying degrees with all its neighbours.

The **core area** of Wenglish, which has a total population of well over a million, corresponds neatly with the South Wales Valleys area (and also the South Wales coalfield), comprising, starting in the West:

1. **The Gwendraeth Valleys**
2. **Llanelli and Eastern Carmarthenshire**
3. **Ammanford and the Amman Valley**
4. **The Swansea Valley, including the smaller valleys to the west of the Tawe (Twrch, Llynfell, Llwchwr and Lliw)**
5. **The City of Swansea**
6. **Neath and the Neath Valley**
7. **Port Talbot and the Afan Valley**
8. **Bridgend and the Llynfi, Garw and Ogmore Valleys**
9. **The Ely Valley**
10. **The Rhondda Valleys**

11. **The Cynon Valley**
12. **Pontypridd, Merthyr Tydfil and the Taff Valley**
13. **The Rhymney Valley**
14. **The Western Valleys of Monmouthshire (Sirhowy, Ebbw)**
15. **The Eastern Valley of Monmouthshire**

The first eight of the above (Gwendraeth Valleys to Bridgend, Llynfi, Garw and Ogmore Valleys) together comprise the **Western Area** of Wenglish. Welsh is spoken widely in the first four of these, and so the influence of Welsh on Wenglish is at its greatest in these four areas. These four areas may be referred to as the **Far Western** part of the Wenglish core area.

The Ely Valley through to the Rhymney Valley together comprise the **Central Area** of Wenglish.

The Western and Eastern Valleys of Monmouthshire together comprise the **Eastern Area** of Wenglish.

These distinctions are of course arbitrary but, as we will see later, are useful in describing some of the variations in Wenglish which are characterised by the speech of these three geographical areas.

All of these areas have many features in common. They all share a long and distinguished industrial history, with coal mining as the main unifying factor. Other heavy industries such as iron, steel and other metals were also very significant in some parts of the area. Because of rapid industrialisation during the nineteenth century, they all experienced a very significant influx of people from other parts of Wales, other parts of the British Isles and indeed further afield, who came in search of work in what has been described as the 'British Klondike'.

The fusion of native South Wales Welsh (*Gwenhwyseg*) and the various forms of English spoken by the incoming workers, together with some influence from Standard English, led to the development of a distinctive new form of English. This was the melting pot from which Wenglish evolved.

This new speech form retained the sounds and intonation of South Wales Welsh and borrowed a large number of words and expressions from Welsh – either directly or with minor modifications. It also took over some important constructions from Welsh, usually in directly-translated form, and retained Welsh word order in certain instances.

It took on vocabulary from the dialect forms of English spoken by the incoming workers. The West Country dialects, and in particular the dialect of the adjoining Forest of Dean (itself having a long history of mining) certainly lent a significant quantity of vocabulary to Wenglish – for example the well-known term 'butty', meaning 'workmate'. In fact, accent and intonation apart, a significant number of expressions current in the West Country (e.g. Bristol) are shared with Wenglish, probably as a result of an influx of workers from Gloucestershire and Somerset during the nineteenth century. Of course, during this period Wenglish also began to generate words and expressions of its own.

1.4 A BRIEF HISTORY OF WENGLISH

It is interesting to consider a language in terms of its different phases or periods of development. The development of Wenglish is closely linked with the industrial and social development of South Wales. For detailed discussion of the industrial history of South Wales, the reader would be well advised to consult one of the many excellent works covering this fascinating period. In the brief summary that follows, many important events and some entire fields of industry are not covered. However, the purpose of this summary is merely to set the scene and establish the context for the development of Wenglish.

At the close of the eighteenth century it would have been virtually impossible to predict how the shape of the Valleys – physically, socially and linguistically – would change so dramatically over the course of the next fifty years. The **initial period** of Wenglish corresponds to the initial phases of industrial development in South Wales, from the late eighteenth century up to about 1840.

It was the **iron industry** that brought the first major influx of workers to the area from outside. Up to the end of the eighteenth century, the South Wales Valleys were still overwhelmingly rural, agricultural and Welsh-speaking. In the second half of the eighteenth century, however, there was a vastly increased demand for iron for domestic and industrial purposes, and all the raw materials necessary for its production were found in a narrow strip at the north-eastern part of the South Wales coalfield. The invention of the 'puddling' process of refining iron ore by Henry Cort in 1783, ended the iron industry's reliance on charcoal, at that time in increasingly short supply throughout Britain. Coal could now be used in place of charcoal and the coal to be found in South Wales provided high quality, readily available fuel. Investment capital flooded in, bringing to South Wales an influx of experienced ironmasters and their workers, mainly from the Midlands, to supply the technical expertise to produce high quality iron.

Workers flocked in from all parts of Britain, many coming from the Welsh-speaking farming districts of Carmarthenshire, Cardiganshire, Breconshire and Radnorshire. Over the next few decades, the production of iron in South Wales grew rapidly and, by 1827, South Wales was producing half of Britain's iron exports. Merthyr Tydfil was the epicentre of the iron industry in South Wales and at this period was the largest town in Wales in terms of population.

Copper smelting was also significant in the lower Swansea Valley, the first copper works having already been established in the first half of the eighteenth century. By 1800 nine copper smelters were in operation and by 1860 the lower Swansea Valley was smelting two thirds of the copper ores imported to Britain.

In subsequent years it was the **coal industry** that was to provide the main impetus for the industrial development of the Valleys as a whole, and thus indirectly also to the development of Wenglish. In the first half of the nineteenth century the demand for coal increased dramatically. It was required as a fuel to drive the steam engines that powered machinery in the new industrial centres in England, as a domestic fuel in these fast developing urban centres, and also as a fuel for ships, as steam replaced sail and iron replaced wood in shipbuilding.

With industrialisation came a dramatic increase in population – from approximately 500,000 people in the 1750s to over 1,600,000 in 1851 and 2,600,000 before World War I.

A **period of further industrial and linguistic development and consolidation** began around 1840 with the rapid development of the railways, both in Britain and America. This created further and unprecedented demand for coal and iron. The discovery by David Thomas at the Ynyscedwyn Iron Works, Ystradgynlais, that the hot blast could be also used to smelt iron ore with anthracite, transformed the Swansea Valley, where ample supplies of anthracite were to be found.

As workers from other parts of Wales and from all over the British Isles sought employment in the coal and other industries, they brought with them their own forms of speech. During this initial period, Welsh was still the dominant language in the Valleys but gradually, the forms of English spoken by the incoming workers were fused with the intonation of the Welsh language, from which many words and expressions were borrowed. This process was effectively the birth and early development of Wenglish.

From the middle of the nineteenth century, following various reports by Royal Commissions on Education in Wales during the 1840s, the imposition of English at Board Schools and in some cases repressive measures such as the 'Welsh Not' to counter the use of Welsh, contributed to the adoption of English as the main medium of communication in the Valleys. Although its use was stigmatised, Welsh was still a major force throughout the Valleys area but inevitably English became increasingly important during this period. For many speakers in this period, English was still a foreign language which had to be learned. It is because of this that Wenglish contains many loan words from Welsh. Wenglish also retained several features of Welsh pronunciation. For example, in this period, speakers would trill the letter 'r' in all positions in a word (as in Scottish English), not just in initial position or before a vowel as is normal in Wenglish today.

However, by about 1900 Wenglish had reached a plateau of development and was now a formidable medium for the expression of matters relating to family and home life, to work and to the local community.

We can consider the period from 1900 to the end of the World War II as the **'Classical'** period of Wenglish, with the inter-war years (1914-1939) as perhaps the **'Golden Age'**, before the influence of Standard English increased considerably.

It was in the early part of this 'Classical' period that English replaced Welsh as the dominant language in the Valleys, though this had of course happened earlier in some places. The adoption of English clearly had economic and social reasons behind it. English was regarded as the language of progress, knowledge of which was necessary if one wanted 'to get on'. Speaking English at this time must also have carried some social prestige, as it was obviously regarded as more fashionable to speak in 'modern', 'progressive' English rather than in 'backward' and 'old-fashioned' Welsh.

The process of adopting English as the main language of communication often took rather bizarre forms. For example, my grandparents and my wife's grandparents (who were all born during the first decade of the twentieth century) all spoke English (i.e. Wenglish) with their spouses but Welsh to their brothers and sisters. This type of situation must have been replicated all over the Valleys, thus dramatically changing the entire linguistic landscape.

In education, the use of English was greatly encouraged, generally to the detriment of the use of Welsh. Many people born in the inter-war period – the 'Golden Age' of Wenglish – have a good passive understanding of Welsh from hearing their parents and grandparents speak but are often reluctant to speak Welsh themselves because they think their Welsh is 'not good enough'. One major reason for this is the great emphasis placed on the role of English in this period.

However, the form of English that they spoke – at home, on the street, in the village – was not Standard English but Wenglish. There is no doubt that this spoken form of English was subjected to systematic 'correction' in schools, as it did not conform to the norms of Standard English. Wenglish was given absolutely no recognition as a dialect or alternative form of English rather condemned outright as 'bad English' which needed to be corrected.

The later part of the 'Golden Age' of Wenglish – the 1930s – was a period of relative prosperity in the Valleys, following the harrowing experiences of the General Strike in 1926. In the 1930s the Valleys communities gained a new confidence and assurance. It is generally the case that prosperity leads to a measure of cultural prestige. This in turn leads to an increase in the prestige and confidence – at least in the community itself – of its manner of speech.

Radio had led to the exposure to Standard English during the inter-war period, but the influence of Standard English increased sharply with the outbreak of war, as the British government's propaganda machine swung into action. All news bulletins and official communications were given in ultra-standard BBC English, the intonation and vocabulary of which differed markedly from Wenglish: this was generally understood as how English 'should be spoken'.

After the war, a '**Postclassical**' period of Wenglish began, lasting through to about 1980. During this 'Postclassical' period, Wenglish was subjected to massive influence from Standard English via the mass media. The diffusion and huge popularity of American films brought Wenglish speakers into contact with American English. Later, the advent of television brought an even greater and daily exposure to Standard English. The consumer boom of the 1960s with its new products (cars, washing machines, fridges, record players, etc.) was heralded in and communicated via the medium of Standard English. In fact, all contact with 'modernity' ever since has generally involved Standard English. The net result of this increased contact with Standard English inevitably meant some loss of distinctive Wenglish forms. Some of the most 'fragile' in this respect were old loan words from Welsh, which by now was a minority language in the Valleys. Also, some of the general characteristics of Standard English, such as diphthongisation of simple vowel sounds, began to gain a small foothold in Wenglish, particularly among younger speakers. Nevertheless, in general Wenglish of this 'Postclassical' period was not radically different from that of the 'Classical' period.

1.5 MODERN WENGLISH

The '**Modern**' period of Wenglish began in about 1980 and continues to the present day. During this period, the influence of Standard English has continued to be felt. The 'Modern' period has also been one of radical structural change in the South Wales Valleys' industrial and employment base. The traditional industries, particularly coal but also steel, which to a great extent helped shape the Valleys communities, have experienced massive contraction during this period. Although some new industries have come in to take their place, the net effects have been an increase in unemployment, an exodus of many of the younger, better educated, economically active people (even if only as far as Cardiff). There has also been a significant reduction in the general level of prosperity and in the range of facilities available locally in Valleys communities.

The dramatic structural change in the industrial profile of the Valleys, and, in particular, the rise in unemployment, has undoubtedly taken its toll on the self-confidence and self-esteem of Valleys communities. In the relatively prosperous 1930s the Valleys communities were thriving and confident, and had a wide range of cultural facilities available locally. This was in turn reflected in the confident way in which Wenglish was used in community life. The opposite would seem to have been the case at the beginning of Wenglish's 'Modern' period: lack of confidence and self-esteem in the Valleys communities arguably led to Wenglish having even lower prestige and being even more prone to influence, primarily from Standard English, but also from American English via television programmes, films and music.

However, it was not all doom and gloom. There developed an increasing realisation among some people resident in the Valleys and others who had returned to the Valleys after living and working elsewhere, of the value of Wenglish and the social and cultural heritage it represented. The publication of John Edwards's **Talk Tidy** in 1985 put down a clear marker that Wenglish was not the same as Standard English; and the differences were not only interesting and often humorous but also something to be celebrated, and something to be proud of.

It is from this time that Wenglish began to regain some of its former dignity. It is hoped that this book will assist further in increasing recognition of the value of Wenglish, and restoring pride in this unique speech form.

Among the linguistic developments in Wenglish during this 'Modern' period, four are worthy of note:

First, there has been further **loss of older loan words** and loan constructions from Welsh, a trend which had begun even in the 'Classical' period.

Secondly, **use of extended contractions in verb forms** has become more prevalent (e.g. the 'Classical' Wenglish and colloquial Standard English *I'm not going* being rejected in favour of **I in't goin'**, and *I don't want to go* by **I doh wannw go** by certain (but by no means all) Wenglish speakers.

Thirdly, the process of **diphthongisation** has continued slowly, changing the pronunciation of once pure vowel sounds: e.g. the **-ow** of **tomorrow** being pronounced in the standard English way, rhyming with **mow**, not just a long pure **o** as in 'Classical' Wenglish.

Fourthly, and most recently, among younger speakers particularly, the process of **glotalling** has just begun to have some influence on the pronunciation of the letter **t** (and occasionally **d**) at the end of words, and between vowels in certain cases. Glottalling is the process of introducing the glottal stop, that is, a tension in the vocal folds in the throat, in place of certain consonants, especially **t**. For example, the word *little* is pronounced **li'l**, the word *digital* is pronounced **digi'al**, where the apostrophes denote the glottal stop. It is a marked feature of Cockney speech. It must be stressed that at the time of writing, the phenomenon of glottalling has had a fairly minimal effect on the pronunciation of Wenglish, and then only among some speakers. However, it will be interesting to see if this phenomenon becomes more widespread over the coming decades.

Diphthongisation and glottalling have almost certainly spread as a result of the influence of another form of English, 'Estuary English', the archetypical form of which is Cockney, on the spoken English of other parts of Britain. There are several reasons for this: television programmes such as *EastEnders* and 'The Bill' to name just two, have tended to increase exposure to, and street credibility of, this form of English, thus enhancing its status and prestige. Also, this form of English is spoken by many leading influencers in the media and in sport: the speech forms of the hip and trendy are, naturally enough, copied. A further possible reason is the economic dominance of London and the South East of England in the British context. Because of these reasons, certain features of Estuary English have been adopted by speakers of English far removed from London. Diphthongisation (the process of changing simple vowel sounds to combinations of vowel sounds) and glottalling (introduction of the glottal stop) are far advanced in Estuary English and can be heard in the spoken English, especially of younger people, in many parts of Britain where they would not traditionally have been heard. They are historically alien to Wenglish and would never have been heard from Wenglish speakers in the 'Classical' period. However, these features have certainly gained a firm foothold in the speech of younger people in Cardiff and it seems only a matter of time before they become more widespread among younger Wenglish speakers too.

There have also been a number of recent developments which could have a very positive effect on the use and status of Wenglish in the future. Following a second referendum, Wales gained some measure of autonomy from London with the setting up of the National Assembly for Wales. This immediately gave Wales greater prominence on the national and international stage and served to boost consciousness of being Welsh and pride in Welshness. There were also a number of other factors which tended to make Wales and being Welsh trendy and a source of pride. The completion of the flagship Millennium Stadium and the staging of the Rugby World Cup tournament in 1999 further raised the profile of Wales on the world stage. The immense popularity of Welsh pop bands like Catatonia, the Manic Street Preachers and the Super Furry Animals, not just in Wales but also outside, led to the coining of the term 'Cool Cymru'. It should also be noted that these groups actively promoted their Welsh origins and did not disdain speaking in Wenglish and deliberately singing in Welsh to non-Welsh-speaking audiences. Catherine Zeta Jones also became a global superstar who was proud of her Swansea origins. At that time, she made no attempt to cover or adapt her accent, rather in interviews making the tones of Wenglish known to audiences who otherwise might never have even heard of Wales.

In Education, there has rightly been new interest in regional forms of English since their inclusion as a topic in English on the National Curriculum. There seems, at last, to be some recognition of the value of regional speech forms and their importance as part of regional cultural identity. How this will develop in future remains to be seen but it is not unreasonable to think that greater emphasis should be given to Wenglish in schools in the South Wales Valleys. This would not only help the young people of the Valleys to appreciate and value their social and cultural heritage but also help them to understand how Standard English differs from Wenglish. It is hoped that this book will help in this process.

Wenglish has not changed radically since the 'Classical' period but, as we have seen, there have been, and continue to be, interesting developments. Language inevitably changes over time and it will be interesting to see how Wenglish develops during this third millennium.

1.6 VARIATIONS WITHIN WENGLISH

While Wenglish has an identifiable core area, there are some significant **geographical variations**.

The **Western Area** (Gwendraeth Valleys through to Bridgend and the Llynfi, Garw and Ogmore Valleys) tends to retain many more Welsh loan words than the Central and Eastern Areas. Generally speaking, the further west one travels, the greater the frequency of Welsh loan words and expressions in Wenglish. It must be remembered that Welsh is still an important and natural medium of communication in East Carmarthenshire including the Gwendraeth Valleys, Llanelli, Ammanford and the Amman Valley and also in the Swansea Valley and its offshoots. It is therefore natural that Welsh loan words and expressions should be much more prevalent in the Wenglish of this Far Western part of the core area.

In the **Far Western** part of the Wenglish Core Area, there is a tendency for many words to be used almost interchangeably between English (i.e. Wenglish) and Welsh (i.e. Colloquial South Wales Welsh). In this way Welsh continues to supply lexical material to Wenglish in an active way, which is not really the case in the Central and Eastern Wenglish areas. Also, it is quite usual for speakers to alternate between English (i.e. Wenglish) and Welsh (i.e. Colloquial South Wales Welsh) in the same conversation. The Wenglish generally contains many direct loan words and expressions from Welsh, while the Welsh tends to contain many loan words from English, especially in terms of 'technical' vocabulary. While in these circumstances the two languages are converging, it is nevertheless clear from the syntax and sentence structure as well as the 'dominant' vocabulary, which one is being spoken. However, as there is a tendency to alternate between languages, conversations would not always be readily understood by 'foreigners'.

Another feature of the Western Area is that the use of the present tense of verbs formed with **to do** (e.g. **I do do**, **they do say**) is relatively limited. Again, the further west one travels, the less frequent this feature becomes. It is virtually unknown in the speech of the far western part of the core area.

Western Wenglish thus differs from Central and Eastern Wenglish in its much more extensive use of Welsh loan words and also the speech rhythms and intonation of the Welsh language. That is not to say that these elements are completely lacking in Central and Eastern Wenglish, rather that they are particularly striking features of Western Wenglish.

The **Central Area** (Ely, Rhondda, Cynon, Taff and Rhymney Valleys) probably has the greatest concentration of 'urban expression', because of the sheer dominance of coal mining in these valleys and the linear settlement patterns (long terraces of houses) which characterise these valleys.

The use of the present tense formed with **to do** (see above) is very typical of this Central Area.

Proximity to Cardiff, and the fact that many thousands of people commute to Cardiff for work may leave this area more open to the influence of the speech forms of the capital. As a result there is some incipient diphthongisation of certain sounds among certain speakers but at the moment this is not very prominent.

The Central Area uses many words and expressions which would be unknown in the Western Area. Examples are **craxy** (annoyed, irritable), **wanged out** (exhausted), **moithered** (confused), **bosh** (sink). Generally, these words are derived from English dialects or English colloquialisms and not from Welsh.

The speech of the **Eastern Area** (Western and Eastern Valleys of Monmouthshire) shows a much lower concentration of Welsh loan words and some tendency to diphthongisation of certain vowel sounds by some speakers. However, as with the Central Area, this is not especially prominent. The Eastern Area tends to have more expressions from English dialects (e.g. Gloucestershire, Midlands) because of past migration patterns and also the relative proximity of these areas.

It should also be noted that certain words and expressions in Wenglish are peculiar to one particular valley or community and might be completely unknown only a short distance away.

There is also variation of speech **according to age**. Older speakers tend to be more conservative in their speech and are thus more likely to speak a form of Wenglish nearer to that of the 'Classical' period.

Younger speakers of any language tend to use a different vocabulary, reflecting their particular concerns and interests (e.g. pop music, computers, going out). Older speakers may be unaware of the specialist vocabulary relating to these areas, as they have little or no interest in them.

Younger speakers also tend to be more subject to influence by external factors and to social and peer pressure: if it is considered hip and trendy to pronounce a word in a certain way, they are more likely to do so. Diphthongisation and glottalling may well be accelerated by this.

Younger people may also consider the speech of older people as unfashionable and thus to be avoided.

In work and interview situations, speakers of broad dialects may well be disadvantaged as their speech may give out the 'wrong signals'. They may be perceived as 'stupid' and unable to express themselves properly in Standard English. This is another important factor working against the retention of dialect in Britain as a whole.

There is also variation on **socioeconomic and educational lines**. While Wenglish itself arose out of the everyday speech of ordinary working people, its use today is not restricted to any particular socioeconomic group. However, certain features used by some speakers of modern Wenglish (such as advanced verbal contractions like **I in't goin'** for *I'm not going*, and **'e doh wannw go** for *he doesn't want to go*) and pronunciation of intervocalic **t** as a trilled **r** (e.g. **she gorrw go**, for colloquial Standard English *she has got to go*), are no doubt more prevalent among lower socioeconomic groups.

However, it must be stated that the use of such features is actually becoming more common, even among speakers from higher socioeconomic groups. These features may not occur on all occasions but their use would appear to be more widespread. They were practically unheard of in Wenglish's 'Classical' period.

It would be generally true to say that better educated people would be less prone to use features like this. It is likely that they will be more aware of the correct forms in Standard English, and so carry these over into their Wenglish. Nevertheless, many speakers of Wenglish are graduates and belong to the higher socioeconomic groups. Indeed, it must be stressed that the use of Wenglish is not restricted to any particular social group.

Historically, the use of non-standard forms of English was frowned upon, and often considered downmarket and ignorant. The situation may not be so bad these days but prejudices still exist. This speaks volumes about Britain's London-centred and imperialist-minded government and society during the nineteenth century and the greater part of the twentieth century.

However, the use of dialect need not be looked down on. In Switzerland, for example, the use of Swiss German is part of national identity. Its use carries no social stigma and it is used actively at every level of national, community and social life. In Norway and Luxembourg too, dialect is accorded a high status in all aspects of national life. These three countries, incidentally, are among the richest per capita, in the whole of Europe.

As we have seen, Wenglish owes its origins to the coming together of workers from all parts of the British Isles, in search of employment in the industries of the Valleys. As a result, Wenglish shares a warmth, humour, intimacy and a directness of expression, with other dialects which have arisen among ordinary working people, such as Geordie and Brummie.

1.7 THE RANGE OF WENGLISH

No-one can deny that a good knowledge of Standard English is essential for international communication in the modern world. However, that does not mean that regional speech forms, including Wenglish, do not have a value and function of their own. In the sphere of domestic and family life, for example, Wenglish has a much richer and 'warmer' mode of expression than Standard English. For example, the Wenglish phrase: *'Come by 'ere an' 'ave a cwtch with Mam'* with all its emotional connotations, cannot easily be translated into Standard English.

Wenglish is an excellent vehicle for the discussion of the important matters of everyday life such as family, friends, human relationships, home life, the workplace, sport and community life.

It is a spoken language of great vitality. Its origins among the speech of ordinary working people give it a directness, warmth and force which Standard English simply does not possess.

On the other hand, it is sometimes said of dialects generally that they lack precision of expression. There may be some truth in this assertion, at least in connection with particular fields of activity. I do not think, for example, that Wenglish would be a particularly good medium for technical or scientific discourse: it has never been used in these fields, and as such lacks the precise technical vocabulary and mode of expression that is required in these areas. Standard English, in contrast, is an excellent medium for such topics.

The vocabulary of Wenglish, as with all dialects, is much smaller than that of Standard English. Because it originated as the everyday language of working people, it has a good range of expressions to cover the occurrences of everyday life. Wenglish prefers simple, vivid, concrete expressions to complex abstractions and, in general, Latin-derived expressions are avoided. For example, **flat shot** would be used in preference to the Standard English's *disappointment*, and **feeding** in preference to *nutritious*.

1.8 THE RELATIONSHIP OF WENGLISH TO STANDARD ENGLISH

Wenglish is not as different from Standard English as, for example, Swiss German and Bavarian are from Standard German. However, there are important differences in grammar, vocabulary, syntax and sound, which set it apart from Standard English, and give it a distinct identity and feel.

It could not be claimed that Wenglish is a completely separate language from Standard English (as could legitimately be claimed for Scots – the language that is, not just Standard English spoken with a Scottish accent). However, Wenglish is certainly different enough to be given the status of a dialect of English.

Speakers of Wenglish have no difficulty at all in understanding Standard English and other major varieties of English, such as Cockney, which are given exposure via television, films and radio.

Although Wenglish grammar and syntax differ from Standard English, these factors would not present special difficulties of comprehension for speakers of Standard English. However, vocabulary and expressions peculiar to Wenglish would cause more problems. For example, a speaker of Standard English would probably not ordinarily come across Wenglish words like **clecs** (gossip), **cwtch** (1. place/spot 2. cuddle/hug), **didoreth** (slovenly in housekeeping, denoting strong disapproval), **ware teg** (fair play), **mitching** (playing truant), and so on.

The relationship between a dialect and a standard language is always interesting. Two opposing tendencies tend to operate, which bring about changes in the dialect, and occasionally in the standard language itself.

The first is a tendency on the part of the dialect to copy or borrow certain features from the standard language, often under the influence of mass media. As a result, the dialect tends to lose some of its distinctive features. This can be seen in Wenglish in the process of diphthongisation which has begun to affect certain vowel sounds.

The second is a tendency on the part of the dialect to generate new and different forms. An example of this in Wenglish is the tendency to contract further already contracted verb forms, and/or render the expression of a negative, in a different way, e.g. **I an' seen**, or **I never seen** where Standard English would require *I haven't seen*.

Generally speaking, especially under the influence of mass media in Standard or American English, the stronger tendency is for Wenglish to absorb some of features of the standard language.

There is also the question of gradation from dialect to standard language. Clearly, language is not homogenous and differs from speaker to speaker. Some speakers tend to use more 'typical' dialect features than others, while at the other end of the scale, some speakers use relatively few dialect features, yet retain the accent and intonation of the dialect. This is certainly the case with Wenglish.

Of all aspects of language, vocabulary can most easily be transferred from standard language to dialect. This is for several reasons: first, the word stock of a dialect tends to be smaller and so vocabulary borrowing from the standard language is sometimes necessary for clarity of meaning in certain fields of activity, such as motor mechanics; secondly, vocabulary is relatively superficial when compared with grammatical structure or idioms, and is thus more easily transferable. This is also the case between different languages.

1.9 THE RELATIONSHIP BETWEEN WENGLISH AND OTHER SOUTH WALES SPEECH FORMS

Wenglish is perhaps the most well-known and distinctive of the forms of English spoken in South Wales. It must be stressed that all the forms of English spoken in South Wales have features in common, and Wenglish, because of the central geographical position of its Core Area, shares features in varying degrees with all its neighbours.

We have seen that the Wenglish Core Area corresponds to the South Wales Valleys, from the Gwendraeth Valleys in the west to the Eastern Valley of Monmouthshire in the east.

The speech of three neighbouring areas, Western Carmarthenshire, Gower and the Vale of Glamorgan, shares much in common with Wenglish so could justifiably be termed as the **Extended Wenglish Area**. These areas have a total population of some 200,000. Thus the core and extended

Wenglish areas have a combined population of some 1.2 million.

The speech of **West Carmarthenshire**, including Carmarthen and the Tywi Valley, differs comparatively little from that of the extreme western part of the core area. The Welsh accent is, if anything, stronger and the use of Welsh loan words more prevalent. However, certain of the 'urban expressions' characteristic of the Central and Eastern parts of Wenglish core area may be unknown in this western frontier area.

These 'urban expressions' include expressions relating to the world of work and industry, especially coal mining, and to everyday life in close communities, especially living in the characteristic terraced housing to be found in the Valleys. Examples would include **butty** (workmate, partner), **mandrel** (pick-axe), **dram** (small wagon used to transport coal from the coalface in a mine), **tommy-box** (miner's food container), **gwli** (lane behind terraced houses in Valleys) and **bosh** (kitchen sink).

The speech of **Gower,** at least of natives of the peninsula who do not purport to come from the Home Counties, also differs little from that of the Western core area, though the accent may be slightly lighter; there may be some evidence of diphthongisation, and some of the 'urban expressions' typical of the Central and Eastern parts of the core area would not be generally known.

The speech of the rural **Vale of Glamorgan**, at least of natives of the Vale who do not claim or aspire to hail from deepest Surrey, differs not greatly from that of the neighbouring parts of the core area. However, the accent may be lighter and there is some evidence of diphthongisation of some of Wenglish's pure vowel sounds. Again, some of the 'urban expressions' of the Wenglish Central and Eastern core area would not be used.

The speech of the Vale of Glamorgan's largest town, **Barry**, shares some of the characteristics of the rural area and thus with the Wenglish core area too. The accent and intonation are a little different, however, and the speech has something of a 'swagger' to it. Barry also shares some of the expressions derived from English dialects and colloquialisms of the Central and Eastern core area. Because this area has for many years been highly anglicised, few Welsh loan words and expressions are to be heard. Also, the speech of Barry shares features in common with its larger neighbour Cardiff. Diphthongisation is fairly advanced and glottalling of the letter **t** at the end of certain words may be heard in the speech of some Barry residents, especially younger people.

The inclusion of Barry in the Extended Wenglish Area is rather borderline but I have included it along with the rural part of the Vale of Glamorgan if only for the fact that two of my grandfather's sisters lived there, and they certainly spoke excellent Wenglish!

The other South Wales speech forms, namely **Cardiff**, **Newport**, **Rural Monmouthshire**, **Rural Carmarthenshire**, **North Pembrokeshire**, **South Pembrokeshire** and **Breconshire**, also share features with Wenglish but not to quite the same extent as the Extended Area described above.

The speech of **Cardiff** has traditionally been different from that of the Valleys. Cardiff has long been a cosmopolitan melting pot and numerous influences have shaped the speech of the capital city. Generally speaking, the accent is more anglicised, the vowel sounds are often quite different to those of the Valleys (e.g. the proverbial *Pint of Dairk in Cairdiff Airms Pairk*, in which the vowel sound is repeatedly pronounced as in the first vowel of the word *mare*, where Wenglish would have a long a-sound). Cardiff speech today contains quite a few diphthongs, even triphthongs (combinations of three vowel sounds), in positions where Wenglish would retain pure, simple vowel sounds. Furthermore, the process of glottalling has definitely gained a foothold in the speech of many younger people.

Despite all these factors, the speech of Cardiff still has quite a few features in common with Wenglish. Some of the expressions from colloquial English are shared. There is a slight but noticeable Welsh intonation, and some of Wenglish's (sometimes adapted) loans from Welsh also occur in Cardiff too: e.g. gibbons (spring onions).

The speech of **Newport**, like that of Cardiff and Barry, shares some of the expressions from English dialects and colloquial English with Eastern Wenglish, and some of the background intonation too. However, it also shows a marked tendency towards diphthongisation, and the vowel sounds often differ markedly from those of Wenglish. It also shares some of the features of the speech of Rural Monmouthshire.

The speech of **Rural Monmouthshire** has some aspects of Welsh intonation but also some Gloucestershire features the further east one travels. Diphthongisation is widespread, and the vowel combinations are sometimes quite complex sounds.

In the west, the speech of **Rural Carmarthenshire** shares some features with Western Wenglish but not the 'urban expressions'. The area is predominantly Welsh-speaking so the intonation resembles Welsh quite closely.

The speech of **North Pembrokeshire** has some features in common with Rural Carmarthenshire but has a noticeably different accent. It is perhaps another quarter of a step further removed from the Wenglish of the western core area.

The distinctive speech of **South Pembrokeshire** is different in accent from Wenglish but does share some of the background intonation, vocabulary and turns of phrase. Diphthongisation is quite common. It should be noted that many of the distinctive speech patterns of South Pembrokeshire derive from the speech of Flemish settlers who went there in the Middle Ages. There are therefore numerous expressions peculiar to South Pembrokeshire which are unknown in Wenglish.

To the north, the speech of **Breconshire** shares some of the intonation and vocabulary of Wenglish but not the urban expressions. The further east one travels, the greater the tendency to hear a Herefordshire burr in the accent.

1.10 RESURGENCE OF INTEREST IN REGIONAL LANGUAGES ACROSS EUROPE

Since about 1980 the increase in interest is notable in terms of regional languages and dialects across Europe.

In **Spain**, for example, since Franco's death and the introduction of democracy, the central government's repressive policy towards regional autonomy and regional languages (regarded rightly as an integral part of distinctive regional identity) has changed radically. Today Catalan, Galician and Basque enjoy official status in their respective regions, and, arguably, Catalan has supplanted Standard Spanish (Castilian) as the dominant language of Catalonia.

In **France**, where, even before the Revolution at the end of the eighteenth century, government policy had been highly centralist, the official language of the Republic – Standard French – was imposed throughout the country, regardless of the existence of regional languages and cultures. In practice, this led to the active suppression of regional languages such as Breton, Occitan and Alsatian. However, rather belatedly, in more recent years there has been a realisation of the value of linguistic and cultural diversity. As a result there are now varying degrees of official recognition of, and support for regional languages.

In **Italy**, there is renewed pride in the various regional languages and dialects, with many dictionaries, grammar and course books being published.

In **Britain and throughout the British Isles**, too, there has been increasing official recognition and support for regional languages. In **Wales**, measures such as the establishment of Welsh-medium schools, the Welsh television channel S4C, the passing of the Welsh Language Act and the establishment of the Welsh Language Board have all helped to safeguard the position of Welsh in various ways. The British-Irish Council (which brings together the government of the United Kingdom and the devolved administration of Wales, Scotland and Northern Ireland, the governments of the Republic of Ireland, the Isle of Man Jersey and Guernsey) has resolved further to promote the use of Welsh, Scottish Gaelic, Irish, Manx, Jèrriais (Jersey's Norman French), Guernesiais (Guernsey's Norman French) and Ulster Scots. However, all this is fairly recent and until about 1980, the current was most definitely in favour of Standard English in virtually all aspects of life in Britain.

The development of a Standard English began, arguably, with the advent of printing and the mass diffusion of books, notably the Bible and Book of Common Prayer. Because of its political, economic and cultural significance, the speech of educated people in London and the South East was increasingly identified with how English 'should' be spoken.

In the days of the Empire, the 'King's English' became a well-known and accepted concept. During the nineteenth century, repressive measures were introduced in schools systematically to eradicate regional languages such as Welsh and Gaelic. Many readers will be familiar from history lessons with the 'Welsh Not', a wooden or slate board hung around the neck of school pupils if they spoke Welsh at school. This repressive and insidious device could be passed on from one pupil to another if he or she heard another pupil speaking in Welsh. The child wearing the 'Welsh Not' at the end of the day would be punished by the teacher. The survival of the Welsh language in such repressive conditions is all the more remarkable.

Albeit in a much less extreme way, Wenglish, too, has always suffered at the hands of the educational establishment. It has never been recognised as a valid dialect form of English, with intrinsic value of its own, rather it has been dismissed without much thought as 'bad English' which needs to be corrected. There is no doubt that all through the twentieth century, in schools throughout the Valleys, Wenglish speech forms have been ridiculed and 'corrected' to Standard English, sometimes constructively, sometimes violently.

It is of course true that Wenglish is not the same as Standard English: there are important differences in grammar, vocabulary, syntax and pronunciation. However, this does not mean that Wenglish does not possess an integrity and consistency, indeed a harmony and beauty, of its own.

1.11 THE QUESTION OF WHAT IS 'CORRECT' WENGLISH

There is no standard form of Wenglish. However, as there exist variations within Wenglish, the question arises as to which forms are 'correct'. In short, they are all valid forms of Wenglish but some have a wider currency and have been established for much longer. In general, the forms recommended in this book are those which have a wide currency throughout the Wenglish core area and are understood and used by the majority of speakers. In cases of doubt, Wenglish of the 'Classical' period is used, not because it is 'better' but rather because it is generally understood by the majority of speakers and is usually distinctively Wenglish. However, variant forms are covered in the Grammar section. In general these are only used by some speakers and have not become established as characteristic features throughout Wenglish. Nevertheless, it is important to recognise and understand the more frequently occurring variant forms.

1.12 THE PROBLEMS OF WRITING IN DIALECT

It is generally recognised that attempts to write in a dialect of any language bring a particular set of problems. There are several reasons for this:

Dialects are by their very nature spoken forms of language. The Welsh for dialect is *tafodiaith* (literally 'tongue language') and in German, dialect is known as *Mundart* (literally 'mouth form'). Because of this, there are generally no agreed norms for representing the sounds of the dialect. Using the spelling system of the standard language can often be misleading as the dialect pronunciation often differs greatly from that of the standard language.

One solution to this problem would be to use phonetic script. However, this presupposes a specialist technical knowledge on the part of the reader and is tantamount to having to read and write in a different alphabet. In my experience, the use of phonetic script is more of a hindrance than a help to the general reader, and so is not used at all in this book.

Another problem arises in that dialects are by no means uniform. There are often important internal differences in speech, for example, between different geographical areas. Unlike a standard language, there are no agreed norms for spelling or pronunciation.

In order to make practical progress in this rather anarchic environment, three main approaches have been adopted in attempts to write in the dialects of the major European languages.

1. To remain as far as possible with the spelling system of the standard language, indicating divergence from the standard by means of apostrophes and similar devices. The advantage of this approach is that it makes what is written more or less comprehensible to all speakers of the standard language. The big disadvantage of this approach is that it does not always accurately reflect the particular sounds of the dialect, especially when they differ from the sounds suggested by the spelling of the standard language. (This is the approach adopted by Frank Vickery in his plays. It is true that plays are meant to be performed – and thus heard – rather than read, so the adoption of near-standard spelling is not a problem).

2. To adopt a radical approach to reflect the particular sounds of the dialect. While this approach generally succeeds in this aim, the big disadvantage is that it is often difficult to read, as words are spelled in an unfamiliar way and use has generally to be made of accents and signs to modify the sounds of the letters to reflect those of the dialect. The extreme form of this approach is the use of phonetic script, however, this is tantamount to writing in another alphabet is of little practical use in material for the general reader. (John Edwards experiments with a quasi-phonetic system in some of the exercises in **More Talk Tidy**. While these are just for fun and are quite interesting in suggesting the pronunciation intended, the 'words' or 'sound pictures' he devises look strange and are open to interpretation).

3. A middle way based primarily on the familiar spelling system of the standard language but to be read following detailed explanation of the sounds which the standard spellings represent in the dialect. Where the standard spelling, even in the light of these instructions and despite the use of apostrophes and similar devices, does not accurately reflect the dialect pronunciation, the words affected may be spelt differently in order to fulfil this requirement. An example of this in Wenglish would be **innit?** to represent the advanced contracted form of **isn't it?**, and **gorrw** to represent the pronunciation of **got to** by some speakers.

This third approach has the distinct advantage of using the familiar spelling system of the standard language for the most part and thus not breaking up familiar 'word pictures'. However, the flexibility to deviate from standard spelling where this does not reflect dialect pronunciation, goes a long way to represent the sounds of the dialect as accurately as possible. To a large extent, this third approach combines the advantages of Approaches 1 and 2 above, and so has been adopted in this book.

1.13 THE PRONUNCIATION OF WENGLISH

Wenglish has a characteristic sound and lilt and is spoken with a marked Welsh accent. Essentially, it is English spoken with the characteristic intonation and stress of South Wales Welsh (*Gwenhwyseg*).

There are many examples of vocabulary loans from Welsh, while several commonly used constructions derive directly from Welsh. Such features would just not be possible in Standard English.

The intonation of Wenglish is much more 'sing-song' than Standard English, with the tone usually rising, then falling again at the end of a sentence. This is characteristic of the intonation of the Welsh language.

Stressed elements are normally placed first in a sentence and are spoken with rising intonation. A secondary stress, also with rising intonation, may occur at the end of a sentence.

1.13.1 Consonants

Generally, the consonants are similar to those of Standard English (SE). However, there are some important differences, and these should be noted carefully to achieve an authentic Wenglish pronunciation.

Letter	Pronunciation	Example
b	• Generally as in SE • Occasionally silent as in SE	barber lamb
c	• Generally as in SE, 'hard' (k-sound) before a, o and u • 'soft' (s-sound) before e, i, y • In Welsh loan word pronounced 'hard' in all positions.	cup centre clecs
ch	• Generally as in SE, but in Welsh loan words pronounced as the guttural sound in the Scottish 'loch' or the name of the German composer *Bach*. • There is a tendency not to pronounce the **ch** at the beginning of Welsh loan words e.g. **ware teg** (fair play) not *chwarae teg* as in Standard Welsh. • Some Wenglish speakers, particularly in the Central and Eastern areas, tend to pronounce this **ch** as **k** or **ck**, e.g. in place names (e.g. **Llanbradach** pronounced as **Lanbraduck**).	church bach
d	• Generally as in SE • There is a tendency not to pronounce **d** in final position. • Some speakers pronounce intervocalic **d** as a trilled **r** in a few circumstances. • Some speakers have a tendency to replace final and intervocalic **d** with a glottal stop (not as common as glottalisation of **t**).	dram ol', tol' I dirrent do it
dd	• Mostly as in SE • In Welsh loan words it is pronounced as **th** in **the**.	ladder as old as Adda
f	• As SE • In Welsh loan words it is pronounced as a **v**.	fancy Pont-Rhyd-y- Fen

ff	• As SE • In Welsh loan words it is pronounced as SE **f**.	**Taff** **Griffith**
g	• Normally as in SE ('hard'), but • can be 'soft' (**j**-sound) where 'soft' in SE. • In Welsh loan words it is always pronounced 'hard'. • Silent when silent in SE.	**get** **gen'rally** **gambo** **gnome**
h	• Generally not pronounced at all except in the name of the letter, **haitch**, and words which contain this name.	**have ('ave)** **haitch TV**
j	• As in SE	**jam**
k	• As in SE • Silent when silent in SE	**kokum** **knife**
l	• As in SE	**lamb**
ll	• As in SE • In Welsh loan words, the characteristic aspirated **l**, as in Welsh. However, many Wenglish speakers, especially in the Central and Eastern areas, simply pronounce this as a normal **l** (e.g. **Llanbradach** pronounced as **Lanbraduck**).	**mill** **Llanelli**
m	• As in SE	**men**
n	• As in SE	**name**
ng	• Generally as in SE • Where southern Standard English has the pronunciation **ng-g** as in *finger*, this is retained in Wenglish. It is not applied to words ending in **-ing** as in northern English pronunciation (e.g. *somethingg*, *runningg*). • In words ending in **-ing**, these letters are pronounced **-in** except monosyllables like **thing**, **sing**.	**bang** **finger** **running** **(runnin')**
p	• Normally as in SE • Silent when silent in SE	**park** **psalm**
ph	• F-sound, as in SE	**Caerphilly**
qu	• As in SE	**Queen**

r	• In initial position and before vowels and **y**, it is trilled as in Scottish English. Note that the following vowel need not belong to the same word. It is also generally trilled in Welsh loan words and in Welsh place names (but not always, e.g.**Caerphilly** is usually pronounced **Cuffilly**). **r** was also trilled in all positions during the Initial and development periods of Wenglish, and by quite a number of (especially older) speakers in the 'Classical' period too. Today this trilled pronunciation in all positions is usually heard only from the very oldest speakers. • There is a tendency among some speakers, especially in conversation with people from outside the Wenglish-speaking area, to 'soften' the **r**-sound nearer to the sound used in southern SE (a sort of semivowel). This was unknown in Wenglish of the 'Classical' period and is not recommended. • In all other positions it is not pronounced at all but generally indicates that the preceding vowel is long. It is in most cases interchangeable with the letter **h** to indicate vowel length (e.g. **door** could be written **doh**).	**run, dry, over it** **Merthyr, car, four, door**
rh	• In Welsh loan words **rh** is normally pronounced exactly as **r,** although the **h** should strictly speaking be pronounced too.	**Rhys, Rhydfelin**
s	• Generally as in SE it is pronounced as z where southern SE has this pronunciation. However, this pronunciation is never used in the word **us** as is the tendency in North Wales and Lancashire.	**sing houses (houziz)**
sh	• As in SE	**shop**
si	• In Welsh loan words as **sh**	**siop popeth**

t	• Generally as SE	train
	• There is a tendency not to pronounce **t** in final position. In such instances there is no substitution of **t** by the glottal stop. This is particularly the case in negative verbal contractions (e.g. **won't, don't, haven't**), especially if something follows directly after this contracted word.	**wha', tha', won', don' lo' (lot), ge' (get) (where the apostrophe represents the glottal stop)**
	• Some speakers have a tendency to pronounce intervocalic **t** as a trilled **r.** It should be noted that the two vowels between which the **t** stands need not be in the same word. This is **not** common to all speakers.	
	• Final and in some cases intervocalic **t** is replaced by a glottal stop. This is quite a new development and is by no means universal in Wenglish. At the moment it is restricted mainly to some younger speakers.	**gorra lorra, burrer, we gorrw, gerroff!**
th	• Unvoiced, as in SE *thin*	**thick**
	• In Welsh loan words **th** is always unvoiced	**carthen**
	• Voiced, as is SE *the*	**that**
	• In a few words as **t,** as in SE	**Thomas**
	• Initial **th** is not pronounced by some speakers in the definite article, **the**, in demonstratives (**this, that**) and **there**, especially in unstressed situations.	**'e (the), 'ere (there), 'em (them)**
v	• As in SE	**van**
w	• As in SE	**wall**
wh	• As **w** – the **h** is never pronounced	**white**
x	• As in SE	**fox**
	• when SE pronunciation differs e.g. **z**-sound, Wenglish follows	**xylophone**
y	• As in SE	**yellow**
z	• As in SE	**zoo**

1.13.2 Vowels and Diphthongs

There is a noticeable difference in the vowel sounds of Wenglish and Standard English. The following guidelines are important for accurate pronunciation and should be studied carefully.

For practical purposes there are 24 vowel sounds in Wenglish, 7 short, 8 long and 9 diphthongs. The vowels, whether long or short, are all simple sounds – the quality of the sound does not vary during pronunciation. The diphthongs are combinations of two vowel sounds. Complex triphthongs do not exist in Wenglish. In general the range of vowels and diphthongs in Wenglish is far less complex than in southern Standard English. The vowels and diphthongs of Wenglish correspond closely to those of South Wales Welsh.

The general tendency towards diphthongisation, which is a marked feature of southern Standard English, has historically been quite alien to Wenglish, and would not have been heard in the Wenglish of the 'Classical' period. However, under influence from Standard English, especially via the media, there is now a tendency among certain speakers to diphthongise certain pure vowels in 'Classical' Wenglish. These tendencies are covered in the explanation below.

Diphthongisation is already a marked feature of the speech of Cardiff and Newport, and seems to be getting more widespread in Wenglish. However, for the purposes of ensuring an authentic and distinctive Wenglish pronunciation, use of pure vowels, as in 'Classical' Wenglish, is recommended.

Short Vowels

Vowel	Pronunciation	Example
a	• A simple short **a**, as in northern English. The **a** of southern English pronunciation of *man* (tinged with an e-sound) is to be avoided.	mam, marry
e	• As in SE *hen*	pen
i	• As in SE *pin*	shin, houziz (houses)
o	• As is SE *pot*	pot
u	• Rounded, as in SE *put*. Note that u only has this rounded pronunciation where southern SE does, not in all positions as in northern English. • Unrounded vowel, as in SE *but*. Note that this pronunciation is used where southern SE has it.	(1) hook, put bun, but, enough, Merthyr
murmur vowel	Various spellings. It is an indistinct but commonly occurring vowel between short **a** and short unrounded **u**. It corresponds to the vowel sound of **-er** at the end of **later**, and the vowel in **the** as normally pronounced before a consonant. It is quite similar to the unrounded **u** but pronounced slightly further forward and with lips slightly more closed.	later, the, Merthyr

There is no tendency at all to diphthongise short vowels.

Long Vowels

Vowel	Pronunciation	Example
a	As in southern SE *car* and *aardvark*. There is no hint of **r** in this pronunciation.	can't, are, car, shark
e	• A long, pure vowel, equivalent to **e** with an acute accent – **é** – in French, and the long, pure **eh** in the German *Mehl*. This sound does not exist in southern SE but is very close to the Geordie pronunciation of *made*. In SE the first vowel sound of *made* is a diphthong **ay**, and *made* thus shares an identical pronunciation with *maid*. 'Classical' Wenglish differentiates this pair of words but nowadays there is a tendency among certain speakers to diphthongise as in SE.	made, Mary
	• A long, pure vowel, equivalent to **e** with a grave accent – **è** – in French. It is similar to the vowel sound in SE *hair* but without any hint of diphthongisation.	hair, mare, share, there
i	• A long pure vowel, similar to the **ee** in SE *keen*, but without any hint of colouring with another vowel sound.	mean, seen, been, paraffin, receive
o	• A long pure **o**-sound, like in the French *Beaune* and the German *Mohn*. This sound does not occur in SE, where long **o** is diphthongised to **-ow**. This tendency also exists in Wenglish among some speakers but did not exist in the Wenglish of the 'Classical' period.	bone, moan, stroke, four, hoe, yellow, tomorrow, Porth
au, aw	• Long **a** coloured with **o**, similar to the vowel sound in SE *paw* but with no variation in quality. The sound is produced in the front of the mouth.	Porthcawl, saw, Morgan, claw, for
u, oo	• Long pure oo sound. Similar to oo in SE but without any hint of colouring with another vowel sound.	shoot, hose (hooze), through, too, two, to
long murmur vowel	• The vowel in SE *girl*. Similar to German **ö** but without lip rounding.	fur, chauffeur, girl, her

Diphthongs

The diphthongs of Wenglish are combinations of two vowel sounds. The stress is on the first of these vowels.

Diphthong	Pronunciation	Example
ai (a + i)	• This only occurs in Welsh loan words. It is similar to the SE pronunciation of *I*.	**Caerphilly, paish**
ei (e + i)	• Similar to SE sound in *high*, *my* but without any hint of the sound **a**, which tends to be the case in northern English. It is the combination of the **murmur vowel** and a shorter version of the long **i**-sound without any hint of the vowel **a**	**high, my, dry, pile, fire, quite**
ay (a + y or i)	• As in SE *pay*	**maid, paid, pay, they**
ew, iw (i + u/w)	• This combination does not exist precisely in SE but is close to the vowel sound in SE *you*. It is the same as the Welsh diphthong **iw**, which could also be used in transliterating the sound. It is a combination of the short **i**-sound and the rounded **u**. This sound is characteristic of Wenglish.	**new, you, fruit, recruit, Jerusalem, queue**
ow	• As in SE *know, show* • As in SE *brown*	**know, show brown, frown, around**
oy	• As in SE *boy*	**boy, boil, poen**
i + long murmur vowel	• Does not exist in SE but similar to diphthong sound in SE *here*.	**by here, hear, year**
wy	• Only occurs in Welsh loan words. It is a combination of short rounded **u** and a shortened version of long **i**. It should be pronounced as the diphthong in *pwy* in South Wales. Welsh and should not be pronounced almost as separate sounds, as in North Wales Welsh.	**clwy, Clwyd**

PART TWO

WENGLISH IN ACTION

2 WENGLISH DIALOGUES, TEXTS AND SENTENCES

As well as providing examples of Wenglish in use, these dialogues, together with the sentences and texts in the Exercises in Part Four, can be used as reading passages.

2.1 SPELLING AND PRONUNCIATION

The pronunciation and grammar of Wenglish are covered in some detail in Parts One and Four respectively. In writing Wenglish I have adopted a 'middle way', which for the most part follows Standard English spelling, uses apostrophes to indicate minor differences from Standard pronunciation but also remains free to depart from the Standard English spelling if the Wenglish pronunciation varies markedly from the Standard, especially when these differences are not in line with the general rules of pronunciation given in Part One.

This 'middle way' has the advantages of easy recognition and readability of words while retaining the flexibility to deviate from the standard spelling when this is helpful. With this approach, it is important to have a good understanding of how to pronounce Wenglish and the reader is advised strongly to study the Pronunciation section of Part One carefully.

Of course, other approaches to writing Wenglish are possible. Frank Vickery uses Standard English spelling. While some 'missing' letters are indicated by apostrophes, there is in general little accommodation to reflect Wenglish pronunciation. One has to have some idea of the sound of Wenglish to get the full flavour of the text. It is of course true that plays are really to be performed and heard rather than read so the use of standard spelling is not a problem.

John Edwards experiments with another approach in **More Talk Tidy**, that is, use of a sort of 'phonetic' system based on words and sounds in Standard English spelling. 'Decoding' the words may be good fun but this is not a system I would advocate – it presupposes a knowledge of how the 'Standard English' words and sounds should be pronounced and is prone to inconsistency.

It would be possible to write Wenglish in standard phonetic script. However, as indicated in the section on pronunciation, this is tantamount to using a different alphabet and is not much good for the general reader.

2.2 WENGLISH DIALOGUES

2.2.1. Gladys an' Dilys

Gladys: Hiya Dil! How you keepin?

Dilys: Very good, thanks, gull but our Albert's back 'ave been givin him a lot a gyp, an there's no sign of him goin up the garden to rise 'em spuds.

Gladys: Ne' mind, gull. He'll come.

Dilys: I hope he do. An then there's our Elsie. Been baad under the doctor a good month now. Thing is, 'ey don't know what it is she've got. She haven't been right since she come back from 'at crewse. Somethin she've eaten, I 'xpext.

Gladys: Aye, sure to be. I can't abare forrin food. It don't agree with me and do repeat on me.

Dilys: Our Albert do love a curry. 'otter the better. He was out in India durin the war, you know.

Gladys: Well I won't keep you now, love. I know you gorrw go up the Post Office to rise youer pension. Of goin up the village, will you get a pint of milk for me from the Cop?

Dilys: Aye, course I will, love. Pay me after.

Gladys: Right-o, gull. See you now jest. Come in for a cup o' tea when you get back.

2.2.2 Fetch my specs, will you?

Albert: Dil! Come by 'ere now, gull! Fetch me my specs, will you? I wannw read 'e Echo. They're on the mantelpiece in the parlour, I think.

Dilys: Aright, love. I'll bring them up to you now in a minute.

Albert: Woss for dinner today, 'en, love? Egg an chips?

Dilys: No. I gorrus some of the butcher's best pork sausage. We'll 'ave 'em with a bit o' ponjin an onion gravy. Aright for you, love?

Albert: Aye, grand, love.

Dilys: How's youer back today, 'en, love?

Albert: Iss a bit better, I think.

Dilys: When you think you'll be able to go up 'e garden to rise 'em potatoes?

Albert: I don't know. We'll aff to ask Ivor to help. He'll be 'ere on 'e weekend.

Dilys: I spose I could ask Billy nextdoor.

Albert: No, less wait till Ivor do come. He can rise the ool lot for us 'en. (*Doorbell rings*)

Dilys: Better go an answer the door. Might be the doctor. (*Shouts up to Albert*) Albert, you got a visitor.

Albert: Who is it?

Dilys: Iss Billy nextdoor.

Billy: Shwmai wuss! How's youer back?

Albert: Well, to tell the trewth iss nosso good. Ass all I've 'ad since retiring.

Billy: I think you could put in for compo off the Coal Board.

Albert: 'Ere's no point, Billy. They won't pay nothing 'less you can prove it was workin down 'e pit 'at done it.

Billy: Watchin 'e rugby on Sat'day?

Albert: I'll be watchin' it by here on the box. You goin'?

Billy: No, I'm watchin it down the club. There's a lot of the boys goin down to Cardiff to watch it, 'ough.

Albert: Tell you what, I'd be goin down with 'em if I could! Can't move at all with this bloody back. 'e doctor can't do nothing about it. Says I jes' gorrw rest it. One thing, 'ough, I don't aff to go up 'e garden to rise 'em spuds. We'll aff to get Ivor to do it when he do come on 'e weekend.

2.2.3. Playin up Nan's back

Mam: Peter! Come by 'ere now, will you?

Peter: Wha' for, Mam?

Mam: Look at you! Filthy you are after playin up Nan's back! Gerrin by 'ere an 'ave a bath before youer father do come 'ome!

Peter: Aright, Mam. We was playin in the gwli an then we went up 'e mountain. We was aimin stones at thar old tree up by the quarry. After that we come down to play up Nan's back.

Mam: Di' she see you?

Peter: Yes, course she did. She give us a drink of squash an some pics to eat.

Mam: What she say about you bein so dirty?

Peter: Nothin reelly. Nan don't mind about things like that.

Mam: Well I do, so you better get up 'em stairs an run 'at bath!

2.2.4. C'mon Ponty!

Dai: C'mon Ponty! Stick it up theyer aaf!

Shwn: Opeluss they are 'is season! 'Aven' won a game yet. An 'ey was so good las' season an all!

Dai: Aye, but they've lost all thayer top players: Dai John 'ave gone to play for Cardiff – poached 'im they 'ave – an John Walters 'ave gone to play for Bridgend. Waldron and Huw Jones is injured – Waldron will be out till Christmas, by all account!

Shwn: Waldron's a chopsy ol' bugger but they're missin 'im in the scrums and lineouts.

Dai: Come on ref! Tha' was forward!

Shwn: 't was an all! 'e've given a scrum. Our put-in.

Dai: Come on Ponty!

Crowd: Ponty! Ponty! Ponty! Shove!

Shwn: Our ball! Gowon Charlo! Gerrit out to Pricey!

Dai: ''E 'ave an'all! 'e's in! Try!

Crowd: Ponty! Ponty! Ponty!

Shwn: 'E've kicked it an all! Ass more like it! We're in with a chance now!

Dai: Aye! Ebbw are not much cop this season either.

Shwn: No, but we might manidge to win now!

2.2.5. Ystrad dogs

Gwyn: Hiya Brian! Fancy goin down the dogs in Ystrad tonight?

Brian: Aye, aright, Gwyn. I 'aven't been down the dogs frages. It'll be a nice change. Had a good tip 'en, Gwyn?

Gwyn: As a matter of fact I have. 'ere's iss bloke in work gorra dog runnin in the third race. Reckons iss 'e best dog he've seen runnin in years.

Brian: Oh aye?

Gwyn: Aye.

Brian: Wossit called?

Gwyn: Penderyn Flyer.

Brian: Sounds more like a bloody steam engine than a dog!

Gwyn: Aye, well it can go like one an all, by all account!

Brian: Been down the booky's today?

Gwyn: Aye. I had a little flutter in the 3.30 at Kempton Park. Fell he did, 'ough! A flat shot.

Brian: Well maybe youer luck will pick up a bit down Ystrad.

Gwyn: I 'ope so. Mind you, I don't think our Elsie will be too 'appy with me goin down there.

Brian: Well, she'll be 'appy enough if we pick a couple of winners!

2.2.6. Valleys Lines

Tannoy: The next train to arrive on Platform 2 will be the delayed 8.08 service to Barry Island, calling at...

Mr. Jones: Late again!

Mr. Evans: Aye, as usual!

Mr. Jones: An packed it'll be now, you'll see! Won't get a seat on this one. No chance. Awful, mind. We should't have to pay for this sort of service, you know.

Mr. Evans: I know, but what can we do about it?

Mr. Jones: Not much. But what I can't understand is why they can't put 4 carridges on this one. There's always 4 on the 9.08 an iss always aaf empty. The 8.08 is always a 2 carriage job an iss 'eavin.

Mr Evans: Here it comes.

Tannoy: Your attention please. The train arriving on Platform 2 will now be non-stop to Cardiff. Would passengers for all stations to Pontypridd please wait for the next train, which will follow in ten minutes' time. Valley Lines apologises for any inconvenience that this may cause.

Mr. Jones: I reelly don't know what they're playing at. I bet that next train will be delayed an all.

2.2.7. Howells's Sales

Blod: Hiya Bron! Been down Cardiff for the sales?

Bron: No, not yet. You been?

Blod: Aye. Picked up some tidy bargains in Howells's sale an' all. Leather 'ambag quarter price and a couple o' shirts for Ivor. I din buy no sospans, ough. Too pricey they was.

Bron: I'll be goin down there on Sat'day with Brenda. Probly go on 'e train.

Blod: Cardiff's pricey gone 'ese days, you know.

Bron: Aye, but iss better than Swansea for shoppin.

Blod: I remember we use' to go one Sat'day to Cardiff an' one Sat'day to Swansea shoppin for years when Brenda was a girl.

Bron: Them was the days!

Blod: Aye, different world!

Bron: Iss 'ard now we're getting older, innit?

Blod: Iss not 'e same no more. An' there's nothing in town no more.

Bron: No, only old charity shops are in Maesteg these days.

Blod: No, iss not like it use' to be, Bron.

2.2.8. Tidy Job

Dan: You done a tidy job b' there, Bill.

Bill: Thanks, Dan. 'At wall took a bit o' buildin, I can tell you.

Dan: I can see.

Bill: 'At sment you give me was good stuff.

Dan: Aye, well I thought you might as well 'ave it 'cos we've finished ouer alterations now.

Bill: Aye. Looks nice an' all that porch you've got.

Dan: Yes. Annie's 'appy now. She'd been on to me frages to do it. I had to do it in the end or I wouldn't have had no peace.

Bill: I know what you mean.

Dan: Anyway, goin down the 'Colliers' tonight?

Bill: Aye. See you there, then. I owe you a pint from las' time.

Dan: What time you goin down?

Bill: I want to catch the Welsh news first and I'll be down after that.

Dan: Right you are, then! See you later!

2.2.9. Holidays

Maggy: Where you goin on youer 'olidays this year, then, Nell?

Nell: Down Trecco as usual. We're 'avin a lend of Bruce's trailer again. Nice down b' there, mind. You always meet loads of people you know.

Maggy: They've got a nice club down there now, they do say, with a show on evry night, neely.

Nell: A comedian or a singer usually. They've spent a tidy bit doin the place up, you know. New swimming pool, 'eated it is, an' new amusement arcades.

Maggy: Aye. It's aright for the kids but not much good for us oldies, Nell!

Nell: Where you goin, then, Maggy?

Maggy: We're off to Spain again on the bus. Ferris 'olidays. Very reasonable. Lovely 'otel we 'ad las' time. Food was aright, an' all. Full English breakfast for 'em 'at wanted it, an' you could 'ave fish an' chips or a roast dinner evry night. We found a Welsh pub an' all. Couple from Lantwit Major keeping it. Been out there for five years now. Doin a roarin trade. Don was landed.

Nell: Next year we might come with you. I'll have to work on Brian but he do love it down Trecco. He do love to meet up with 'is 'ol butties from Nanty.

Maggy: Mind you, you always meet people you know out in Spain an' all.

2.2.10. Come by 'ere an' 'ave a cwtch with Mam

Mam: Wossa marra, love? Come by 'ere an' 'ave a cwtch with Mam!

Christopher: "Em big boys 'ave taken the sweets Anty Vi give me. Said 'ey'd 'it me if I din give 'em to 'em.

Mam: Nasty ol' bullies 'ey are. We'll 'ave to teach 'em a lesson on of 'ese days. I bet that Nigel Jones was one of 'em. Nasty piece of work, he is. Just like 'is mother. Hikey ol' piece she was an' all. An 'is father's always up to no good. Sellin dodgy meat from 'is van he is. Nobody knows where he gets it from. Butcher reckons it's pet food reelly. Well, ne' mind, bach. I'll take you down Jackie's shop an' get you some more sweets.

Christopher: Mam.

Mam: Yes, love.

Christopher: Can I 'ave a Scaletrix for Christmas? All the boys in my class are 'avin one.

Mam: We'll see, love. You know we're saving up for a new cooker. Iss not been easy since youer father was laid off from the steelworks.

Christopher: But Mam...

Mam: We'll do our best, I'm shewer.

PART THREE

ALPHABETICAL GLOSSARY OF WENGLISH WORDS AND EXPRESSIONS

Alphabetical Glossary of Wenglish

The glossary of Wenglish words and expressions that follows is the most complete listing of Wenglish vocabulary ever compiled. Most of the words and expressions identified by John Edwards in the **Talk Tidy** books have been included, to which I have added as many additional entries. All the definitions and examples of usage given in this glossary are of course my own.

Not all of the words and expressions listed are exclusive to Wenglish – some are colloquialisms to be found in other English dialects. It is not always easy to decide on what should be included and what should not be, though the general rule I have adopted is that if the word or expression does not occur in Standard English, or is used particularly frequently or with a different meaning or nuance in Wenglish, it should be included in the listing.

The glossary contains many Welsh words and expressions, some taken over directly into Wenglish, some slightly changed and others changed considerably. These words and expressions deriving from Welsh have an important part to play in Wenglish. As they could not be used in Standard English, they are key differentiators between Wenglish and Standard English. Their use is greatest in Western Wenglsh, especially in areas where Welsh remains an important medium of communication. Indeed, many of these expressions are used interchangeably in the Wenglish and colloquial Welsh of these areas.

As stated earlier, the letter 'h' is not generally pronounced in Wenglish, except for the name of the letter itself – 'Haitch' and in combinations where this is found, such as 'Haitch P sauce' and 'Haitch TV'. Thus words beginning with 'h' in Standard English are generally listed under 'h' though some may also be listed under the second letter of the word preceded by an apostrophe.

The ending '-ing' in the present participles of verbs (e.g. 'walking') is generally pronounced '-in' in Wenglish. This may be written '-ing', '-in" (with an apostrophe to denote the unpronounced 'g') or simply '-in', without an apostrophe. All these spellings are acceptable in Wenglish.

The long 'a' sound is generally represnted by 'aa' or 'â' as in Welsh. However, in some writing in Wenglish, the sound can also be represented by 'ar' or 'ah'. It should be remembered that in these cases the 'r' or 'h' is merely an indication of vowel length and there is no hint of an 'r' or 'h' in the pronunciation.

Some of the words listed have bracketed letters, e.g. 'shw(d) mae?' This is to indicate that the word may be spelled and pronounced with or without the bracketed letter.

The 'rules' and norms of Wenglish pronunciation are covered in some detail at the end of Part One. If the reader is aware of these norms of Wenglish pronunciation, there is little need to change the spellings of the Wenglish words. Thus in general the Standard English spelling has been maintained so as to retain the familiar 'word pictures' and remain comprehensible to the majority of readers.

In some of the entries, the spelling of the Standard English word has been modified to reflect the typical Wenglish pronunciation, especially where this differs from Standard English. Since Wenglish has no official spelling system, such departures from the norms of Standard English Spelling are permissible, and indeed helpful, in indicating the correct pronunciation of the word in Wenglish. However, as stated above, I have tended to avoid excessive and unnecessary departure from the norms of Standard English orthography.

In some entries an acute accent has been placed above a vowel. This is merely an indication that the accented vowel is stressed. The stress pattern is different from that in Standard English in these words (e.g. 'interésting').

NOTE ON THE CATEGORISATION OF ENTRIES IN THE GLOSSARY

The categorisation of entries in the Glossary according to parts of speech (noun, adjective, preposition etc.) follows the generally accepted pattern. In the case of single words, this is simple and clear.

In the case of entries consisting of more than one word – i.e. phrases – an indication of the function of the phrases is generally provided. For example, a phrase which functions as a noun is termed a 'nominal phrase', a phrase that functions as an adverb is termed an 'adverbial phrase', and so on.

Phrases introduced by prepositions are called 'prepositional phrases'. Their function may be adjectival or adverbial. This function is indicated where appropriate.

In this Glossary, all verbs that require other words (e.g. prepositions, adverbs, nouns etc.) to convey their meaning, are termed as 'phrasal verbs'.

Expressions consisting of full sentences (including a verb) are generally called 'expressions' in the listing.

A

a (preposition)

Of: 'She's a bag a nerves gone.' Also **o'** and **o**.

aa pass (expression of time)

Half past: 'It was aa pass leven an' I hadn't done the smoothin' when she landed here.'

aaf / 'alf (noun and adjective)

Half. See also **half: on half**.

abear (transitive verb)

To bear, to tolerate: 'I can't abear it!', or 'She can't abear old long 'air.' Generally used with 'can't'.

about (adverb)

Out and about: 'I seen her about when I was down the village'. A variant is **about the place**. See also **place: about the place** for another meaning of this expression.

acessories

See **assessories**.

ach

(1) See **ach-y-fi**.

(2) See **tych**.

ach-a-fi! / ach-y-fi! (interjection)

An expression of disgust: 'I couldn't eat that cawl of 'ers – ach-y-fi!' (Welsh)

Ach-y-fi was also used as a noun (plural **ach-y-fis**) during the Second World War and subsequently as a derogatory term for evacuees, with which it rhymes approximately.

accidunt (noun)

Accident.

according to (preposition)

Depending on: 'Are you going out?' 'Well, it's according to how Bill is feelin'.'

account: by all account (prepositional phrase, used adverbally)

So they say, it is rumoured, apparently, it seems: 'Dai Jones 'ave won the pools by all account.'

acid (adjective)

Acidic, sharp: 'These oranges are a bit acid, a'n' 'ey?'

act (transitive or intransitive verb)

To operate, to work, to function: 'Fetch it by 'ere now and I'll show you how to act it.'; 'I don't know how it acts – we'll hafto send it away to be mended.' See also **work**.

act up (phrasal verb)

(1) To behave badly: 'He's been acting up again – I'll afto tell 'is mother when I see 'er.' 'My radio's been acting up again – can't get a sound out of it.'

(2) To substitute at work at a higher grade: 'When Marilyn goes on maternity leave, I'm goin to be acting up.'

Adda: as old as Adda (idiomatic expression)

As old as Adam, very old indeed. 'Adda' (pronounced as in Welsh, the 'dd' having the same sound as 'th' in the word 'then', is the Welsh for Adam.

adúlt (noun)

Adult. The stress is on the second syllable, as in American English.

Aelwyd (noun)

A Welsh word meaning 'hearth' or 'home' but when used in Wenglish it almost exclusively refers to Aelwyd yr Urdd, the local branch of the Urdd, the Welsh League of Youth. Thus 'Aelwyd' is more or less synonymous with 'Welsh speaking youth club'.

afford (transitive verb)

To be able to risk, take the chance that. Generally used in the negative, introduced by 'can't'. 'She've 'ad a cough frages so she can't afford to catch a chill on top of it.'

affto

See **have to**.

afraid to open my mouth (adjectival phrase)

Afraid to speak because one fears some sort of criticism: 'I'm afraid to open my mouth gone!'

after (adverb)

Afterwards, later on: 'Are you goin' down youer Nan's after.'

afto / affto

See **have to**.

aftrim, aftrer, aftrus, aftrem/aftrum (contractions of preposition + pronoun)

After him, after her, after us and after them respectively.

afu (g)las (nominal phrase)

Gizzard (of poultry). A generally evil-smelling dish! Welsh, literally 'blue liver', and pronounced as in Welsh. (Western Wenglish) See also **giblet soup**.

again / agen (adverb)

(1) At some time in the future: 'If you haven't got it on you now, you can give it to me agen.' See also **now jest**.

(2) In addition: 'That's another pair agen she've got.'

(3) Once more, as in Standard English: 'You'll afto do that work again' can sometimes mean 'you'll have to re-do that work', as in Standard English but meaning (1) above is more common.

against (preposition)

By the time (that). This is a literal translation of the Welsh 'erbyn'. 'I got the dinner ready against them comin' 'ome.'

age

See **no age**.

agen

See **again**.

ages: frages / 'issages (adverbial phrase)

For a long time: 'I 'adn't seen 'er frages.'

See also **this long time**. All these expressions mean much the same thing.

aggravate (transitive verb)

To cause annoyance to: 'Stop aggravating Dacu with youer shoutin'.'

agony (noun)

Severe pain: 'I was in agony after fallin' off tha' ladder.'

aim (transitive verb

To throw: 'Them kids was aimin' stones at ouer green'ouse agen'.' See also **bricks**.

air (transitive or intransitive verb)

To air clothes. Wenglish housewives were very strict on this practice – clothes had to be aired, after washing and drying, before being worn: 'I've put them shirts to air.'

airin(g) cubbud (nominal phrase)

Airing cupboard. Place where clothes were aired and stored.

'alf

See **aaf** and **half**.

all account

See **account: by all account**.

all along (adverbial phrase)

From the outset: 'I knew all along 'e wouldn't come.'

all came back

See **come back**.

all fuss and feathers

See **fuss: all fuss and feathers**.

all hands on deck (expression)

Everybody has to muck and help, no-one can be idle: 'It was all hands on deck so we could get the job finished.'

all jaw

See **jaw**.

all right!/? / awright!/? / alright!/? / aright!/? (interjection/greeting in form of adverbial phrase/adverb)

How are you? See also **shw mae?** and **hiya!**

all right / awright / alright / aright (adverbial phrase/adverb)

Alright, in a satisfactory manner, OK.

all taken away

See **take away**.

all over (adverbial phrase)

Typically, essentially: 'That's you all over – promise the earth but then forget about it!' See also **thass typical**.

all over you (prepositional phrase, used in predicate with 'to be')

Obsequious, giving a lot of fuss and attention to: 'Tha' Brenda was all over you when you won the bingo, but she ignored you completely in the club las' night.'

all show / all swank (phrase used in predicate with 'to be')

Showy, flashy, superficial, lacking true substance.

all the time (adverbial phrase)

Always, continually. Possibly influenced by the Welsh 'trwy'r amser'.

all there (adverbial phrase, used predicatively with 'to be')

In full possession of one's mental faculties. Generally used in the negative – **not all there**: 'I can't understand why he didn't go on 'olidays when they offered to take 'im – 'e's not all there, mun!' See also **never all there**.

all up with (adverbial phrase, used predicatively with 'to be')

Having reached the end, having come to a situation of no hope: 'It's all up with old Mrs Jones – she 'aven't been right since she buried 'er 'usbunt.'

alley (noun)

A marble. **To play alleys** means 'to play marbles'.

alley bomper / alley bop (nominal phrase)

A large clear glass marble, so called because it was the stopper of the very old style of pop bottles. These were not always perfectly round. To say that something was like an 'alley bop' would imply that it was big, e.g.: 'He had a bump on his head like an alley bop.' **Bomper** could also mean 'a big one': 'They got a bomper of a baby' means that they have a big, bonny baby.

almond (noun)

Almond. The 'l' is always clearly pronounced, unlike in Standard English, Received Pronunciation.

along

See **all along**.

alright

See **all right**.

alter (transitive or intransitive verb)

(1) To make alterations on items of clothing.

(2) To change one's ways or appearance. 'I didn't recognise him – he've altered a lot.' See also **stroke: to alter your stroke**.

always on (adverbial phrase, used predicatively with 'to be')

Always referring to, or speaking about something, generally in an annoying way: 'She's always on about 'er grandson.'

always on the road

See **road**.

always the same (phrase used predicatively with 'to be')

Of the same disposition: 'He's always the same – never loses 'is temper with no-one.'

'ambaag / 'ambarg (noun)

Wenglish pronunciation of 'handbag'. An example of the assimilation of the consonants 'nd' / 'nt'' before 'b'.

amount

See **any amount (of)**.

amynedd (noun)

Patience: ''E's got plenty of amynedd – that job would be too much of a potch for me.' (Welsh) (Western Wenglish)

an / an' (conjunction)

And.

an' all / an all (adverbial phrase)

Also, and all. Added to the end of a sentence or phrase.

'and

See **lend (a) 'and**.

and odd / an' odd (adverbial phrase)

Approximately: 'I give 'im twenty an odd yesterday – 'e's spending money like water gone.'

and that / and 'at / an 'at (adverbial phrase)

And so on.

and there was me thinking

See **think**.

Andrews' (noun)

A proprietory brand of effervescent salts (Andrew's Liver Salts). See also **elsolse**, **Eno's** and **Epsom solse**.

anch / ansh (noun)

A bite (of something edible): 'I was dyin' for an anch a thar apple!'

'anes

See **hanes**.

'anky

See **hanky**.

annibendod (noun)

A mess, untidiness: 'There's annibendod in theyer 'ouse!' (Welsh) (Western Wenglsh)

Annibynwyr (noun, plural)

Members of the Welsh Congregational Churches (Independents). This Welsh word literally means 'Independents'. A member of the Independents is known as an **Annibynnwr**, feminine **Annibynwraig**. The **Annibynnwyr** are sometimes jocularly referred to as the **Annibynns**. (Welsh) (Western Wenglish)

answer the door (phrasal verb)

To go and see who has knocked at the door/rung the doorbell.

antie / aunty / auntie (noun)

Aunty, whether real or a 'Welsh auntie', i.e. a neighbour or any friendly adult female.

any amount (of) (adjective + noun)

Plenty (of): 'There's any amount of swedes in the garden, if you wunt them.'

anyhow / anyroad (adverb)

Anyway, in any case: 'She was goin' to Cardiff anyhow, so she didn't mind givin' me a lift.' **Anyway** is much more common these days.

apartments (noun, plural)

Rented accommodation. Generally pronounced 'partmunts'. 'To live in 'partmunts' was to have separate rooms while sharing someone else's house, as opposed to 'living through and through'. This term is now more or less obsolete. See also **through and through: to live through and through**.

appro: on appro (prepositional phrase)

On approval (merchandise).

apron (noun)

(1) A pig's caul, used in making faggots.

(2) As in Standard English. See also **brat** and **ffedog**.

apt (adjective)

Likely to, having a tendency to: 'It's apt to spill over if you warm it too quick.'

'aputh (noun)

A ha'porth, a halfpennyworth, a very small quantity of.

arbed (transitive verb)

To save, in the sense of to avoid causing wear and tear: 'I covered the table to arbed the wood.' 'I did a hand wash to arbed putting the washing machine on.' (Welsh). (Western Wenglish)

'ard

See **hard**.

Arglwydd! / Arglwydd Mawr! (interjection)

Lord! Good Lord! 'Arglwydd Mawr' literally means 'Great Lord!'. (Welsh) (Western Wenglish)

aright

See **all right**.

arm / back / knee / leg went

See **went**.

arweinydd (noun)

Conductor (musical), especially a visiting conductor at a Cymanfa Ganu (q.v.) (Welsh – mostly Western Wenglish)

arweinydd y gân (nominal phrase)

Musical director in a Welsh chapel. (Welsh, pronounced as in Welsh – mostly Western Wenglish)

arswyd y byd! (interjection)

A mildish expletive. It was probably coined/introduced to avoid saying 'Arglwydd' (Lord), as in strict nonconformist circles, any hint of taking the name of God in vain was generally to be avoided. 'Arswyd y byd!' literally means 'Terror/dread of the world!' (Welsh) (Western Wenglish)

'art

See **heart**.

'artburn

See **heartburn**.

arthritus (noun)

Arthritis.

article (noun)

Individual, person: 'Funny article he is – he's always tryin' some trick or other.'

as good as look at you

See **good**.

as if

See **like as if.**

ash / ashman (noun)

Refuse collector: 'The ash will be round tomorrow: better put the bin out ready.'
See also **scavenger.**

asma / assma (noun)

Asthma.

asmatic / assmatic (adjective and noun)

Asthmatic.

aspestos(s) (noun)

Asbestos.

aspestosis (noun)

Asbestosis.

ass / 'ass (contraction of demonstrative + verb form)

Possible spelling and pronunciation of **that's**: 'I was jest lookin, 'ass all.'

assessories / acessories (noun, plural)

Accessories, such as handbags, belts etc. Note the pronunciation.

assma

See **asma.**

assmatic

See **asmatic.**

'at / 'a' (demonstrative adjective and pronoun)

That.

attack

See **bilious attack.**

attenshun (noun)

Attention.

atto / attw (contraction of verb form + preposition)

Had to.

aught (noun)

Naught, zero.

aunty / auntie

See **antie.**

awa (noun)

Uncle – the masculine of **bopa** (q.v.). (Central Wenglish – not current)

awake

See **wise: awake before he's wise**.

away (adverb)

Not local(ly), not (from) round here: 'is wife is not from round 'ere – she's from away somewhere.' 'They're livin' away – up England somewhere.'

awful (adverb and adjective)

Awful(ly), extreme(ly): 'The baby was cryin' awful.' The double form **awful awful** can also be used for emphasis. 'It was awful awful. The sergeant atto take 'im down the plice station.'

awful for (adjective + preposition)

Over fond of, over reliant on: 'I'm awful for chocolate gone!'

a-willing (adjective)

Willing, prepared to (do something).

awright

See **all right**.

aye (adverb)

Yes. **Aye aye!** is sometimes used as a greeting or as a reply to **shw mae?**, **awright?** or **hiya! Aye** or **aye aye** can also function as a means of emphasising an affirmative when making a statement: 'Well aye mun, thass ovious, innit!!' The single form can also be added to the end of a statement for emphasis. 'There were loads a people there, aye!' See **all right?**, **shw mae?**, **hiya!**.

B

baad / bard (adjective and adverb)

(1) Ill, suffering: 'uncle Dai was baad agen las' night – they atto call 'e doctor.' 'I was baad with my leg.' See also **sick and baad**.

(2) Badly: ''E've 'urt 'imself baad.'

baad-minded / bard-minded (adjective)

Thinking the worst of others.

babi / babi lol / babi loshin (noun/nominal phrase)

A baby, someone craving attention, an over-indulged child. (Welsh)

bach / fach (adjective; can also be used as noun)

Dear, little: 'ow's Dai bach, then?' The soft mutated form, beginning with 'f' (pronounced 'v' in Welsh) us used in the case of feminine singular nouns. In Wenglish, this adjective, which means 'small' or 'little' in Welsh, is more generally used an expression of endearment – 'dear'. As a noun, it can be translated as 'dear'. See also **boys bach**.

back back (phrasal verb, transitive or intransitive)

To reverse (of vehicle): 'Let me back back a bit so I can turn the car tidy.'

back and fore (adverbial phrase)

Back and forth: 'He's a real pest – back and fore all the time.'

back (noun)

Back garden, rear of house.

back kitchen (nominal phrase)

Scullery, small kitchen.

back passage (nominal phrase)

The anus/rectum. See also **front passage**, **passage** and **stoppage**.

back went

See **went**.

backward

See **dull and backward**.

bad job

See **job**.

badly (adverb)

Urgently, desperately. The position of the adverb differs from that in Standard English, e.g. 'The lawn needs cutting badly' is quite permissible in Wenglish and means 'The lawn urgently needs cutting'. In Standard English, this sentence would call into question the quality of the mowing!

bag of nerves / bag a nerves (nominal phrase)

A nervous wreck: ''E've been a bag of nerves since that business down the club.' See also **bundle of nerves**.

bagsa (expression of quantity)

Lots of. Possible spelling and pronunciation of **bags of**.

bailey / beeley / bili (noun)

The back yard, or the area in front of a house, depending on its configuration: 'I'll 'afto go an' sweep the beeley – it's full of old dust after the roadworks.' In

Western, Welsh-speaking parts of the Wenglish area, this might be pronounced as 'beeley', the local Welsh pronunciation of the word.

baet / bait (noun)

An annoying person, someone who irritates, someine who nags. : 'He's an old bait – he always on to me about the shed.' (Welsh, and pronounced as in Welsh) (Western Wenglish)

bake beans (nominal phrase)

Baked beans.

bald-headed (adjective and adverb)

(1) Reckless(ly).

(2) Over-vigorous(ly).

(Central and Eastern Wenglish)

bancyn (noun)

Bank or hill. Also used in colloquial South Wales Welsh. (Western Wenglish)

bankin(g) (noun)

(1) Small coal used to build up a fire. See also **glo mân** and **ribbling**.

(2) See **bancyn**.

bar (preposition)

(1) Except: 'They won all theyer games bar one.'

(2) See **tools ar y bar**.

bar cwtch! (interjection)

A warning for others to stay away from one's **cwtch** (spot, place) while picking blackberries etc. Obsolete or at least obsolescent. However a recently opened bar/restaurant in Cardiff Bay is called 'Bar Cwtch'.

bara bit (nominal phrase)

A very small bit: 'Dwtty she was – no bigger than a bara bit.' (Central Wenglish – probably now obsolete)

bara caws (nominal phrase)

Bread and cheese. (Welsh) (Western Wenglish)

bara jam (nominal phrase)

Bread and jam. (Welsh) (Western Wenglish)

bara llâth / bara llaeth (nominal phrase)

Bread and (hot/warm) milk. (Welsh) (Western Wenglish)

bara menyn (nominal phrase)

Bread and butter. (Welsh) (Western Wenglish)

bara sâm (nominal phrase)

Bread and dripping. (Welsh) (Western Wenglish) See also **sâm / saim.**

bard

See **baad**.

bard-minded

See **baad-minded**.

bare week / bare fortnight (nominal phrase)

A week/fortnight but no more. (Central and Eastern Wenglish)

barges: like canal barges (phrase used predicatively with 'to be')

Much too big: 'These shoes I got are like canal barges on me!'

bash (noun)

A try, a go: 'I'll give it a bash.'

batch (noun)

A small round loaf of bread.

bathers (noun, plural)

Swimming trunks, swimming costume.

battleship

See **enough ... to sink a battleship**.

battry (noun)

Battery.

bawl

See **shout and bawl**.

bays: the bays (noun, plural)

The beach (somewhere on Gower generally implied): 'We can go down the bays in the 'olidays – it'll be nice.' (mostly Western Wenglish)

be for your life (phrasal verb)

To be very careful: 'When Brenda an' the kids was 'ere, I atto be for my life with 'em – into everything, they were!' Only used in the infinitive. (Central Wenglish)

beanfeast (noun)

A large meal, often on a festive occasion: 'We 'ad a real beanfeast in Diane's weddin'.'

Glossary

beans

See **bake beans**, **kidney beans** and **full of beans**.

beautiful / bewtiful (adjective, occasionally as adverb)

Excellent, very nice, very good. Its use in Wenglish is much wider than in Standard English. The double form **beautiful beautiful** is another example of the tendency, taken over from Welsh, to repeat an adjective to intensify its meaning. See also **lovely lovely**.

It can also be used as an adverb: 'Them kidney beans are comin' on beautiful with you.'

Beatress / Beatruss (proper noun)

Beatrice, the female name.

beauty / bewty (noun)

A fine specimen: 'Them caulis of youers are reel bewties.' Can also be used ironically to signify 'a fine one' in a derogatory sense.

beauty of it / bewty of it (nominal phrase)

The particular advantage: 'The beauty of it is, it's so easy to do.'

Bedyddwyr (noun, plural)

The Baptists. 'A Baptist' is **Bedyddiwr**, feminine **Bedyddwraig**. (Welsh)

beef

See **corn beef**.

beeley

See **bailey**.

beer

See **small beer**.

before (preposition)

In preference to: 'Give me 'olidays down Trecco before Gower anyday.'

beholden (adjective)

Indebted: 'If we ask 'im to 'elp, we'll be beholden to 'im.'

be'ind (noun, preposition and adverb)

Behind.

bein(g) I was (verbal construction)

Since I was (in any case): 'Bein' I was goin' to town, I thought pick up some things in the market.' See also **of going**.

beirniad (noun)

Adjudicator in an eisteddfod competition. (Welsh – mostly Western Wenglish)

beirniadaeth (noun)

Adjudication – the result and comments from the 'beirniad' – in an eisteddfod competition. (Welsh – mostly Western Wenglish)

belfago (adverb)

Loudly: 'They was singing real belfago after a couple a pints.' (Central Wenglish)

bell on/in every tooth (nominal phrase)

Someone who has a bell on every tooth is a loud and frequent speaker: 'You can hear 'er from the other end of the village – she's got a bell on every tooth.'

Belli's (proper noun)

Generally pronounced 'bell eyes'. The name of an Italian **caffy** (q.v.) See also **Bracchi's**.

bellyful (noun)

More than enough 'I've had enough – I've had a real bellyful of this now.'

belonging (adjective)

Related: 'They're belonging to us – my grandfather an 'er uncle were first cousins.'

below

See **down below**.

belter

A heavy blow or beating: 'You'll 'ave a belter if you don't stop that nonsense!'

Bessie (noun)

A fusspot, especially of a man: 'He's a bit of an old Bessie but 'is 'eart's in the right place.' See also **paish, Nancy** and **Mary Jane**.

better (adverb used in place of verb)

Had better: 'You better do it quick.'

bev(v)ied up to the (h)ilt (adjectival phrase)

Having had a great deal to drink. A relatively recent addition, probably influenced to some extent at least by colloquial English via TV.

bewtiful

See **beautiful**.

bewty

See **beauty**.

bewty of it

See **beauty of it**.

beyond (adverb)

Extremely: 'She's cheeky beyond: she must be the most naughtiest girl in the hool class.' This word always follows the adjective and is a direct translation of the Welsh 'tu hwnt'.

bicarb / bicaab (noun)

Bicarbonate of soda, sodium bicarbonate. This versatile substance was used medicinally, as a cooking ingredient and for cleaning purposes.

big

See **ugly big**.

big member

See **member: big member**.

big noise

See **noise: big noise**.

big huge / big 'uge (adjectival phrase)

Very big. An example of the Welsh duplication of adjectives carried over into Wenglish.

bili

See **bailey**.

bilious attack (nominal phrase)

A horrible – and horrible-sounding – bout of nausea etc. The expression was heard quite commonly a generation or two ago, even used in Welsh conversation. A bilious attack might be cured by a dose of **elsolse** (health salts) such as Andrew's Liver Salts or similar.

bird

See **dicky bird**.

bished (adjective)

Exhausted, very tired.

bit: a bit (adverbial phrase)

To some extent: 'She can sing a bit.'

bit of (adjectival/partitive phrase)

(1) In a modest (or sometimes not so modest) way: 'He's a bit of an athlete', or 'They've got a bit of garden in theyer new 'ouse.'

(2) Some: 'I'm off to have my bit of dinner, now' and 'I managed to get a bit of fish for my dinner.'

bit pushed

See **pushed**.

black pat (nominal phrase)

Cockroach.

blacklead (noun)

Pencil.

bladder (noun)

Balloon. (Now obsolete)

blaenor (noun)

An elder in the Presbyterian Chuch of Wales, more commonly knwn as the Calvinistic Methodists. Broadly similar in function and role to **deacon** (q.v.) in the Baptist and Congregagtional Churches. (Welsh) (mostly Western Wenglish)

blaggud (noun)

A blackguard, a bully.

blaggudy (adjective)

Rough, dirty (e.g. of a football/rugby team): 'They're an old blaggudy team, them Leeds United.' (An adjective formed from **blaggud**.)

blas (noun)

Taste (Welsh): 'I like something tasty – something with a bit of blas on it.' Note the use on 'on' after 'blas', following the use of 'ar' (on) in Welsh.

blas halen / blas 'alen (nominal or adjectival phrase)

Savoury (literally 'salt taste'): 'I don' like old cakes an' ice-cream – give me something blas halen any day!'

blemmer / brammer (noun)

An excellent specimen: 'Them tomatoes I got are real brammers.'

blew (adjective)

Possible pronunciation of 'blue'.

blewyn (noun)

A hair: 'I've got a blewyn on my nose.' (Welsh) (Western Wenglish)

block (noun)

A log of firewood: 'I've brought in another block for the fire.'

blockage (noun)

An unspecified medical blockage: 'She've got a blockage somewhere down below.'

blodyn (noun)

Flower (Welsh). A term of endearment. Also **blodyn tatws** (potato flower).

bloke / bloak (noun)

Man: 'Tha' bloke was down the club agen las' night.'

blue

See **cry blue murder** and **yell blue murder**.

bogey

See **gambo (2)** and **bwgi (2)**.

boilt (past participle, used as adjective)

boilin(g) (adjective)

(Feeling) very hot: 'iss boilin in the kitchen – I carn stand it no more!' See also **roasting**.

boilt

Boiled. A common form of the past tense and past participle of the verb 'to boil'. 'The kettle 'ave boilt – come and 'ave a cup a tea in the 'and.'

bolshy (adjective)

Awkward, not cooperative, militant. See also **obstropalous**, **strobulous** and **conchy**. It can also be used as an adverb: 'He's actin bolshy agen – look out with 'im!'

bomper (noun)

Big, or a big one: 'They've had twins – and one of them's a real bomper.'

See also **alley bomper**.

bonc / bonk (noun)

A knock, or blow. (Welsh)

bonclust (noun)

A blow or clip to the ears. (Welsh)

bondo (noun)

A canopy or roof giving shelter. This Welsh word literally means 'eaves'. (Western Wenglish)

bone: in the bone (adverbial phrase)

In essence, essentially, at heart: 'He's an old waster in the bone.' (Welsh – a transfer of the idiom 'yn y bôn', meaning 'in essence') (Western Wenglish)

bono

See **gambo (2)**. (Western Wenglish)

boo nor bah (nominal phrase)

Anything at all: 'She's too frightened to say boo nor bah to no-one!'

book (transitive verb)

To have one's details taken by the police, e.g. in connection with a parking or similar offence: 'The copper booked me for parking on double yellows.'

booky / bookie (noun)

Bookmaker, turf accountant. It can also mean the bookmaker's shop.

booky's / bookie's (noun)

The bookmaker's shop: 'Been down the booky's, Dai?' 'No, but I'm goin down now after – I've 'ad a good tip for the 3.15 at Newmarket.'

boomy (adjective)

Booming, reverberating (e.g. of voice).

bopa (noun)

An auntie – either relative or a friendly female neighbour or acquaintance. (Central Wenglish – obsolescent)

bore da! (interjection)

Good morning! (Welsh)

born in a field (adjectival phrase/idiomatic expression)

A critical remark made to people who leave doors open: 'Shut that door! I think you must have been born in a field!'

bosh (noun)

The kitchen sink, generally a Belfast-type or metal sink: 'Better have a swill in the bosh before you go out.' See also **swill**. (Central and Eastern Wenglish)

botch (noun and transitive verb)

As a noun, a mess, or poorly done job. As verb, 'to mess up', 'to do a bad job of'. (See also **potch**)

bound to (be / come etc.) (adverbial phrase)

Very probably, almost certainly: 'There's bound to be some bargains in the sales.' 'E's bound to come – 'e've never missed before.' See also **sure to be**.

bout (noun)

An attack, especially of an illness: 'He's had another bout of flu, poor dab.' See also **pull (1)**.

boy

See **could: it could be a boy or it could be a girl, good boy, old boy** and **nancy boy**.

boy 'n' aaf / boy narf / boy-and-a-half (nominal phrase)

A character, especially of the amusing kind: 'He's a boy ' aaf – he's always up to some tricks!' The 'boy' could occasionally be a girl!

boys bach (nominal phrase and interjection)

As a nominal phrase, it is a familiar and friendly way of addressing several people, similar to the American English 'guys': 'Come on, boys bach, it's time to go!' As an interjection, it means something on the lines of 'good grief!' or 'bloody hell!', to express surprise or sometimes dismay: 'Boys bach! That wasn't right at all!' (Colloquial Welsh – in fact a hybrid, using the English word 'boys'. The 's' in 'boys' is pronounced as 's', not voices to a 'z'.) (Western Wenglish)

Bracchi's (proper noun)

A generic term for an Italian café in the valleys, even though the proprietor's surname could be Belli, Sidoli, Berni etc. See also **Belli's**. (Central and Eastern Wenglish)

brack (noun)

Imperfection, damage caused by wear and tear: 'I've had this sweater this years and there's not a brack in it at all.'

brammer

See **blemmer**.

brasserie (noun)

Brassière, bra.

brassier (noun)

Brazier.

brat (noun)

Apron (Welsh). Obsolete or obsolescent. See also **ffedog** and **apron**.

brau

See **broi**.

brazen (adjective)

Arrogant and/or impudent, caring nothing about local opinion: 'What do you think of that Georgina – goin' into work after all that fuss as if nothin' 'ad 'append – brazen's not the word for it!'

Brazils (noun, plural)

Brazil nuts, once a Christmas treat.

bre(c)kfass / bre(c)kfuss (noun)

Breakfast

Brewce (proper noun)

Wenglish pronunciation of 'Bruce'.

brewer's goitre (nominal phrase)

A beer belly.

brewse / brewze (noun)

Bruise.

bricks (noun, plural)

Stones: 'Stop aimin bricks!'

broderie onglay (nominal phrase)

Broderie anglaise: 'She 'ad a lovely top in broderie onglay.'

broi / brau (adjective)

Tender (of meat), raw-feeling, tender (of body): 'I'm feelin all broi after the op'. 'Broi' is the colloquial South Wales pronunciation, while 'brau' is the Welsh standard. (Welsh) (Western Wenglish)

broke (past participle, used as adjective)

Broken. See also **bust**.

brought up under a tub (adjectival phrase/idiomatic expression)

Brought up in an unsatisfactory manner: 'You can't go out with youer 'air like that – people will think you've been brought up under a tub.' See also **dragged up**.

brush

See **dull**.

bucked (adjective)

Cheered up, encouraged: 'She was bucked when they told 'er she wouldn't 'ave to go back to the 'ospital till June.'

budge (transitive or intransitive verb)

To move: 'I couldn't budge that tank – it was too 'eavy,' and, 'I ate so much I couldn't budge.' The use of 'budge' is more widespread than in Standard English and the use of 'move' generally less so.

buggered up (adjectival phrase)

(1) Very tired. Not to be used in polite conversation.

(2) Spoiled, of no use.

bump (noun)

A (generally) minor crash (car), a minor blow (person): 'They had a bump in the car coming down here tonight.'

bun fight

See **tea fight**.

bundle of nerves (nominal phrase)

A very nervous person. See also **bag of nerves**.

bunk

See **do a bunk**.

bury his wife / bury her husband (transitive phrasal verb and idiomatic expression)

A common local expression to show that someone has been bereaved: 'She buried her husband last month.' Strangers have been known to enquire whether the bereaved spouse actually carried out the interment! (From Welsh 'claddu', 'to bury'.)

bus

See **on the bus** and **lose the bus**.

bust (transitive verb)

(1) To break, hence **busted** means 'broken'.

(2) To burst, to be dying to urinate: 'Cmon I'm bustin! I gorrw gerrw the toilet!'

bust / busted (past participle used as adjective)

Broken.

butt

See **butty (1)**.

butt in (phrasal verb)

To interrupt: 'Scuse me buttin' in, but iss neely time to go.'

butty

(1) A friend or workmate: 'John loves to see 'is butties down the 'stute.' This usage is also found in West Country dialect and reached South Wales via the Forest of Dean, itself an area with a long history of mining.

(2) One of a matching pair: 'Where's the butty to this black boot?'

(3) A sandwich or filled roll. This usage of the word has been borrowed from other dialects (e.g. Scouse, Lancashire), probably through exposure via TV. 'I'd love a chip butty now, aye!'

buzz off! (intransitive verb, imperative)

Go away!

bwci-bo / bwgi-bo (noun)

Ghost or bogey man. (Welsh)

bwgi (noun)

(1) Head louse: 'Dai Jones 'ave got bwgis in 'is 'air. The nit nurse 'ave been in to school agen.'

(2) Bogeys (i.e. in nose).

bwyll

See **pwylla**.

by (adverb)

(1) Aside: 'You don't have to take it now, I'll put it by for you.'

(2) Away: 'Put it by before mammy come home.' (from Welsh 'dodi (he)ibo')

(3) See **by here** and **by there**.

See also **tell by him/her**.

by all account

See **account: by all account**.

by you (preposition + pronoun)

According to you, as in: 'What's the time by you?'

by here / by 'ere (adverbial phrase)

Here, over here. 'By' is very commonly added. **Over by here** is also to be heard: 'Come over by 'ere for a minute.' See also **by there**.

by rights (adverbial phrase)

According to what is just and proper: 'He should 'ave 'ad that dresser after his cousin by rights!'

by the look / by the looks of it

See **look: by the look**.

by there (adverbial phrase)

There, over there. 'By' is very commonly added. **Over by there** is also to be heard. It is sometimes pronounced 'b'there' as opposed to two separate words. 'That's the one youer looking for – over by there'. See also **by here**.

bychan (noun)

My lad. It could be a corruption of 'bachgen' (boy) or the adjective 'bychan' (small): 'Der 'ma bychan! Come and see the ci bach.' (Welsh) (Wesrern Wenglish) See also **'mychan i**.

C

cabbage

See **short: too short to cut cabbage** and **cawl cabbage**.

cabitsien (noun)

Cabbage. A term of endearment. (Welsh) (Western Wenglish)

cabolach

See **cawlach**.

cach / cachu (noun)

Shit. Not to be used in polite conversation. 'He's in the cach now – he should never have done that in the first place'. (Welsh)

cachu (transitive and intransitive verb)

To shit. Not to be used in polite conversation. 'He's cachu'd in his pants again!' 'I was cachu-ing bricks – I jus' din know worrw do.' (Welsh. These examples show the addition of English verb endings to the Welsh verb. Using the Welsh form 'cachu' may be considered slightly milder and less offensive than the English.)

cack handed / coggy handed (adjective)

Left handed. See also **llaw bwt**.

caffy (noun)

Café. Many of these were run by Italian families and have become something of a Valleys tradition.

caib (noun)

A type of pickaxe or mattock. (Welsh) See also **ceibo: shwd mae'n ceibo?** and **meddw caib**.

calennig (noun)

A New Year's gift. (Welsh)

call

See **what you call**.

call on (phrasal verb)

To call (aloud) to, to shout to: 'Call on John, will you? The food's ready. This is a direct translation of the Welsh 'galw ar'. See also **shout on.**

call someone everything / call someone rotten (phrasal verb)

To run someone down by saying unpleasant or abusive things: 'Calling you everything, she was, when she come 'ome an' found the mess you'd left for 'er to clear up!'.

calling you (present participle + pronoun)

Expected of you: 'We can have a spell after dinner – there's nothing calling us now we've finished the job.'

cam bwyll

See **pwylla.**

Cam-bryan (proper noun)

The way 'Cambrian', a common name for a pub/hotel in the Valleys, is pronounced by some Wenglish speakers.

cân actol (noun)

Action song, popular in Welsh nursery schools. (Welsh)

canal

See **barges: like canal barges.**

cant (intransitive verb)

To gossip maliciously.

canting (noun)

Gossip, often malicious in nature.

can't abear / carn abear

See **abear.**

can't afford / carn afford

See **afford.**

can't miss him/her / carn miss him/her

See **miss.**

caper (noun)

A trick, ruse or exploit: 'We can't let them get away with caper – it's a damn cheek – puttin' on us they are!'

cap: to cap it all (phrasal verb, set expression)

In addition to, over and above everything: 'After all them hours of travellin', to cap it all, we could't find the key of the 'ouse when we landed back!'

car

See **in the car**.

cariad (noun)

Love, darling. (Welsh) A term of endearment.

cards: to have your/his etc. cards (phrasal verb)

To be dismissed from a job, to get the sack. The allusion is to getting one's official documents returned.

carn (modal verb, present tense, in negative)

Possible Wenglish pronunciation and spelling of can't. See also **can't abear**, **can't afford** and **can't miss him/her**.

carridge (noun)

Carriage: 'Funny they don't put more carridges on the 8 o'clock from Ponty.'

carry clecs

See **clecs**.

carry on (noun)

Fuss, bother.

carry on (phrasal verb)

(1) To continue speaking about, to refer to repeatedly in conversation: 'You've been carryin' on about this since we got 'ome – can't you give it a rest for a bit?'

(2) To have an illicit affair/relationship: 'She've been carryin' on with a bloke from Nanty, by all account.'

cart (transitive verb)

To transport, to carry: 'After buying them things, we atto cart 'em all 'ome.'

cart: llwyth cart

See **llwyth cart**.

case (noun)

An amusing character: 'She's a case – never know what she's goin' to do next!'

case: in case

See **in case** and **fear: for fear**.

catch

See **ketch** and **change: caught on the change**.

catch easy (intransitive verb + adverb)

(Of woman) To fall pregnant easily.

catched (past tense/past participle of verb)

Possible past tense and past participle of **to catch**: 'He catched a cold after playin in the rain.' **Caught** is however more common. See also **ketched**.

caught on the change

See **change: caught on the change**.

cauli

See **colly**.

cawl (noun)

(1) Soup, especially the traditional Welsh **cawl cennin** – leek soup, which also contains other vegetables (potatoes, carrots, sometimes swedes and parsnips) and also lamb, occasionally beef.

(2) A mess. Sometimes means a difficult situation: 'They're in a real cawl with all that work they've got going on in their house', and 'He's made a real cawl of that job.' (Welsh for 'soup'.)

cawl cabbage (nominal phrase)

An awful mess: 'When 'er boys 'ad taken theyer boots and kit off after playin' football, it was all cawl cabbage in the kitchen! Awful awful it was! I don't know 'ow she can put up with it!' (Hybrid Welsh and English – 'cawl' is Welsh for soup.)

cawl cennin

See **cawl (1)**.

cawlach / cabolach (noun)

A mess, a mix-up, a botched job. The form **cawlach** is more commonly heard in the Western, Welsh-speaking part of the Wenglish area. (Welsh) See also **cawl** and **cawl cabbage**.

caws

See **bara caws**.

caws wedi pobi / caws weti popi (nominal phrase)

Roasted cheese, oven cooked. (Welsh) (Western Wenglish)

ceffyl blaen / ceffyl blân (nominal phrase)

A leading light, a prominent member, someone who takes the lead. Welsh for 'lead or front horse'. (Western Wenglish)

ceibo: shwd mae'n ceibo? (idiomatic expression)

How is work progressing? A polite enquiry as to how the work/job is coming on. (From colloquial Welsh, literally, 'How is the work with the **caib** going?') See also **caib**. (Western Wenglish)

cera (o 'ma)! / cer (o 'ma)! (intransitive verb, imperative)

This is the South Wales version of the command form of the Welsh verb 'mynd', 'to go'. 'o 'ma' means 'from here'. The expression means 'get on with you!', 'get away!' as a gentle, teasing sort of reproach.

cerdd dant (nominal phrase)

A type of Welsh musical arrangement where one melody is sung while another is played, usually on the harp, as accompaniment. (Welsh – literally 'tooth music')

chalk: miss a chalk (phrasal verb and idiomatic expression)

To fail to take advantage of an opportunity: 'I could 'ave signed up for the lottery syndicate the day before they won – I missed a chalk there, that's for shuer!' (Central and Eastern Wenglish)

chance (noun)

Opportunity: 'I aven't 'ad a chance to mend them tools yet.' 'It'll be a good chance frim, goin' to college.'

change: caught on the change (adjectival phrase, based on part participle)

Caught out by menopausal irregularities: 'They say that Mrs Isaacs 'ave 'ad another baby – she gorrw be neely 50, you know! Caught on the change she've been, poor dab.'

chapel losin / chapel loshin (nominal phrase)

A long-lasting hard sweet, generally mint-humbug or mint imperial, so called because they were often taken to chapel and surreptitiously eaten, possibly in order to sweeten the sermon! See also **llyfyr ime**. (Central Wenglish)

cheap tack (nominal phrase)

Goods of inferior quality.

cheek (transitive verb)

To be cheeky to, to be rude/insolent to: 'That kid is always cheekin the teachers!'

chesty

Arrogant, boastful: ''E's always so full of himself – real chesty 'e is!' (Central and Eastern Wenglish)

chew bread (phrasal verb and idiomatic expression)

To know well, be well acquainted with (often humorously): 'We know 'er well – 'er sister used to chew bread for ouer ducks.' (Central and Eastern Wenglish)

chick / chickeroo

See **click (2)**.

chimney

See **fire half way up the chimney.**

china (noun and adjective)

Ceramic, china, porcelain.

See also **tea: for all the tea in China and all the coal in Wales.**

chips: to have your/his etc. chips (phrasal verb)

To have reached a generally unsatisfactory conclusion in a matter with no prospect of improving the situation, to be beyond repair, to have 'had it': 'That sofa's had its chips – we'll have to chuck it out.'

choclate / chocolet / chocklet / choclet (noun)

Chocolate.

choier (noun)

Possible pronunciation of 'choir'. The 'ch-' is pronounced 'k' as in Standard English.

choke off (phrasal verb)

To put someone in their place, to rebuff: 'Fancy 'im tryin' to get us to sign them papers! I wasn't 'avin none of it, though: I choked 'im off straight away!'

choked (adjective)

Sad, so sad as to be unable to speak: 'I was choked when I 'eard about Bob's accident.'

choops

See **chwps.**

chopped (adjective)

Possible – and fairly widespread – pronunciation of 'chapped'.

chop sticks (phrasal verb)

To cut firewood.

chops (intransitive verb)

To talk a lot, to be very talkative.

chops (noun)

Mouth, especially of a talkative person.

chopsy (adjective)

Garrulous, talkative.

Chrissmass / Chrissmuss / Crissmass / Crissmuss (proper noun and adjective)

Christmas.

Chrissmassy / Chrissmussy / Crissmassy / Crissmussy (adjective)

Christmassy.

chutes / shutes / shoots (noun, plural)

Drainpipes, guttering. See also **troughing**.

chware teg

See **ware teg**.

chwilmentan

See **wilmentan**.

chwps / choops (adjective and adverb)

As an adjective it generally means 'in a mess', 'soggy' or 'mushy', e.g. 'Them tomatoes are chwps gone.'

As an adverb it means 'beyond measure', 'to excess', 'to an extreme degree' or 'in an extreme state'. There is often – but not always – a pejorative implication: 'Dai was knockin' 'em back alright – by the end of the night he'd drunk 'imself chwps.' However, 'The new baby's so lovely I could squeeze her chwps,' has no pejorative connotations. Here the meaning is something similar to the American expression 'I love her to death'.

ci (noun)

Dog. (Welsh)

ci bach (nominal phrase)

Puppy. (Welsh)

cidna bêns

See **kidney beans**.

ciff / cyff / kiff (adjective)

Not feeling very well: 'I thought he was over that pull, but he don't seem very ciff today agen.' Pronounced 'kiff'.

cigrette / cigurette (noun)

Cigarette

cil: to cil to cwat / to kill to cwat (phrasal verb and idiomatic expression)

See **cwat**.

cilbwt / crec (noun)

Ailment, illness: 'She's always goin' down the surgery – there's some crec with 'er all the time!'

classes

See **night classes**.

clatsien / clatshen (noun)

A blow, a smack: 'Stop it now, or I'll give you a clatsien!' (Welsh) (Western English)

clatsh on with (phrasal verb)

To progress with, to continue with, to get on with: 'I'd better clatsh on with it to get it finished before it comes to rain.' (From Welsh 'clatsio' – 'to hit', 'to strike')

clean: to go clean out of his/her head (adverb, used with phrasal verb)

To forget completely: 'I told 'er I'd 'elp 'er las' week but it went clean out of my 'ead this mornin'.'

clec / cleck (intransitive verb)

To gossip, to inform on someone: 'She's down 'er mother's agen, cleckin no doubt.' 'He've clecked on us – Mammy will be mad – we better watch out!' (From Welsh)

cleckerbox

A person who 'clecks' habitually.

clecs (noun)

Gossip: 'Tell me the clecs, then! What did that June 'ave to say?' **To carry clecs** means ' to carry tales'. (Welsh)

clecshun (noun)

Collection: 'E showed me 'is stamp clecshun the other day – 'e've got loads, aye!'

click (noun)

(1) Clique, intimate – possibly conspiratorial – group. People can be described as **clicky**.

(2) Generally in the plural, a term for 'head-lice': 'That girl's 'air was full of clicks.' Also called **chicks** and **chickeroos**.

click (intransitive verb)

To be successful, particularly in the context of a relationship: 'Our Billy seems to 'ave clicked with Mary, Jane Williams's daughter.' This seems to be the most common context in which this expression is used: 'He's clicking with her' means they are courting, dating, going out etc. 'It's clicked with him now' means 'the penny's dropped' or 'he's got the hang of it now'.

clicky (adjective)

Forming intimate, conspiratorial groups, somewhat hostile to 'outsiders'. From **click (1)**.

clip / flip (noun)

A blow, generally by way of punishment: 'A clip you'll get if you don't shut up!' Though less common, the word **flip** could be used in a similar way.

clobber (noun)

Clothing, belongings: 'I'll 'ave to go up 'is 'ouse to get all my clobber.'

clock: every ... like the clock (adverbial phrase)

With unfailing regularity: "e do never miss a game – 'ere every Wednesday like the clock, 'e is!'

clod (noun)

Praise, glory: 'I done all the 'ard work but she'll get the clod for it, you'll see'. Pronounced 'clode', with a long, pure 'o'. (Welsh) (mostly Western Wenglish)

clodges (noun, plural)

Lumps of grass with earth attached.

clodhoppers (noun, plural)

Heavy, clumsy boots or shoes.

clodhopping (adjective)

Big and awkward.

clonc (noun)

Gossip, chat. (Welsh) See also **clecs**.

close (noun)

The normal pronunciation of **clothes**.

clwb claddu (nominal phrase)

Savings for a funeral, literally, 'burial club'. (Welsh)

clwy

See **eli for every clwy**.

cmon! / c'mon! (verb imperative and interjection)

Possible spelling and pronunciation of **come on!**

cnec / cnecu (intransitive verb)

To fart. to break wind: 'What a niff! Have you just cnecked/cnecu'd?' Use of this Welsh form in Wenglish would be considered less offensive than the English equivalent.

cnec (noun)

A fart. Use of this Welsh form in Wenglish would be considered less offensive than the English equivalent.

coal

See **colse, small coal, glo mân** and **tea: for all the tea in China and all the coal in Wales**.

coat

See **whose coat is that jacket?**

cob (noun)

A knot in one's hair.

cob (transitive verb)

See **cop**.

cochen (noun)

A red-headed female. (Welsh) (mostly Western Wenglish)

cochyn / cwchyn (noun)

A red-headed person. (Welsh)

cock their nose (at) (phrasal verb)

To show disdain for, to reject arrogantly: 'After all I've done for them – all they can do is cock their noses!'

coddles (noun, plural)

Rubbish; nonsense: 'That's a load of old coddles you're givin 'er to eat!'

coggy handed

See **cack handed**.

cold

See **full of it (2)**.

colder: overcoat colder

See **overcoat colder**.

collery (noun)

Colliery, mine.

colly / cauli (noun)

The favoured local word for 'cauliflower'.

cols / colse (noun)

The burnt, or partly burnt, pieces of coal/ashes after a fire. This is an Anglicised Welsh word derived from 'coals'.

come (intransitive verb)

To get better: 'He's been real bard and under the doctor frages, but I think he'll come now.' (Welsh 'dod')

come back (nominal phrase)

(1) Repercussions, consequences: 'Was there any come back after you'd lost the keys?'

(2) See **nice: It's nice to go and nice to come back.**

come for (phrasal verb)

(1) (Of clothing or other items) To be capable of use by, generally as a hand-me-down: 'That suit of Jack's will come for Gary.'

(2) To come on behalf of: (e.g. in a shop) 'Can I help you?' 'I'm just lookin', thanks. I've come for my mother.' This does not mean 'I've come to collect my mother', rather 'I've come to look at some clothes on behalf of my mother.'

come off (phrasal verb)

To succeed: 'Dai'll be landed if that job comes off!'

come on to (phrasal verb)

To approach someone (to speak to them): 'I was down the village and guess 'oo came on to me!'

come out with (phrasal verb)

To say, to utter: 'You never know what 'e's goin' to come out with next!'

come over (phrasal verb)

To affect, to influence, to cause to behave out of character: 'I don't know what came over me – I should have known better than to trust him.'

come to (phrasal verb)

(1) To regain consciousness. The accent is placed on the word 'to'.

(2) See **when it came to.**

come to go (phrasal verb)

To take one's leave, to depart: 'It's time for us to come to go.'

come (on) to rain/snow (phrasal verb)

To begin to rain/snow.

come up a treat (phrasal verb)

To improve in appearance or quality: 'That door should come up a treat with a lick of paint.'

coming: no coming (nominal phrase)

No (likelihood of) improvement in health: ''Es 'ad a bad chest for weeks – 'e jus' can't shake it off – there's no coming to him.'

common (adjective)

Vulgar, morally reprehensible: 'There's common it is when people go to bingo.' The Welsh expression s**obor o gomwn/gomon** (very common indeed) is also used. 'You know what she's like – sobor o gomwn.'

compass (noun)

Note Wenglish use of singular – **a compass** – where Standard English would require 'a pair of compasses'.

compliance: out of compliance (prepositonal phrase)

No longer entitled: ''E's been off work for over six months – 'e's out of compliance for sick pay now.'

compo / composation (noun)

Compensation: 'He've 'ad 'is compo off the Coal Board for thar accident las' year.'

cone (noun)

A cornet (ice-cream).

conflab (noun)

An long and involved discussion.

conk (noun)

Nose, especially a big one.

considrate (adjective)

Considerate.

consid(e)rin(g) (present participle, used as an adverb)

When all is considered: 'The boys done aright, considrin!'

contrary (adjective)

Awkward and uncooperative. The accent is on the penultimate syllable.

convalassunt (adjective)

A possible pronunciation of 'convalescent'.

coom (noun)

Possible pronunciation of 'comb'.

coopy down (phrasal verb)

To squat, to crouch. (Central and Eastern Wenglish)

See **twti down, cwat/quat**.

conchy (noun)

In the Second World War, conchy was short for 'conscientious objector'. Later, anyone who made objections and acted bolshy (q.v.) tended to be called a conchy. A Welsh conchy was a disparaging term for a Welsh nationalist.

cop (noun)

Value, use, usefulness, utility, quality: 'That play wasn't much cop – borin' it was, I thought.' See also **up to much**.

Cop / Cwop (proper noun)

The Co-operative Society Store.

cop / cob (transitive verb)

To catch (e.g. a ball) or to receive punishment: 'You'll cop it from your father when he gets home!'

coppish (noun)

Flies, zip (on trousers). From 'codpiece'.

cord (noun)

String: 'We need to buy some cord to mark out the rows in the garden.'

'cordin(g) to (preposition)

According to, from what someone says.

corn beef (nominal phrase)

Corned beef.

cos / 'cos / coz (conjunction)

Because

costic (noun and adjective)

Caustic soda, caustic.

costiff (adjective)

Constipated.

cost him/her etc. somethin(g) (phrasal verb)

To be very expensive indeed: 'That new motorbike must 'ave cost 'im somethin', I bet.'

could: it could be a boy or it could be a girl (expression)

This obvious statement of fact concerning an impending birth was/is often uttered with deadly earnestness, as though it were some revelation. Similar sentences were/are also to be heard. It seems the speaker is thinking aloud.

couple: a couple of/a (nominal phrase, partitive usage)

A small, generally unspecified quantity of: 'Put me have a couple of pears, will you?'

course: a course (adverbial phrase)

Of course.

course: on a course of tablets / tabluts

See **tablets/tabluts: on a course of tablets/tabluts**.

courtin(g) (strong) (present participle + adverb)

Having a serious relationship, generally with marriage in prospect: 'Ouer Billy and Geraldine from Union Steet are courtin' strong – it'll be weddin' bells before long, I 'xpect.'

coz

See **cos**.

crachach (noun, collective)

Snobs, posh people, or people who like to think they are posh. (Welsh for 'the elite')

crackin(g) laughin(g) (present participles)

Laughing heartily. Also **roarin(g) laughin(g)**.

craxy (adjective)

Irritable: 'The baby's reeal craxy – 'e's keepin' us up all night!'

crazy on (adjective + preposition)

Crazy about.

create (intransitive verb)

To make a fuss about something: 'She was creatin' about me not turning up to the meetin' last week. I told 'er I couldn't 'elp it coz there was no buses, but it din make no difference to her!'

crec

See **cilbwt / crec**.

credit (transitive verb)

To believe: 'You wouldn't credit all he done for 'em – he done 'em proud, 'e did!'

cree (noun)

Place of safety in children's games.

creed: (the) creed / cryd: (the) cryd (noun)

Shivers, a fever, goosepimples: 'It gives me the creed when I think of it!', and, 'She's not feelin very well – she's got the creed.' (Welsh) (Western Wenglish)

crem (noun)

Crematorium.

crewse (noun)

Cruise.

crewshal

See **crueshal**.

crib (intransitive verb)

To complain, to moan: 'He's always cribbing about something or other – he's real miseryguts!'

crimpalene (noun)

Crimplene.

crimped up (adjectival phrase)

Slumped, stooping: "E 'obbles along all crimped up.'

Crissmass / Crissmuss (proper noun)

Christmas.

Chrissmassy / Chrissmussy (adjective)

Chritmassy.

cronjy / crogie (noun)

A very short haircut. (Central Wenglish)

crop (noun)

A haircut. 'Where's Dai, then? He've gone down Edlyn's for a crop.'

crosho (transitive and intransitive verb; also noun)

Wenglish for 'crochet': 'Nan have crosho'd a lovely shawl for the baby.'

crosst (transitive verb, past tense and past participle)

Past tense and past participle of 'to cross': 'I crosst the road down by Tesco's.'

crot / crwt / crotyn /crwtyn (noun)

A boy, young lad. The plural is **crots** or **crwts**. (Welsh)

croten (noun)

Girl, lass. (Western Wenglish)

crowd (noun, collective)

A company of people: 'We met a great crowd of people when we were on holidays', means 'We met a congenial group of people when we were on holiday.'

crown (transitive verb)

To hit by way of punishment, generally uttered as a threat only, after discovering a misdemeanour: 'I'll crown 'im when I ketch 'olt of 'im!'

crueshal / crewshal (adjective)

Crucial.

crwt / crwtyn

See **crot**.

cry like the rain (expression)

To cry a very much.

cry out for more (phrasal verb)

To demand urgently: 'The crowd couldn't get enough of 'im – they were cryin' out for more!'

cryd

See **creed**.

cubbud (noun)

Cupboard. See also **airin' cubbud**.

cuecummer (noun)

Possible spelling and pronunciation of **cucumber**.

cun (modal verb)

Possible spelling and pronunciation of **can**: 'You cun do it if you reelly try 'ard.'

cup

See **up for the cup**.

cup of tea in the hand (nominal phrase)

(To drink) tea in an informal manner, usually while chatting: 'Have a cup of tea in the hand while I put myself ready to go!'

curling box (nominal phrase)

A large scoop for carrying coal when a load had been delivered. The small coal was then **riddled** (sieved). The pieces that were too big to go through the sieve were called **curlings**.

cut

See **short: too short to cut cabbage**.

cut out

See **work cut out**.

cut sticks (phrasal verb)

To chop firewood.

cut up (adjectival phrase)

Upset, distressed: 'She was cut up when she 'eard the new about 'er mother!'

cute (adjective)

Crafty, cunning: 'She's cute like that – you never know what she's reelly plannin' to do.'

cwat / quat (intransitive verb)

To squat, to crouch. (from Welsh 'Cwato', meaning 'to squat'). See **twti down** and **coopy down**.

cwat / quat (transitive verb)

To hide, to conceal (from the Welsh 'cwato', meaning 'to hide'). The expression **to cil to cwat** may occasionally be heard. It draws on two Welsh verbs, 'cilio', 'to 'flee, to run away', and 'cwato', 'to hide, conceal oneself'. It means 'to run away and hide'.

cwchyn

See **cochyn**.

cwm (noun)

Valley. Not in general use for 'valley' but used to designate a specific steep bank or drop down to a river or stream: 'He's thrown it down the cwm.' 'He's kicked the ball over the fence down the cwm.' (Welsh)

cwrdd clecs (nominal phrase)

A gossiping session Literally, it means a 'gossip meeting'. (Welsh)

Cwrdd y Mawr (nominal phrase)

A series of special services in Welsh Baptist and other Welsh non-conformist chapels, involving one or more guest preachers. The services would be held for a number of consecutive days, perhaps beginning on a Sunday but continuing on weekday evenings. Although the form **Cwrdd y Mawr** was, and is, used in colloquial Welsh, the official designation of these services in Welsh is 'Cyrddau Mawr' (literally 'big meetings') or 'Cyrddau pregethu' ('preaching meetings/

services'). (Welsh) (Western Wenglish)

cwtch (noun)

(1) A place or spot, especially for storage. This can be made more specific by adding further descriptive words, e.g. **the coal cwtch** or **cwtch glo** (place where coal is stored) or the **cwtch under the stairs** or **cwtch dan stâr** (the glory hole or storage place under the stairs). Derived from the Welsh 'cwt'. Another example: 'It was awful down Swansea – I couldn't find a cwtch to park nowhere.' See also **bar cwtch**.

(2) A cuddle, hug, snuggle: 'Come by 'ere and 'ave a cwtch with mam!'.

cwtch (transitive and intransitive verb)

(1) To cuddlle and hug: 'Cwtch up to mam an' you'll be warm!'

(2) To lie down, as in a command to a dog: 'Cwtch!'. This could be a command to the dog to go to its **cwtch**. See **cwtch** (noun) (1).

(3) To conceal: 'Keep that cwtched in by there now – we don't want no-one to see it before it's finished.'

cwtyn y saint (nominal phrase)

A big mess: 'The place was like cwtyn y saint after they'd been 'ere!' (Welsh)

cyd-adrodd / cyd-atroth (noun)

Group recitiation in Welsh, a popluar item in eisteddfodau. (Welsh – mostly Western Wenglish)

cym bwyll

See **pwylla**.

Cym Cym (noun)

A somewhat jocular abbreviation of 'Cymry Cymraeg', meaning Welsh-speaking Welsh people. In use in Welsh-speaking circles in English (Wenglish) too, hence its inclusion here. Pronounced as in Welsh (i.e. like the English words 'come come'). The plural is **Cym Cyms**.

Cymanfa Ganu (nominal phrase)

A Welsh hymn-singing festival. Sometimes just called a **Cymanfa**. These were traditionally held around Easter (Good Friday or Eatser Monday) or sometimes at Whitsun, by the various nonconformist denominations. A Cymanfa Ganu is also held annually at the National Eisteddfod.

cymer bwyll

See **pwylla**.

cynhyrfu (transitive verb)

To annoy, to provoke, to work someone up: 'All that nonsense 'ave cynhyrfu'd me.' Note use of English verb endings on this Welsh verb. (Welsh, and pronounced as in Welsh)

cystadlu (intransitive verb)

To compete in an eisteddfod (Welsh): 'When did you cystadlu in the Urdd?' (Pronounced as in Welsh – Western Wenglish)

cythraul / cythral / cythrel (noun)

A devil. Also used in the interjection **beth cythrel!** (What the devil!) (Welsh)

D

da bo! (interjection)

All the best! Goodbye! (Welsh) (Western Wenglish)

dab (noun)

Creature, fellow. Generally used in the phrases **poor dab** (signifying pity or sympathy for the person referred to) and **lucky dab** (signifying that the person referred to has been fortunate in some way). 'Weddol 'e was yesterday but worse he's getting evry day, poor dab.' 'She's off on 'er 'olidays to Spain on the weekend, lucky dab!'

dab hand / dab 'and (nominal phrase)

An expert or skilled person: "E's a dab (h)and at 'ome brewin'!' See also **gamster**.

dadcu / tadcu / dacu (noun)

Grandfather. Usually heard in the soft-mutated form **dadcu** with accent on the last syllable. The 'u' is pronounced as in Welsh, rhyming with the '-ey' of 'key'. Sometimes further shortened to **dacu**, again with the stress on the last syllable. (South Wales Welsh)

dai-cap (noun)

A flat cap popular with miners in the past and still popular with many older males in the Valleys.

daioni / joni (noun)

Good. Used in the phrasal verb **to do daioni / joni**, meaning 'to do one good': 'Have a hot drink now – it will do you joni.' It is a direct translation of the Welsh 'gwneud daioni'. The form **joni** is another example of the marked tendency in colloquial South Wales Welsh for initial 'di-' to be pronounced as 'j'. (Welsh) (Western Wenglish)

dal (noun)

Substance, quality, durability, reliability. Generally used with an introductory negative such as 'not much' or 'no'. 'There's not much dal on this material,' means that there is not much substance to the material in question, or one cannot rely on it. 'There's no dal on him' means 'He's unreliable or unpredictable'. See also **depends**, which means much the same. (From the Welsh 'dal', meaning 'to hold', 'to keep')

dal(a) slac yn dynn (Welsh idiom)

To spin a job out, to twiddle one's thumbs, to kill time. Welsh idiom, literally 'to hold the slack tight'. (Western Wenglish)

dampers (noun)

Spoiling, extinguishing (of enthusiasm): 'That'll put the dampers on theyer plans, them.' See also **kybosh** and **moch / mockers / molochi**.

dandelion and burdock / dandylion and burdock (nominal phrase)

Dandelion and burdock, a popular flavour of 'pop' (q.v.), brown in colour.

danted / daunted (adjective)

Exasperated, frustrated, weighed down with troubles. Can sometimes mean 'weary': ''E must 'ave felt danted when they told 'im 'ow much more work 'e 'ad to do.'

dap (noun)

(1) A gym shoe or plimsoll.

(2) Shape and size: 'He's the same dap as his father exactly!' See also stamp.

(3) Something appropriate or pleasing: 'Just my dap, that kind of job!'

dap down (phrasal verb)

To put down carelessly: 'iss ovious why you've lost youer keys agen – you're always dappin' 'em down somewhere or other.'

daro! (interjection)

Dash it all! 'Daro, 'eve done it agen!' (Welsh)

daunted

See **danted**.

day

See **for every day, pass the time of day** and **give the time of day**.

dayry (noun)

Dairy, shop selling butter, eggs etc and often bread and cakes as well.

days

See **these days**.

ddrwg

See **o ddrwg i wâth**.

de!

See **Duw!**

deacon (noun)

An elder in a Welsh nonconformist chapel. Sometimes the Welsh form **diacon** (pronounced as in Welsh) is used. 'Ivor was deacon in Carmel when 'e was 23.' See also **blaenor**.

deal (intransitive verb)

To patronise (a shop etc): 'I don't deal in Idwal's no more — 'e's too pricey for me gone.'

dear (adjective)

Expensive. More commonly used than 'expensive' and generally even more used by the older generation. See also **pricey** and **salty**.

deceiving (adjective)

Misleading: 'It's deceiving – it looks lovely out but it's quite nippy reelly.'

decency (noun)

Common courtesy: 'They din 'ave the decency to tell us that the shop was closin' early, an' they knew we'd all been waitin' 'ere for ages.'

decent (adjective)

Suitable: 'I haven't got a decent pair of shoes to wear to the wedding.'

deck

See **all hands on deck**.

deep (adjective)

Deep-thinking (of person), abstruse, difficult to understand (of thing): 'The vicar's a lovely man but when he starts off, I can't follow 'im – he's too deep for me.'

deerane

See **diraen**.

deers (noun, plural)

The generally heard plural of **deer**, as opposed to 'deer' in Standard English.

deesive (noun and adjective)

Adhesive.

degree: one degree under (phrase used predicatively with 'to be')

Not feeling quite right, though not seriously ill.

depends (noun)

Dependability, reliability: Always intoduced by 'no'. 'There's no depends on 'er – she might come or she might not.' See also **dal**, which means much the same.

der 'ma / dere 'ma (verb imperative)

Come here. (South Wales Welsh)

deuce

See **jiws**.

deuce annwl

See **jiws annwl**.

dew!

See **Duw!**

dewrin

See **durin**.

di' (verb, past tense)

Possible pronunciation of **did**.

diabetus (noun)

Diabetes.

diacon

See **deacon**.

diawch! / diawch eriôd (i)! / diawch erioed (i)!

See **jawch!** and **myn jawl (i)!**

diawl!

See **jawl!** and **myn jawl (i)!**

diawl

See **jawl**.

diawledig / diawletic

See **jawledig**.

dibs (noun, plural)

Contribution, subscription.

dib up (phrasal verb)

To pay one's subscription, contribution or debts.

Dicky show your light (nominal phrase)

Formerly, a children's game, similar to hide-and-seek, using a candle and tin can.

didoreth (adjective)

Sloppy, slovenly, not proficient at household duties. A Welsh word but given extra meaning and currency in Wenglish. Perhaps not as common now as in the 'Classical' period of Wenglish.

different: not to know no different/diffrunt (phrasal verb)

To know no differently, not to know otherwise.

diffrunt (adjective and adverb)

Different, differently.

di-hwyl (adjective)

Unwell. (Welsh) 'Uncle Dai's feelin a bit di-hwyl today.' Note that the **h** is not normally pronounced. (Western Wenglish) See also **hwylus**.

diod fain

See **jovain**.

diflas (adjective)

Miserable. (Welsh) The expression: **as diflas as pechod**, literally 'as miserable as sin', is a good example of a Welsh-English hybrid.

dim ots (nominal phrase and interjection)

It doesn't matter, it makes no difference. 'Well, dim ots, if it's booked up, we'll 'ave to find somewhere else.' (Welsh) See also **no matter**.

dim perswâd / no perswâd (nominal phrase)

No persuading him/her, no changing his/her mind: 'Well you know what she's like – dim perswâd once she's got an idea in her 'ead!' (Colloquial South Wales Welsh) (Western Wenglish)

dim siâp (nominal phrase)

No method, inefficient, ineffective. The expression is generally used as a self-standing comment on someone's lack of organisation or inefficiency. The form **no shape** also exists. (Welsh) See also **di-siâp** and **shape**.

din (verb, past tense, negative, extended contraction)

Extended contracted form of **didn't**.

diniwed (adjective)

Harmless, innocent (Welsh): 'Diniwed 'e is – wouldn't 'urt a fly.'

dinner: like a dog's dinner (phrase used predicatively with 'to be')

Dressed up, made up. The expression implies a pejorative view of the person referred to. 'Dressed up like a dog's dinner, she was, for the Christmas party!'

dinnit? (verb, past tense, negative question form, extended contraction)

Possible pronunciation of **didn't it?**

diolch / diolch yn fawr / diolch i chi (noun/nominal phrase)

'Thanks', 'Thanks very much' and 'Thank you' respectively. (Welsh) See also **thank you fawr**.

di-olwg (adjective)

Ugly, not good-looking. This would be used in preference to the word 'ugly' to soften its meaning a little. (Welsh) (Western Wenglish)

diprish (adjective)

Slovenly, untidy. Obsolescent or obsolete.

diraen / diraan / diran / di-rân (adjective)

Not looking at its best, i.e having no **grain / graen** (q.v.): 'Them pillowcases are diraan with you gone.' (Welsh)

di-shaap

See **di-siâp**.

di-shift (adjective)

Awkward, unable to manage, disorganised (colloquial Welsh). (Western Wenglish) See also **shift**.

di-siâp / di-shaap (adjective)

Having no shape (q.v.) about him/it etc., awkward, disorganised. (Western Wenglish) See also **dim siâp**, **shape**, **shift** and **di-shift**.

diw!

See **Duw!**

diwedd y byd! (interjection)

Gosh! Goodness gracious! A mild Welsh interjection, changing 'Duw' (God) into the first element of 'diwedd'. The expression literally means 'end of the world!'. (Welsh) (Western Wenglish)

diwrin

See **durin**.

diws / deuce / dukes

See **jiws**.

diws annwl / deuce ynnwl

See **jiws annwl**.

do (noun)

Social function, party: 'We're 'avin a bit of a do for 'er sixtieth.'

do a bunk (phrasal verb)

To abscond: 'They say Bill Jenkins 'ave done a bunk – up to 'is years in debt 'e was by all account.'

do a Martha and Mary (phrasal verb)

One person doing all the work while the other sits back. From the Bible story of Mary and Martha being visited by Jesus.

do anything with him / her (phrasal verb)

To be able to approach/deal with someone – indicating someone's amenability: 'You can do anything with him.'

do daioni / do joni (phrasal verb)

To do one good: 'A good rest will do joni to you.' Direct translation of the Welsh 'gwneud daioni'. See **daioni / joni**.

do my 'ed in (phrasal verb)

To give cause for frustration, to exasperate, to annoy.

do up (phrasal verb)

To renovate, to improve, especially of a building etc.

dock (transitive verb)

To deduct: 'They docked 'im a tenner for turnin' up 'alf hour late.'

doctor

See **under the doctor**.

documunt (noun)

Document.

dodge (transitive verb)

To avoid: 'We left early to dodge the traffic.'

dodge (noun)

Trick, ruse. Generally used in the plural. 'There's no flies on 'im – 'e knows all the dodges.'

dog-end (noun)

Cigarette stub. See also **tod-end** and **nip**.

done in / done up (adjectival phrase)

Tired out. See also **bished**, **wanged out**, **fagged out** and **buggered up**.

don't look!

See **look**.

don't say stories! (verb, negative imperative)

Don't tell lies.

don't talk! (verb, negative imperative, and idiomatic expression)

This is a difficult phrase to translate into Standard English. It implies a sort of intimacy/solidarity with the person being addressed. It means something on the lines of 'I know what you mean (and agree with you) – there's no need to tell me more.' 'Don't talk! My son's always on the computer – can't get 'im off it!'

doolally / doolally tap (adjective/adjectival phrase)

Mad, touched, insane.

door

See **knock: the door was knocking, door went** and **stand on the door.**

door went (noun + verb)

Someone has knocked the door or rung the doorbell.

dosbarthu (transitive verb)

To share out, to distribute. 'We can dosbarthu the cards after we've had a cup a tea.' (Welsh, and pronounced as in Welsh) (Western Wenglish)

dose (noun)

A bout of illness: 'The 'ool famly 'ave 'ad a nasty old dose of flu.'

dose up (phrasal verb)

To take medicine/tablets: 'You dose yourself up – I don't want you to miss the show!'

doss (noun)

A nap, a sleep: 'I was so tired I had to have a little doss.'

double B (nominal phrase)

The big brass bass (musical instrument).

dout (transitive verb)

To extinguish a fire etc. The word – a contraction of 'do' and 'out' – exists in several other English dialects.

down (preposition)

The preposition is used to mean 'down in' or 'down towards': e.g. 'I seen him down Swansea last night'. See also **up**.

down below (adverbial phrase)

In one's private parts, withour being very specific. Often uttered confidentially, in hushed tones. See also **front passage** and **women's problems**.

down belows (nominal phrase)

Those parts of the anatomy 'down below' (q.v.).

down in the dumps (prepositional phrase)

Depressed, sad, dispirited.

drafers

See **dravers**.

drag (noun)

(1) A difficult journey: 'It's a long old drag up to Edinburro.'

(2) The **main drag** means the main road.

dragged up (adjective)

Rude, badly brought up. See also **brought up under a tub**.

dram (noun)

A small truck or wagon, generally running on rails, used in the colliery to transport coal from one underground location to another, to the surface or above ground. The Standard English is 'tram'.

drama (noun)

A theatrical production.

dramway / tramway / dramroad / tramroad (noun)

The railway line – and later the route of the railway line after the tracks had been lifted up and removed following the closure of a colliery – on which the 'drams' (q.v.) carrying coal ran. This could refer to an underground railway in a mine or tracks on the surface, especially those linking a mne to a yard or depot.

drash / trash (transitive verb)

To cut hedges. (Eastern Wenglish)

dravers / drafers / drovers (noun, plural)

Long underwear. (Welsh usage)

draw (transitive verb)

(Of shoes) To make one's feet hot and sticky: 'These new shoes do draw my feet awful.'

draw (intrabsitive verb)

(Of fire) To begin to light (by drawing in air).

drefl / drev(v)le (intransitive verb)

To dribble. 'The baby was dreflin' all over the shop.' Note again the use of English verb endings on the root of a Welsh verb (Colloquial Welsh 'dreflan' – 'to dribble')

drefl(s) / drev(v)le(s) (noun)

Dribble: 'The baby's bib was all drefls'. (Colloquial Welsh 'drefl' – 'dribble')

dressed up to the eyeballs

See **eyeballs**.

drev(v)le

See **drefl**.

drev(v)le(s)

See **drefl(s)**.

dribs and drabs: in dribs and drabs (adverbial phrase)

Bit by bit, in small quantities: 'They were still comin' in in dribs and drabs until about ninish.'

drovers

See **dravers**.

dry (adjective)

With a wry sense of humour, witty.

dry dinner (nominal phrase)

A dinner of meat and two vegetables served without gravy.

drysu (transitive verb)

To confuse, to fluster (Welsh): 'Comin 'ere and drysu-in' me – I can't abear it!' 'She drysu-ed me with all her talking.' (Note use of English suffixes on the root of the Welsh verb-noun – an excellent example of a hybrid!) (Western Wenglish) See also **moither**.

dukes

See **diws**.

dull (adjective)

Stupid, slow on the uptake. Note the expressions **as dull as a brush** and **as dull as a sledge**. See also **dwl**.

dull and backward (adjectival phrase)

Educationally subnormal, retarded. Once used – generally unkindly – to refer to remedial classes at school, those who attended them or those – in the opinion of the speaker – should attend/have attended them. This expression would be most politically incorrect these days.

dumps

See **down in the dumps**.

dunno (verb, present tense, negative)

A possible spelling and pronunciation of **don't know**.

durin / diwrin / dewrin (preposition)

During.

dust: the dust (noun)

Silicosis.

Duw! (interjection)

God! Variant forms/euphemisms include **de!**, **dew!**, **diw!**, **jew!** and **jiws!**

Duw (h)elp

See **pity (h)elp**

Duw mawr! (interjection)

Good God! (Welsh, literally 'Great God!')

dwl (adjective)

Dull, stupid, slow on the uptake. (Colloquial Welsh version of 'dull')

dwt / twt (noun)

A little one, especially a little child.

dwtty (adjective)

Tiny.

dwy 'wech am swllt (nominal phrase an Welsh idiomatic expression)

The literal translation of this Welsh idiom is: 'two sixpences for a shilling'. It is used to signify that one is not feeling very well. 'I'm not feelin' too good – I'm like dwy 'wech am swllt today.'

dynn

See **dal(a) slac yn dynn**.

E

early days yet (adverbial phrase)

In its early stages, thus difficult to predict the outcome: 'It's early days yet – there's a long way to go.'

'eart

See **heart**.

'eart an' soul

See **heart and soul**.

'eartburn

See **heartburn**.

east (noun)

Yeast.

east cake (nominal phrase)

Yeast cake.

easy (adverb)

With ease, with certainty; at least: 'There was easy 'undred down the club las'night – maybe 'undred an' twenty.' 'You should do 'at easy.'

eat: I could eat him (idiomatic expression)

An expression – not to be taken literally – indicating fondness for the the person – often a child – referred to: 'The new baby's so pretty – I could eat 'er!'

eat out of (h)ouse and (h)ome (phrasal verb)

To eat a great deal, possibly all the food in the house (though not really, of course!). 'Them boys are eatin' me out of 'ouse and 'ome.' 'Well they're growin boys, Mary. Our boys were the same.'

'eated (adjective)

Heated: 'They got 'eated swimming pool down 'e Afan Lido.'

'eavin(g)

See **heavin(g)**.

'eavy 'and

See **heavy hand**.

'eavy 'anded

See **heavy handed**.

'eavily fruited

See **heavily fruited**.

ecentric / esentric (adjective)

Eccentric, unusual, unconventional: 'That 'eadmaster 'ave gone eccentric.' The initial 'e' is pronounced 'ee'.

'ed

See **'ead**.

ee-ya boy! / 'ere boy! (interjection)

A command to a dog to 'Come here'. The tendency is to put great stress on the first syllable, which then becomes lengthened.

Echo: the Echo / Echoo: the Echoo (proper noun)

The South Wales Echo, a popular local evening newspaper.

egzackly

See **exackly**.

eisht! / highsht! (interjection)

Be quiet! (From Welsh 'ust')

eisteddfod / 'steddfod (noun)

An eisteddfod – a Welsh (and generally Welsh-language medium) competition of music, literature and the arts. The two primary eisteddfodau are the National, held annually in August, alternately in North and South Wales, and the Urdd Eisteddfod, organised by the Welsh League of Youth, held annually at the end of May/early June, again alternating between North and South Wales. The ceremonies include the crowning and chairing of the successful bard. The plural in Wenglish may be **eisteddfods** or the Welsh form **eisteddfodau**.

'eld up

See **held up**.

elder (noun)

Elderflower wine, a home-made herbal concoction, with medicinal and curative properties. It was even used to bathe wounds – of animals as well as humans! See also **jovain** and **small beer**.

eli for every clwy (nominal phrase)

Another Welsh-English hybrid. It is a partial translation of 'eli i bob clwy' – 'an ointment for every sore'. Used to describe someone who has a ready excuse to cover all eventualities: 'E won't tell you 'ow it 'append – 'e's got an eli for every clwy!'

'ell (noun)

See **(h)ell**.

else (adverb)

Otherwise, if not: 'You've got to give them somethin' to eat – they won't come else.'

elsolse (noun)

Health salts, such as Andrew's Liver Salts, used to cure indigestion and bilious attacks (q.v.).

'em (pronoun and demonstrative)

Them, those.

emty (adjective)

Empty.

emty down / empty down (phrasal verb)

To rain heavily.

'en (adverb)

Then.

end: no end (nominal and adverbial phrase)

Plenty, no shortage: 'There's no end of things you could do in the 'olidays.' 'The tablets 'ave 'elped no end.'

end of the quarter (nominal and adverbial phrase)

The period at the end of a quarter (three month period) when accounts need to be settled and the Co-op (q.v.) dividend was paid. See also **Pencwarter**.

England

See **up England way**.

enough to put years on you

See **put years on you**.

'eol rydd

See **(h)eol rydd**.

Epsom solse (nominal phrase)

Epsom salts. See also **elsolse**.

'er (pronoun)

Her.

'ere

Here. See also **'ee-ya boy!** and **by here**.

ergid (noun)

A blow – physical or emotional: 'She 'ad an ergid – 'er mother died sudden.' (Welsh) (Western Wenglish)

'ers (pronoun)

Hers.

'ese (demonstrative adjective and pronoun)

These.

esentric

See **ecentric**.

et (transitive verb, past tense and occasionally past participle)

Ate. The spelling reflects the way the word is always pronounced in Wenglish.

every ... like the clock

See **clock**.

every: for every day

See **for every day**.

every when?

See **evry when?**

everlasting: for everlasting

See **for everlasting**.

everything

See **into everything**.

evry (adjective)

Every.

evry when? (adverbial phrase)

How frequently? How often?

ewn (adjective)

Cheeky, pushy, over-familiar. (Colloquial South Wales Welsh, the Standard Welsh form being 'eofn')

'ewl rydd

See **(h)eol rydd**.

Ex Lax (nominal phrase)

A proprietory brand of laxative chocolate.

exackly / egzackly (adverb)

Exactly.

expect / 'xpect (intransitive verb in this usage)

To understand, to believe: 'I'll be back before ten, I 'xpect.'

'ey (pronoun)

They.

eye-ah!

See **hiya!**

eyeballs: dressed up to the eyeballs (adjectival phrase)

All dressed up: 'She went out dressed up to 'er eyeballs again.'

eyeful (noun)

(1) A good view of, especially something forbidden: 'I opened the bedroom door and got an eyeful – our Dai was dryin' after his bath!'

(2) A small amount: 'The food in that new restaurant looked lovely but you only got an eyeful of everythin' – I felt reely 'ungry after.'

eyes everywhere (noun + adverb)

Prying, spying, taking it all in: 'The rag-and-bone man 'ad eyes everywhere when 'e came in!'

eyes in the back of your head (nominal phrase)

Need to be vigilant. 'You gorrw 'ave eyes in the back of youer 'ead – you never know what them kids are goin' to do next.'

F

fach

See **bach**.

fagged out (adjectival phrase)

Tired out, exhausted. Perhaps derived from, or influenced by, the Welsh word 'diffygio' which means 'to be tired'. See also **wanged out**.

fair do's (nominal phrase)

Fair dues, fair play: 'Fair do's, 'e've done a tidy job b'there.'

fall

See **fell**.

famly / fam'ly (noun)

Family.

fancy (transitive and intransitive verb)

To think, believe, imagine: 'I'm not sure but I fancy he used to live up Caera.'

fancy man / fancy woman (nominal phrase)

Lover, 'bit on the side': 'They say Dai 'ave got a fancy woman livin' in Bridgend but I don't think he've got it in 'im!'

fault (noun)

Blame: 'I'll have the fault for that now, you'll see!' Direct translation of Welsh 'bai'.

favoright

Possible pronunciation of 'favourite'.

fawr

See **thank you fawr** and **diolch yn fawr**.

feable (adjective)

Ineffective, weak: ''E's feable gone – can't leave 'im to shift for 'imself.'

fear: for fear (conjunction and adverbial phrase)

In case: 'Take your mac for fear it will rain.' 'You'd better take your umbrella for fear.' See also **in case**.

fear: no fear (adverbial phrase)

In no way, certainly not: 'He can't come back here, no fear, not after the way 'e've been carryin' on!'

feathers

See **fuss: all fuss and feathers**.

feed / good feed (noun/nominal phrase)

A hearty meal: 'We'll have a good feed when we get back home.'

feedin(g) (adjective)

Nutritious.

feelin(g) (adjective)

Sympathetic: 'She was a great 'elp after Mam died – she's very feeling.'

feery

See **fiery**.

feet

See **shoes full of my feet**.

fell (down) (transitive verb, past tense)

Dropped: 'I fell my bus ticket on the pavement.' This usage is mostly restricted to the past tense. This expression is not especially common these days, **dropped** now having gained in popularity, following Standard English usage.

feller (noun) .

Man, person, fellow: 'Tidy feller he is, so they say.'

fellum / ffelwm (noun)

A whitlow. (Welsh – 'ffelwm')

ferian

See **san ferian**.

fetch (transitive verb)

To bring: 'Fetch it by 'ere now and I'll show you how to act it.' (i.e. make it work, operate it)

fetch him one (phrasal verb)

To hit him: 'I was getting' so mad I neely fetched 'im one!'

fetcher (noun)

A blow, a knock: 'John give 'im a real fetcher when he started to pick on 'im.'

fetchin(g) (adjective)

Attractive, nice-looking: 'She looks very fetchin' in 'er new dress.'

few

See **quite a few** and **tidy few**.

fewreeuss / fewrious (adjective)

Furious.

ffaeledig / ffeletic (adjective)

Failing, frail, doddery. 'Poor dab, she's very ffaeledig gone.' (Welsh) See also **torri: wedi torri** and **heneiddio: wedi heneiddio**.

ffedog / ffetoc (noun)

Apron: 'Leave me take my ffetoc off and 'ave a swill, an' then I'll be ready to go.' (Welsh – the spelling 'ffetoc' reflects the pronunciation in colloquial South Wales Welsh) (Western Wenglish) See also **brat** and **apron**.

ffelwm

See **fellum**.

ffetoc

See **ffedog**.

fidgety (adjective)

Fussy, pernickety, fastidious: "E've gone fidgety beyond – fussy's not the word!'

ffibledd (adjective)

Feable, fastidious, over-fussy: "E's ffibledd gone – 'e don't like it if somebody reads the paper before 'im.' (Colloquial South Wales Welsh) (Western Wenglish)

ffriwt

See **fruete**.

field

See **born in a field**.

fiery / feery (adjective)

Fiery. Sometimes pronounced 'feery'.

figure it out / figrit out (phrasal verb)

To guess, to discover, to find out: 'No-one told me nothin' about it so I 'ad to figrit out for myself.'

finger: with your finger in your mouth (adverbial phrase and idiomatic expression)

Not having enough money: 'If you want them new close, you'll 'ave to save up – you can't go shoppin' with your finger in your mouth!'

fine one (to talk) (nominal phrase)

Used ironically as a reproach to someone who is guilty of the same fault that he/she draws attention to in others: 'You're a fine one to talk – you'd be out playin' golf too given 'alf a chance!'

fire

See **put (4), fyer** and **on fire**.

fire half way up the chimney (nominal phrase)

A hearty fire in the grate.

first go off / first goin(g) off (adverbial phrase)

At the beginning, at the outset, at first: 'First go off 'e wasn't very good but 'e soon got the 'ang of it and by the end 'e was pretty good, fair do's.' See **last go off / last goin(g) off** and **last lap**.

first thing (adverbial phrase)

First thing in the morning, early in the morning, at the beginning of the (working) day: 'See you first thing.'

fit (adjective)

Assertive, not backward in coming forward, knowing one's way around the system: 'There's fit that Marion is – I don't know 'oo she thinks she is!' A possible variant is **fit for livin(g)**. See also **ewn**.

fit: neely had a fit

See **neely had a fit**.

fit to bust (adverbial phrase)

Very much indeed, extremely: 'The stories John was tellin' us about theyer 'olidays – 'e 'ad us laughin' fit to bust!'

fits: forty fits (nominal phrase)

Great fright, shock or annoyance: 'is mother neely 'ad forty fits when she 'eard he'd been chucked out a the scouts.' See also **haint**.

fix: in a fix (adverbial phrase)

In a predicament, in a difficult situation: 'She was in a proper fix when she found she didn't 'ave nothin' to wear to the party.'

fixed: how are you fixed? (exprression)

To what extent are you able? What is your situation (regarding)?: 'How are you fixed for a lift to the station?' and 'How are you fixed for teabags?' See also **how are you off for...?**

flag (noun)

(1) An unreliable person: 'He'a a bit of a flag – you can't depend on 'im at all!'

(2) A flagstone, a large piece of flat stone flooring.

flagstone

See **flag (2)**.

flannen (noun)

Flannel. Possibly influenced by the Welsh 'gwlanen' as well as the Standard English word. Obsolescent. (Central Wenglish)

flat (adjective)

Disappointed: 'I didn't want to tell her for fear she'd be flat.'

flat shot (nominal phrase)

A disappointment, something which fails to live up to expectations. It could refer to a shot of explosive in a mine which fails to detonate.

flatad (noun)

A disappointment. The Welsh ending '-ad', signifying the action of a verb-noun, is here added to the adjective **flat** (q.v.). 'She've 'ad a bit of a flatad – 'er son 'ave failed 'is exams.' (Colloquial South Wales Welsh) (Western Wenglish)

flea-bite (noun)

A very small quantity: 'I wunted a plateful but they only give me this little flea-bite.'

flicks (noun, plural)

Films, the cinema.

flighty (adjective)

Flirtatious, vain, provocative (generally of a woman).

flip

See **clip**.

fliwt (noun)

Possible spelling and pronunciation of **flute**, as in Welsh.

flummox (transitive verb)

To confuse, to bewilder. (adjective)

flush / flushed

With plenty of ready money: 'He can settle up now he's flush agen.'

fly (adjective)

Cunning, crafty, self-seeking.

flying

See **go flying**.

fooball / foo'ball (noun)

Possible spelling and pronunciation of 'football'.

food

See **get the food going** and **picky with food**.

food poisnin(g) (nominal phrase)

Food poisoning.

foot (noun, singular and plural)

As a unit of measurement, the plural is the same as the singular: 'He's over six foot tall.'

for (preposition)

As well as meaning 'for' as in Standard English, it can also mean 'on behalf of'. See **come for (2)** for an example of this usage in Wenglish.

for everlastin(g) (adverbial phrase)

Constantly: 'She's for everlastin' down 'er mother's for somethin' or other.'

for every day (adverbial phrase)

For use everyday, for routine use/wear: 'I got a new set of dishes for every day.' Similarly, **for round the house, for the lorry**, etc.

for fear (conjunction and adverb)

In case, lest. See also **fear**.

for shame on you!

See **shame**.

for you

See **there's... for you**.

force

See **full force**.

forestry (noun)

Wood, forest.

fork out (phrasal verb)

To pay out, to pay up: 'You'll have to fork out a tidy bit to get them windows fixed.'

forrid / forred (noun)

Wenglish pronunciation of 'forehead'.

forrin (adjective)

Foreign.

forriner (noun)

Foreigner.

forty: forty fits

See **fits: forty fits**.

forty winks (nominal phrase)

A snooze, a little sleep: 'If you can 'ave forty winks on the bus, you won't be so tired when you get to London.'

forward / forwud (adjective)

Advanced (e.g. of child), or presumptuous: 'Nigel is very forward for 'is age – 'e come top in the 'ool class.' See also **knowing**.

fours-and-a-half (noun and expression of shoe size)

Adding an 's' to the number is the way shoe sizes are generally expressed in

Wenglish. With half sizes, **and-a-half** is generally added.: 'I tried fours-and-a-half but they were a bit tight so in the end I got fives instead.'

fox (transitive verb)

To confuse (deliberately): 'You know what these doctors are like – they do fox you with science!'

fra (contraction of preposition + indefinite article)

Possible spelling and pronunciation of **for a**.

frall (contraction of preposition + adjective or indefinite pronoun)

Possible spelling and pronunciation of **for all**.

frazzle: into/to a frazzle (prepositional phrase)

To cinders and, figuratively, to the extreme: 'The bacon was burnt to a frazzle.' 'Mary worked herself up into a real frazzle!'

frem

See **frum**.

frens / frenz (noun, plural)

Possible spelling and pronunciation of **friends**. See also **not friends**.

frer (contraction of preposition + pronoun)

Possible spelling and pronunciation of **for her**.

fresh (adjective)

(1) New, additional: 'You don't want to catch a fresh cold just as you're getting better.'

(2) Cool, cold: 'It's fresh this morning after that frost.'

frew (contraction of preposition + pronoun)

Possible spelling and pronunciation of **for you**. See also **frue** and **for you**.

fried potatoes (nominal phrase)

Boiled potatoes, usually left-overs after a dinner, often sliced, and fried in a frying pan.

friends

See **not friends**.

frightened of (past participle used as adjective)

Concerned about: 'What I'm frightened of is that the dog could run onto the road.'

frim (contraction of preposition + pronoun)

Possible spelling and pronunciation of **for him**.

frit (contraction of preposition + pronoun)

Possible spelling and pronunciation of **for it**.

front (noun)

Front of house, front garden: 'The kids was playin in the front.' See also **back**.

front horse

See **ceffyl blaen**.

front passage (nominal phrase)

The vagina (in quasi medical parlance), as opposed to the **back passage** (q.v.). See also **down below** and **women's problems**.

frue (contraction of preposition + pronoun)

Possible spelling and pronunciation of **for you**. See also **for you**.

fruete / ffriwt / fruit (noun)

Fruit. The spellings reflect the pronunciation of the word in Wenglish. See also **heavily fruited** and **tin fruete**.

frum / frem (contraction of preposition + pronoun)

Possible spelling and pronunciation of **for them**.

frump (intransitive verb)

To sulk: 'David do go to frump awful if 'e can't get 'is own way – I think iss 'is mother's fault, bendin' over backwards to suit 'im she've been ever since 'e was a little dwt!'

fry (noun)

Liver: 'I'll get some pig's fry when I'm in the butcher.'

full

See **hands full** and **shoes full of my feet**.

full force (adverbial phrase)

With all one's strength: 'He hit his head full force on the corner of the mantelpiece.'

full fuss (adverbial phrase)

With great enthusiasm: 'She was tellin' us about 'er trip full fuss.' 'They were full fuss, ready to go on theyer 'olidays.'

full of beans (adjectival phrase)

Full of energy.

full of himself (adjectival phrase)

Full of self-importance, arrogant. See also **chesty**.

full pelt (adverbial phrase)

At full speed: 'She ran out of the 'ouse full pelt.'

funeral

See **rise (2)**.

funny (adjective and adverb)

Odd(ly), peculiar(ly), unconventional(ly): 'He's a funny ol' man' could mean 'He is an amusing senior citizen' but is much more likely to mean 'He is a rather strange chap, I don't really approve of him.' 'He's funny in the 'ead gone!' As an adverb it tends to mean 'in a peculiar way': 'She done it a bit funny'. See also **stick: funny old stick**.

furry (adjective)

Furry. Generally pronounced with a short 'u' and heavily trilled 'rr'.

fuss

See **full fuss**.

fuss: more fuss than the worth of it (nominal phrase)

Not worth the bother: 'It takes me ages to get everythin' ready for 'em – it's more fuss than the worth of it!'

fuss: all fuss and feathers (nominal phrase)

Making a great fuss about something: 'She's all fuss and feathers about goin' to the party!'

fussed on (adjectival phrase)

Keen on: 'I'm not fussed on peas gone.'

fyer (noun)

Wenglish pronunciation of **fire**, with two distinct syllables. See also **on fire**.

G

gafael / gavull / gavel (noun)

Substance, quality: 'There's not much gavel on this material.' It can also refer to female flesh in a voluptuous sense: 'I do rather a woman with a bit of gafael on her, not one of them skinny pieces.' (Welsh, meaning 'grasp' or 'grip'.)

gafferalier / gaffer haulier / gaffer halier (noun/nominal phrase)

The boss, the man in charge. From the term 'for the man in charge of pit ponies at a mine.'

gain (intrasnitive verb)

Improve, get better, making progress (e.g. of health). 'Gaining he is after 'is pull.' Also heard in the form **gaining ground**. See also **lose/losing ground**.

gâm (noun)

Courage: "Na gâm!' means 'What courage!' 'What confidence!' See also **macu gâm**. (Colloquial South Wales Welsh)

gambo (noun)

(1) a home-made cart, often incorporating old pram wheels. This was also sometimes called a **bono** (short for 'boneshaker') or a **bogey**.

(2) a banger of a vehicle.

gammy (adjective)

Lame: 'I can't go very quick with my gammy leg.'

gamster (noun)

An expert, a **dab hand** (q.v.). Pronounced as in Welsh. (Western Wenglish)

gangarene (noun)

Gangrene.

gare / gêr / gear (noun)

Possible spelling and pronunciation of **gear**: 'This engine's got four gares.' 'Shift that gare out of the garidge, will you?' The spelling 'gêr' is that which is standard in Welsh.

garidge (noun)

The usual Wenglish pronunciation of **garage**.

gather (intransitive verb)

(1) To form an abscess.

(2) To meet.

(3) (Of cloth, fibre etc) To form a lump, to run.

gathering (noun)

(1) An abscess.

(2) A meeting.

gear

See **gare**.

genral (adjective and noun)

General. **The Genral** often used to refer to Cardiff General (now Central) Station.

genrally (adverb)

Generally, in general, usually.

gêr

See **gare**.

gerraway! (interjection)

Possible spelling and pronunciation of **get away!** The expression indicates incredulity or surprise.

gerrew/gerrue / gerrer / gerrim / gerrus /gerrem/gerrum (contractions of verb + pronoun)

Possible spellings and pronunciation of **get you, get her, get him, get us** and **get them** respectively, with intervocalic 't' pronounced as a trilled 'r'. Not found among all speakers.

gerrin! (contraction of verb, imperative + adverb)

Possible spelling and pronunciation of **get in!**

gerrw (contraction of verb + preposition)

Possible spelling and pronunciation of **get to.**

get about (phrasal verb)

To go/move out and about: 'He's gettin' on a bit now and 'e can't get about like 'e used to.'

get him/her (transitive verb + pronoun)

To find someone in a sociable/amenable mood, as in: 'There's no depends on if she'll talk to you or no – you never know when you've got her.'

get the food goin(g) (phrasal verb)

To begin to cook a meal: 'The kids will be in from school now in a minute so I better get theyer food goin'.'

gib

See **jib** (verb).

gibbons

See **shibbwns**.

giblet soup (nominal phrase)

A horrible and evil-smelling concoction made from the giblets of poultry, especially the Christmas turkey. See also **afu las**.

girl

See **could: it could be a boy or it could be a girl** and **old girl**.

gis / giss (contraction of verb, imperative + pronoun)

Give us, give me.

giunt (noun and adjective)

Giant.

give (transitive verb)

(1) To punish (or at least threaten with punishment): 'I'll give you – tramplin' my flower bed and I only planted seeds there yesterday!' **What for** is sometimes added. 'I'll give you what for – dirtyin' them clean towels!'

(2) To forecast, especially the weather: 'I seen the weather forecast on the box – they're giving rain today agen.' **To promise** is also used in the same sense.

(3) To give (as an indication of preference): 'Give me cotton sheets any day!'

give in (phrasal verb)

(1) To admit: 'She won't give in even though the teacher knows she done it.'

(2) To surrender, to give up: 'I give in – I don't know 'oo done it.'

give him what for

See **know what for**.

give the once over (phrasal verb)

To scrutinise, to check over: 'I didn't have the chance to give it the once over.'

give the time of day (phrasal verb)

To bother speaking to: 'That old Rowena's ignorant sometimes – she wouldn't even give Joan the time of day this morning down the village.'

giving in (nominal phrase)

Surrendering, yielding, conceding: 'There was one 'ell of a row but she atto do the giving in in the end.'

glad of that (adjectival phrase)

Pleased to have that: 'I was glad of my umbrella when it started to rain.'

glad and sorry: on the glad and sorry (adverbial phrase)

On hire purchase: 'Glad to have it, sorry to have to pay for it.' See also **never-never: on the never-never.**

glassouse

See **greenouse**.

glaw mân (nominal phrase)

Drizzle. 'What was the weather like?' 'Oh, it wasn't too good, old glaw mân most of the time.' (Welsh, literally 'small rain') (Western Wenglish)

glo mân / glo mên (nominal phrase)

Small coal. These tiny pieces of coal were sometimes bound together with cement, formed into **pele** (q.v.) and used as coal. (Welsh – literally 'small coal') (Western Wenglish)

glowty (noun)

Cowshed. (Welsh – Western Wenglish)

glycereen (noun)

The Wenglish pronunciation of 'glycerine'.

go (intransitive verb)

(1) To get to the point (that), to become: 'I'm gone I just don't care no more!' The word order can often be different in Wenglish, mirroring the Welsh 'mae e / hi / nhw … wedi mynd': e.g. 'e's all ffibledd (q.v.) gone.' In such sentences **gone** is added at the end of the phrase to complete its meaning.

(2) To go to: 'Swansea you're goin', is it?' Note use of the verb without the preposition to. This again echoes Welsh usage.

(3) To become unserviceable, to deteriorate: 'My sandals 'ave gone.' (my sandals are no longer wearable). 'The lasric 'ave gone in these pants.'

(4) See **door went**.

(5) See **nice: it's nice to go and it's nice to come back**.

See also entries under **went**.

go by (phrasal verb)

To rely on: 'You can go by him any time.'

go flying (phrasal verb)

To fall awkwardly, to lose one's footing and fall headlong: 'Went flying, I did – I was lucky not to break a leg.'

go in for (phrasal verb)

To decide to proceed with/embark upon: 'He worked for a year in the bank year before decidin' to go in for the law.'

go lost (phrasal verb)

To get lost, to lose one's way: 'They'll be wonderin' where I am – they'll think I've gone lost!'

go on its worse/worst

See **worse / worst: go on its worse/worst**.

go pregnant (phrasal verb)

To get pregnant, to fall pregnant.

go through me/you etc. (phrasal verb)

To upset deeply, to move to pity: 'It went through me when I saw that cut 'e 'ad on 'is 'ed.'

go to come back (phrasal verb)

To go as soon as possible in order to get it over with and then be in a position to return home, generally to begin/resume something else. cf **to come to go**.

God (h)elp

See **pity (h)elp**.

Gog (noun)

Person from North Wales: 'You know that Elsie – the one 'oo married a Gog – she've been rushed into hospital in Bridgend, so they say.' (From Welsh 'Gogleddwr', meaning 'Northerner'.)

goin(g)

See **go (3)** and **thass going**.

golden raisley

See **raisley**.

gomwn / gomon

See **sobor o gomwn** listed under **common**.

gone

See **go (1)**.

gone (past participle, used as adjective)

Vanished: 'When I went to 'unt for it agen – there it was – gone!'

gone clean out of his/her head

See **clean**.

gone lost

See **go lost**.

gonna / gonnw (contraction of verb, present participle and preposition)

Possible spelling and pronunciation of **goin(g) to**.

good: a good... (adverbial phrase)

Definitely, certainly, at least: 'There was a good thirty in there, I'd say!'

good: as good as look at you (phrase)

Without any qualms: 'Iss a bit dodgy in Brazil – some a them would rob you as good as look at you – you gorrw be careful, like.'

good: like a good 'un (adverbial phrase)

Up to his usual standard, as well as ever: "E 'ad a couple a bad games but 'e's playin' like a good 'un agen now.'

good boy (nominal phrase)

My lad: 'Now lissen 'ere good boy – he've been doin that job for years and he knows what he's talking about.'

good feed (nominal phrase)

A hearty meal: 'We'll have a good feed when we get back home.'

good job (nominal phrase)

A well-paid job: 'His wife has got a good job in 3M's.'

good job (adverbial phrase)

It's just as well: 'Good job you brought your mac – it turned out nasty, din it?'

good scholar (nominal phrase)

A child doing well at school.

good with his hands (adjectival phrase)

Skilled at DIY/plumbing/carpentry/building etc.

goods (noun, plural)

Groceries, provisions: 'I'm goin down the Cop for the goods.'

goosegogs (noun, plural)

Gooseberries.

gorra (contraction of verb/verb, past participle + indefinite article)

Possible spelling and pronunciation of **got a**.

gorrer, gorrim, gorrue/gorrew, gorrus, gorrem (contractions of verb + pronoun)

Possible spellings and pronunciations of **got her, got him, got you, got us, got them** respectively.

gorrin (contraction of verb + preposition)

Possible spelling and pronunciation of **got in**.

gorrw (contraction of verb + preposition)

Example of extended contraction. A possible spelling and pronunciation of **got to**.

gotcha / gotchew / gotchue (contractions of verb + pronoun)

Possible spellings and pronunciation of **got you**.

gottw (contraction of verb + preposition)

Possible spelling of **got to**.

graate

See **great**.

grân / graen

See **grain** and **grôs grân**.

grain / graen / grân (noun)

Clean and attractive appearance (e.g. of clothing, washing etc.), good quality: 'There's no grân on 'er washin'.' 'There'a a bit of grân on that work.' In Western, Welsh-speaking Wenglish areas, the pronunciation 'Grân' is usual. See also **grôs grân**. (Welsh 'graen')

gramother

See **granmother**.

grand (adverb)

Splendidly, very well: 'He've learnt to do that grand now.' 'He've come on grand after the opereshun.'

granfar / granfer (noun)

Grandfather.

granmother / gramother (noun)

Grandmother.

granson (noun)

Grandson.

grass'opper / grassopper (noun)

Grasshopper.

grate

See **great**.

great / graate / grate / grêt (adjective and adverb)

Splendid, very good: 'We had a great time – we're really glad we went!' 'He's comin' on great after 'is fall.' The vowel is a long pure 'e', without any hint of diphthongisation.

greenouse / glassouse (noun)

Greenhouse.

Grist

See **Iesu Grist**.

grizzle (intransitive verb)

To complain, to moan: 'Them two are always grizzlin(g) about something or other – they're a proper pair.'

groes graen

See **grôs grân**.

grofen / groven (noun)

Crackling (of pork): 'I love the grofen – it's the tastiest part of the hool joint!' (Welsh 'crofen', meaningr 'crust' or 'crackling'. The soft-mutated form is used in Wenglish.)

grôs grân / groes graen (adverbial phrase)

Against the grain, against one's principles: 'What he did was a bit grôs grân – he should be more considerate.' See also **grain**. (Welsh) (Western Wenglish)

groven

See **grofen**.

gul / gull (noun)

Girl, woman: 'What shoes are you lookin' for?' 'You know gul, the ones I was wearing on Saturday.' Quite often used in familiar address to an adult female.

gummel: to get my/his etc. gummel up (phrasal verb)

To be prepared and be in the right frame of mind: 'I'll get my gummel up and sort that 'eadmaster out!'

guts (noun)

A greedy person: ''E's a real guts – 'e just keeps stuffin' 'is face all the time!'

gutsful: to have a gutsful (phrasal verb)

To have more than enough. Slightly less polite than **bellyful**.

gweddol

See **weddol**.

gweinidog / gweinitoc (noun)

Minister (of religion). (Welsh) (Western Wenglish)

gwli (noun)

The back lanes of Valleys houses, especially terraces: 'We was playin' in the gwli an' John fell an' cut 'is leg baad.'

gwnna / gwnnw (contraction of verb, present participle and preposition)

Possible spelling and pronunciation of **goin(g) to**.

gwt / cwt (noun)

Queue. Literally 'tail' in Welsh. See **shark**.

gyp

See **gip**.

H

Note that initial 'h' is not generally pronounced in Wenglish, except for the name of the letter – 'Haitch' – and words and expressions which contain it, such as 'Haitch P sauce' and 'Haitch TV'.

Words beginning with 'h' could also be spelled with an apostrophe to show the non-pronunciation of the aspirate 'h', though this is not necessary if one bears in mind the pronunciation rule mentioned above. Bracketed (h) in the list below indicates that spellings without 'h', or with an apostrophe in place of 'h', are also permissible.

(h)ad: to be (h)ad (verb, passive)

(1) To be deceived, duped, tricked: 'We've been had – they charged us full whack for the meals, and they should 'ave been 'alf price by rights.'

(2) To be available: 'I went to buy some battries but there was none to be 'ad in the shop.'

(h)aint (noun)

A fit: 'She'll have a haint when she ses the state of this place!' (Welsh, and pronounced as in Welsh) (Western Wenglish)

(h)air: to (h)ave (h)is (h)air off (phrasal verb)

To be angry: 'You're uncle will 'ave 'is 'air off when 'e sees what you done to 'is geraniums!'

(h)air: to keep your (h)air on (phrasal verb)

To keep calm, not to lose one's temper.

(h)alf

See **boy narf**.

(h)alf (h)is time (adverbial phrase)

Much of the time: ''Alf 'is time 'e's down the pub.'

(h)alf: on (h)alf (adverbial phrase)

Halfway through, in an incomplete state, unfinished: 'I had to leave the paintin' on 'alf while I went to fetch the kids.' (Welsh 'ar hanner')

(h)alf 'n' (h)alf (adverbial phrase)

So-so, middling: 'How was the trip?' 'Oh, half 'n' half.'

(h)alf soak / (h)alf soaked (adjectival phrase)

Lackadaisical, lacking in urgency and concentration: 'He's proper 'alf soaked – too slow to catch a cold!'

(h)alf tidy (adjectival phrase)

Quite good, quite acceptable. See **tidy**.

(h)alf: to (h)alf murder

See **murder**.

(h)ammer (transitive verb)

To thrash, to beat convincingly: 'City should hammer Port Vale in the Cup.'

(h)ammer: that's the (h)ammer (expression)

'That's the way! You've got the right idea!' An expression showing approval.

(h)ammer and tongs (adverbial phrase)

Violently, hurriedly: 'They went at it hammer and tongs – they wanted to finish the job before the match.'

(h)ammerin(g) (noun)

A thrashing a convincing beating: 'The Swans give Wrexham an 'ammerin' in the Welsh Cup.'

(h)and

See **turn his hand** and **lend (a) hand**.

(h)ands and knees: on my (h)ands and knees (adjectival phrase)

(1) Begging, asking earnestly: 'On my 'ands and knees I was to 'em but they'd made up theyer mind already, it was ovious!'

(2) Reduced to a state of desperation.

(h)ands

See **good with his hands** and **all hands on deck**.

(h)and's turn (nominal phrase)

Work, participation in a collaborative job: 'He's a lazy old bugger – never does (a) 'ands turn 'round the 'ouse.'

(h)andy (adjective)

Skilful, good at D.I.Y.: 'He's 'andy round the 'ouse – 'e've fitted the kitchen and done all the letrics an' plummin'!' See also **good with his hands**.

(h)anes (noun)

Story, tale, report: 'I told 'im the hool hanes of our trip to London.' (Welsh for 'story' or 'history')

(h)ang on (phrasal verb)

(1) To wait.

(2) To linger to continue (e.g. of cold, cough, illness): 'My cold's been hanging on for weeks.'

(h)anky (noun)

Handkerchief.

(h)a'puth / (h)a'porth (noun)

A halfpennyworth, a very small quantity of.

(h)ard: to (h)ave it (h)ard (phrasal verb)

To have a difficult time of it: 'She've 'ad it 'ard, specially since buryin''er 'usbunt.'

(h)ard lines (nomninal phrase and interjection)

Unfortunate, unlucky; (as interjection) Bad luck! Unlucky!: 'It's hard lines on City, they should 'ave won that game easy!' 'Hard lines! You'll 'ave to try agen.'

(h)ave to / afto / affto (verb + preposition)

Have to, must.

(h)ave someone on (phrasal verb)

To tease, to pull someone's leg: 'You're 'avin' me on, aren't you? You can't be serious!'

(h)ave up (phrasal verb)

To summon to appear before the magistrate/judge: 'He was 'ad up for speeding.' See also **summons**

(h)awk (transitive verb)

To carry with difficulty: 'I had to hawk all the stuff up the hill to my mother's.' See also (h)ump.

(h)ead: bear with a sore (h)ead

See **bear with a sore head**.

(h)ead

See **off his head, do my 'ed in, cool head, funny in the head** (listed under **funny**), **not right in the (h)ead** and **wash my head.**

Glossary

(h)ead: to go clean out of (h)is/(h)er (h)ead

See **clean**.

(h)ead sharang (nominal phrase)

The boss, the chief.

(h)eaps (expression of quantity)

A large number or quantity: 'There was 'eaps a food left after the party.'

(h)eaps (adverb)

Much: ''E's 'eaps better now after 'is opereshun, thanks.'

(h)eapsa (expression of quantity)

Lots of. Possible spelling and pronunciation of **heaps of**.

(h)ear

See **never hear the end of it** and **year**.

(h)(e)art

Desire, motivation: 'I din 'ave the 'eart to mow the lawn after we landed back from ouer 'olidays.'

(h)eavin(g (adjective)

Very crowded: 'It was 'eavin' down Swansea on Saturday – iss better to go in the week when it's quieter.'

(h)eavy hand (nominal phrase)

A difficult time: 'She's 'avin' a 'eavy 'and with 'er kids – Dawn in 'ospital an' Darren with a broken leg!'

(h)eavy handed (adjectivall phrase)

Liberal with, taking a lot of: 'I must have been a bit too heavy handed with the salt – there's a nice taste on the gravy but it's too salty.'

(h)eavily fruited (adjectival phrase)

A cake containing a lot of dried fruit.

(h)ec (intransitive verb)

To hop. (From Welsh: 'hec' means 'a hop', while the verb-noun is 'hecian')

(h)eld up (adjectival phrase)

Delayed: 'We was 'eld up in the traffic.' See (h)old up.

(h)ell

Hell. Commonly found in combinations such as 'ow the 'ell?, what the 'ell!, and so on. See also **(h)ope in (h)ell** and **play (h)ell**.

(h)elp: pity (h)elp

See **pity (h)elp**.

(h)eol rydd / (h)ewl rydd (nominal phrase)

Freedom to act, carte blanche: 'You'll 'ave 'ewl rydd to do what you like on the weekend.' (Welsh) (Western Wenglish)

(h)eneiddio: wedi (h)eneiddio / wedi (h)eneiddio'd (adjectival phrase formed from Welsh intransitive verb)

Having aged, having got older. While the first variant is pure Welsh, the second is a hybrid, incorporating an English past pasticiple ending: 'She's wedi heneiddio'd – she 'ave reely gone to look old now.' (Western Wenglish)

(h)ere's (adverb + verb, functioning as a prepositional phrase)

What terrible: 'Here's weather – the rain 'asn't looked like stoppin' all day!' See also **there's**.

(h)ewl rydd

See **(h)eol rydd**.

(h)ewn

See **ewn**

(h)igh up (adjectival phrase)

Occupying a senior position: 'He's very high up in the Coal Board.'

(h)ighly (h)onoured (adjectival phrase)

Privileged, fortunate: 'I was highly honoured – she let me go into the parlour!'

(h)ightth (noun)

Height: 'There must be a good heightth on that shed of theyers – ten foot at least, I reckon.'

(h)ightth of fashion (nominal phrase)

The pinnacle of elegance. See also **rage: all the rage**.

(h)ikey (adjective)

Conceited, stuck up: 'Hikey piece that Lilian!'

(h)ilt

See **bev(v)ied up to the (h)ilt**.

(h)inder (transitive verb)

To hinder, to delay, especially a housewife in the middle of her tasks: 'That Jinnie called here at leven and hindered me.' 'Don't 'inder me now – I've got a lot of work to do!'

(h)iraeth (noun)

Longing, homesickness (Welsh). 'Hiraeth' has passed into the English language as a word which is not 100% translatable into English. 'I 'ad a pull of 'iraeth for 'ome.'

(h)it (h)im sick (phrasal verb)

To hit violently (or to threaten to do so): 'There's times I could 'it 'im sick.'

(h)iya! / eye-ah! (interjection)

Hello! Probably the most commonly heard greeting these days having to some extent replaced **shw mae?**, **'owbe?** and **awright?**

(h)obble (noun)

Moonlighting, illicit (jobs of) work: ''E's been doin' some hobbles, I know, even though 'e's sposed to be on sick with 'is back.'

(h)og

See **(h)ool (h)og**.

(h)old up (nominal phrase)

Delay: 'There was a big 'old up comin over the bridge.'

(h)old up (phrasal verb)

To delay: 'I don't want to 'old you up.'

(h)olidays (noun, plural)

The plural is generally used in Wenglish whereas the singular is more common in Standard English: 'Where are you goin on your 'olidays this year, then? Down Trecco agen?'

(h)ollo (adjective and adverb)

As adjective, 'hollow'; as adverb 'thoroughly': 'Next time, we'll beat 'em 'ollo!'

(h)olt (noun)

Hold, grip. It is used mostly with the verbs **to ketch** or **to catch**. 'I couldn't ketch 'olt of 'im – 'e was too fast for me.' 'Ketch 'olt of this plank by 'ere for me, will you?' See also **ketch**.

(h)oneycoom (noun)

Possible spelling and pronunciation of 'honeycomb'.

(h)onoured

See **(h)ighly (h)onoured**.

(h)ool / whool (adjective)

Whole, entire. See also **(h)ool (h)og**.

(h)ool (h)og / whool (h)og (adverbial phrase)

All the way, to the full extent.

(h)ool(h)(e)arted / whool(h)(e)arted (adjective)

Wholehearted.

(h)oolmeal / whoolmeal (noun and adjective)

Wholemeal: (e.g., in baker's) 'Give me a small hoolmeal, love, please.'

(h)oolsome / whoolsome (adjective)

Wholesome.

(h)ooze / (h)ooze-pipe (noun)

Hose-pipe.

(h)op: on the (h)op (adverbial phrase)

Unpreparedly, unexpectedly: 'They caught us on the 'op – we 'ad no idea they was comin'.'

(h)opeluss (adjective)

Hopeless.

(h)opes (noun, plural)

Cause for optimism, expectation, hope: 'Now that Waldron and Pricey is fit, there's hopes for Ponty agen.'

(h)ope in (h)ell (nominal phrase)

Absolutely no chance: ''E aven't got a 'ope in 'ell of passin' that exam.'

(h)opping jinny: like a(n) (h)opping jinny (phrase used predicatively with 'to be')

Moving about constantly and annoying others in the process: 'Sit still, mun! You're like an 'opping jinny!' Note that if the 'h' of 'hopping' is not pronounced (as is usual), then the indefinite article that preceeds it turns from 'a' to 'an'.

(h)orse

See **ceffyl blaen.**

(h)ouse room: wouldn't give it (h)ouse room: (expression)

Wouldn't touch it with a barge-pole. An expression indicating disapproval of something and unwillingness to get involved with it.

(h)ouseful (noun)

A lot of visitors: 'We've got an 'ouseful staying.'

(h)ow (are) you keeping? / (h)ow('s) you keeping? (expression)

How are you?: 'How (are) you keepin(g) these days with all this old flu about?'

(h)ow are you off for... ? (expression)

Do you have enough... ? The implied question is often 'Do you need more ...?' 'How are we off for light bulbs?' See also **fixed: (h)ow are you fixed for?**

(h)ow do you sell... ? (expression)

What price is/are... ?: 'How do you sell the carrots, pears, bacon etc.' See also **what's the onions/carrots/apples/oranges?**

(h)ow's it looking? (expression)

What are the chances? 'How's it looking to have a lend of a tenner till Tuesday?'

(h)owbe? (interjection)

How are you? A form of greeting less commonly heard these days, **hiya!** often being preferred. See also **shw mae?** and **hiya!**

(H)owells's / (H)owellses (proper noun)

Howell's, the well-known department store in Cardiff. The apostrophe 's' ending is added to any store name, e.g. Morgans's (the now sadly defunct Cardiff department store, David Morgan's), sometimes (as with both Morgan's and Howell's) adding yet another 's' to the name! 'I do my shopping down Lidl's these days – iss cheaper, see', and, 'Our Dawn do work on the checkout down Tesco's on a Satday.'

(h)uff: in a (h)uff (adverbial phrase)

Pouting unhappily: 'She went off in a huff when I asked her where she'd spent her pocket money.'

(h)ump (transitive verb)

To carry, especially with difficulty: 'We atto 'ump the 'ool lot back 'ome.' See also **hawk**.

(h)undredweight (noun, singular and plural)

The plural of this measurement of weight is the same as the singular: 'I bought three 'undredweight of sment down the saw mills.'

(h)unt for (phrasal verb)

To search for: 'I've 'unted everywhere but I can't for the life of me remember where I put it.'

(h)urdy-gurdy (noun)

(1) A thingumajig, a what's-the-name – a name given something the name of which does not immediately come to mind.

(2) An unpleasant noise: 'What's that old 'urdy-gurdy you're keeping?' See also **keep a noise**.

(h)urt (adjective and adverb)

(1) Incredulous(ly), not believing: 'She looked at me 'urt when I told 'er about it.'

(2) Stupid, ignorant: 'Jawl 'urt!' (Ignorant devil!)

(Welsh and pronounced as in Welsh, i.e. 'hirt') (Western Wenglish)

(h)usbunt (noun)

Husband.

(h)wyl (noun)

Good cheer, good health, good spirits, enthusiasm: 'How's the hwyl today, then, Mrs Jones?' 'Oh, weddol, thank you.' 'I haven't got a lot of hwyl today.' (Welsh) See also **shwd ma'r (h)wyl?**

(h)wylus (adjective)

Well, in good health. It is used in the negative in response to an enquiry about one's health. 'How are you feelin'?' 'Not very hwylus today, gul.' (Welsh, though Wenglish usage of the word is restricted to this context only). See also **di-hwyl**.

I

I: to Dad and I (pronoun)

To Dad and me. A commonly heard error among Wenglish speakers when speaking Standard English, which would require 'me' (the oblique case of 'I') following the preposition 'to', even though the conjunction 'and' intervenes. However, in Wenglish this usage is permissible, and even sounds a bit posh!

icelider (noun)

A custard slice.

Ideal / Ideel (noun, brand name)

Evaporated milk, once very popular to accompany **tin frute** and also taken by some in tea/coffee.

idle (adjective)

Out of work, unemployed.

iechyd da! (interjection)

Good health! (Welsh)

iesgyn! / iesgyn Dafydd! / iesgyn wyllt! (interjections)

Welsh expletives, euphemisms/ways of avoiding saying 'Iesu Grist!' (Jesus Christ!). See note to **Iesu Mawr!**

Iesu (Grist)! (interjection)

Jesus (Christ)! See note to entry below.

Iesu Mawr! (interjection)

A Welsh expletive literally meaning 'Great Jesus!', having something of the same force as 'Jesus Christ!' does in Standard English. In Welsh nonconformist circles, taking the Lord's name in vain was strongly frowned upon, so this expletive was thought almost blasphemous in certain circles and would certainly not be used in polite conversation.

ife? (contraction of verb, question form + pronoun)

Is it? Used in a similar way to **is it?** (q.v.) **ife?** is added onto the end of a phrase or sentence as a question, much as the French 'n'est-ce pas?' and the German 'nicht wahr?' and 'gell?' The Welsh usage has been carried over mainly as **is it?** though the Welsh form can also be heard sometimes. This is colloquial South Wales Welsh – the Standard Welsh form would be 'onid ydy e?' (Western Wenglish) See also **ondife**.

if 'e did! / iffeedid! (interjection)

Wenglish for 'if he did!', meaning 'I should say so!' or 'certainly, he did!', by way of intensifying an oral account of an incident. 'Iffeedid! I soon squared 'im!'

'igh up

See **(h)gh up**.

'ightth

See **(h)eightth**.

'ightth of fashion

See **(h)eightth of fashion**.

ignorant (adjective)

Rude, badly behaved, lacking in manners (rather than knowledge).

'ikey

See **(h)ikey**.

'im (pronoun)

Him.

in, in

See **out, out**.

in by there (adverbial phrase)

In there, in with you, in your house. Generally used when one neighbour refers to another's house: 'How's youer father in by there today?' See also **by there**.

in case (adverbial phrase)

In case it is needed: 'It's not rainin' now but take youer umbrella with you in case.' See also **fear: for fear**, which means much the same.

in the bone

See **bone: In the bone**.

in the car (adverbial phrase)

By car. **in the car** follows the Welsh 'yn y car'. See also **on the bus** and **on the train**.

'inder

See **(h)inder**.

innit? (contraction of verb + pronoun, negative question form)

Isn't it? An extended contracted verb form not used by all speakers.

inshe(e)? (contraction of verb + pronoun, negative question form)

Isn't she? An extended contracted verb form not used by all speakers.

interésted (adjective)

Meaning as in Standard English but often pronounced with a strong stress on the penultimate syllable, as if it were a Welsh word.

interésting (adjective)

Meaning as in Standard English but often pronounced with a strong stress on the penultimate syllable, as if it were a Welsh word.

into everything (adverbial phrase)

Rummaging in and untidying drawers, cupboards etc. Generally used in reference to young children: 'He's lovely, I know, but he's into everything now.'

invaleed (noun)

An invalid. The spelling reflects the normal pronunciation of this word in Wenglish.

invaleed car (nominal phrase)

An invalid carriage. These were often small, light blue coloured three-wheelers, with special controls.

'iraeth

See **(h)iraeth**.

irriz (contraction of pronoun + verb)

Possible spelling and pronunciation of **it is**, not used by all speakers.

is it? (verb, question form)

Is that correct? Often tagged onto the end of a phrase as a sort of interrogative, seeking confirmation of something asked. It is used in the same way as the French 'n'est-ce pas?' or the German dialect form 'gell?' It translates the colloquial South Wales Welsh form **ife?** (q.v.) Thus: 'Going shopping, is it?' or 'Having a bit of dinner, is it?'

iss

Possible spelling and pronunciation of **it's / it is**.

'isself

Possible variant of **(h)imself** or **itself**.

J

jack (noun)

A miner's water jug.

jack it in (phrasal verb)

To give up an activity: 'I atto jack it in coz I din 'ave the time to do all the trainin'.'

jacket

See **whose coat is that jacket?**

jam

See **bara jam**.

jant (noun)

Jaunt, trip, outing.

jasper / rasper

A good specimen, a good one: ''E had a reeal rasper of a penknife!' (Central Wenglish)

jaw: all jaw (nominal phrase)

All talk, all words and no action: 'I wouldn't take no notice – 'e's all jaw – 'e won't do nothin'.'

jawch! jawch eriôd (i)! / jawch erioed (i)! / diawch! / diawch eriôd (i)! / diawch erioed (i)! (interjections)

A mild Welsh expletive, less severe than **diawl!** or **jawl!** (meaning 'the devil!' or 'hell!'. All these forms mean something like 'heck!' or 'heck alive!'. 'Eriôd/ erioed' means 'always' or 'ever' in Welsh.

Another example of initial 'di-' being pronounced as 'j' in colloquial South Wales Welsh.

jawl! / diawl! (interjection)

A mild Wenglish expletive, something like 'hell!': 'Jawl, mun there's no need to lose youer temper!' These words are variants of the Welsh word for 'devil' – 'diafol', which in colloquial South Wales Welsh is 'diawl'. There is a marked tendency in spoken South Wales Welsh for the initial letters 'di-' to be pronounced 'j'. See also **jawch!** which is slightly milder, and **myn jawl (i)!**, which is stronger.

jawl / diawl (noun)

A devil, an awful fellow: There's an old jawl that Evan Roberts is! He wouldn't lend me his spare wheelbarrow, mind!' The Welsh plural **jawled / diawled** is generally used: 'There's jawled those kids are – they been pelting the greenouse agen!'

jawledig / jawletic / diawledig / diawletic (adjective)

Devilish: 'They're jawletic them kids gone.' (Welsh)

Jenny (fedw)

See **Jinny (fetw)**.

jes' / jus' / jess / juss

See **jest / just**.

jest / just (adverb)

(1) Almost, nearly: 'I jest lost the train but if I 'adn't caught it, I'd 'ave 'ad to wait an hour for the next one.'

(2) Only just: 'He've just come – give 'im a minute to 'ave a spell!'

(3) Indeed, really Used to show agreement: 'I've 'ad an 'ard time with 'er.' ''Aven't you just!!' 'I've just 'ad enough – I've 'ad a bellyful of it!'

jest now / just now (adverbial phrase)

A little while ago.

jew! / jiw! (interjection)

God! Gosh! Good Lord!: 'Jew, 'e've put on a lot of weight since I seen 'im last!' Derived from **Duw** the Welsh word for 'God'. See also **jiws** and all the variations listed.

jew jew! / jiw jiw! / wel i jew jew! / wel i jiw jiw! (interjections)

A double form of the above: 'Wel i jew jew! I never thought they'd win!'

jib (noun)

Looks, face: ''E'll be alright in a minute – 'e got one in the jib, but he'll come now.'

jib / gib (transitive and intransitive verb)

To give up/in, to renege: 'He said he was going to do it but he jibbed in the end.'

jibs: to pull / make jibs

To pull faces: 'Why are you pullin' jibs all the time? Stop it or people will think you're a bit funny.'

jidge

See **judge**.

jingalers (noun, plural)

Hanging decorations or jewellery, especially earrings.

Jinny (fetw) / Jenny (fedw) (noun/nominal phrase)

The cane (for punishment) 'Bedw' is Welsh for a birch tree. In this example we see hardening of the intervocalic consonant 'd' to 't' – a typical feature of colloquial South Wales Welsh, and a regular soft mutation of the initial 'b' to 'f' – pronounced 'v' – as the noun is used as an adjective qualifying the feminine singular noun, 'Jinny'.

jiw!

See **jew!**.

jiw jiw!

See **jew jew!**

jiws! / jiwcs! / juice! / jukes! / jews! / diws! / deuce! / dukes! (interjections)

Gosh! Dash! Drat! These are all mild expletives and euphemisms for/variants of, **Duw**, the Welsh for 'God': 'Oh jukes, she's goin' to be late agen.' The forms beginning in 'j' arise as there is a strong tendency in South Wales Welsh to pronounce the letter combination 'di-' as 'j' e.g. 'diafol' (devil) becomes 'diawl' and then 'jawl'.

jiws annwl! / jiwcs annwl! / jukes annwl! / juice annwl! / diws annwl! / deuce ynnwl! (interjections)

Gosh alive! Heck alive! These are all mild expletives and euphemisms for/variants of **Duw annwyl** meaning 'Dear God' in Welsh. See above entry for note on forms beginning with 'j'.

job (noun)

Bother, trouble: 'We 'ad 'ell of a job findin' the 'otel.'

job: bad job (nominal phrase)

A hopeless case: 'I tried to fix it with glue bur it was too fiddly so in the end I atto give it up as a bad job.'

job: good job (nominal phrase)

It's fortunate, lucky, just as well; e.g. '(it's a) good job you brought youer coat, it have gone quite cold now'.

jocose (adjective)

Comfortable, at ease: 'He was sittin' there all jocose while she was workin' ard getting the food ready.'

Joe Blunt (proper noun)

Someone who does not mince words but speaks out even if this may cause offence.

joint: to put your/his nose out of joint (phrasal verb)

To upset someone's feelings, to do something contrary to their wishes: 'I atto do it even if it put 'is nose out of joint.'

jonic(k) (adjective)

Genuine, honest, true: ''E's always 'avin a laugh but it could be jonic this time.' Exists in other English dialects. (Central and Eastern Wenglish)

jokin(g) (adjective)

Artificial: 'Those are not real plants, are they?' 'No, we could only get jokin' ones.'

joni

See **daioni**.

jovain / diod fain (noun/nominal phrase)

A home-made nettle drink, made with yeast, sugar and nettles; fizzy and cloudy in appearance. The spelling **jovain** is another example of the marked tendency in colloquial South Wales Welsh to pronounce 'di-' at the beginning of a word as a 'j'.) See also **small beer**. (Welsh, literally 'fine drink') (Western Wenglish)

joy (intransitive verb)

To enjoy: 'Did you joy down the beach.' (Colloquial South Wales Welsh usage.) (Western Wenglish) See also **enjoy**.

joyo / joio (noun)

Enjoyment: 'I'm looking forward to a bit of joio with my choclates in front of the TV tonight.' (Colloquial South Wales Welsh usage. (Western Wenglish)

jubes (noun, plural)

Fruit pastilles.

judge / jidge (transitive and intransitive verb)

To scrutinise, to observe carefully, to spy: 'She was out the front judging all what was goin on.' The form **jidge** is influenced by the colloquial Welsh 'jijo'.

juice! / jukes!

See **diws!**

juice annwl! / jukes annwl!

See **diws annwl!**

jus' / juss

See **jest.**

just

See **jest.**

just now

See **jest now.**

just the same / jest the same (phrase used predicatively with 'to be')

Unaffected by success or wealth: 'Avril's boy was 'ere on the weekend. 'E've got a marvellous job up in London an' a big 'ouse in Surrey, she was tellin' me, but, I gorrw say there was no swank about 'im at all – 'e's just the same!'

K

keep (transitive verb)

(1) To care for, to maintain (e.g. a child): 'Pretty little boy – she do keep 'im lovely.'

(2) See **how (are) you keeping?**

keep a noise (phrasal verb)

To make a noise, directly translated from the Welsh 'cadw stwr'.

keep his cap straight (phrasal verb)

To keep someone happy (generally somenone in authority): 'Better keep 'is cap straight – 'e can be a funny bugger sometimes.'

keep on (phrasal verb)

To bring up in conversation repeatedly, to speak about repeatedly: 'Shut up, will you' 'You're keepin' on about it all the time!'

keep short (phrasal verb)

Not to give enough money, to withhold money: 'He must be keepin' 'er short – she never seems to 'ave no money on 'er.'

keep youer eye out (for) (phrasal verb)

To maintain a sharp look out (for): 'Keep youer eye out for a nice mac for me in the sales.'

keep your hair on

See **hair: keep your hair on**.

ketch (transitive verb)

To catch, to grip, usually used with **holt** (q.v.): 'You gorrw ketch holt of it tight.'

ketched (verb, past tense and past participle)

Possible past tense and past participle of 'to ketch': 'I ketched 'olt of 'im and give 'im a good talking to.' See also **catched**.

kidney beans / cidna bêns (nominal phrase)

Runner beans. The alternative spelling and pronunciation is a carry-over from colloquial Welsh.

kiff

See **ciff**.

kill: a good day's work would kill him (expression)

He is very lazy.

kill: to kill to cwat

See **cil: to cil to cwat** and **cwat**.

kilt (verb, past tense and past participle)

Killed. A possible form of the past tense and past participle of the verb **to kill**. 'The dog 'ave kilt a mouse agen in the garden.'

king: a king to (nominal phrase)

Much better than: 'I'm feelin' much better – a king to what I was last week, I can tell you!'

kitchen

See **back kitchen** and **scullery**.

knees: on my (h)ands and knees

See **(h)ands: on my hands and knees**.

knee went

See **went**.

knock: the door was knocking (expression)

Someone was knocking at the door.

kokum (adjective)

Crafty, cunning: 'You're kokum, aren't you? Peolple think that butter wouldn't melt in youer mouth.'

knock back (phrasal verb)

(1) To cost, to set one back financially: 'How much did that jacket knock you back?'

(2) To drink heavily: 'He wasn't half knockin' them back down the club.'

know: to know how to take him / her (phrasal verb)

To be unable to predict/undertand someone: 'He's a funny old bugger – can't say I know know how to take him half the time.'

know: not to know no different

See **different: not to know no different.**

know: not to know youerself/himself/herself (phrasal verb)

To experience a great improvement: 'When you've got youer new kitchen, you won't know youerself!'

know all the wrinkles

See **wrinkles: to know all the wrinkles.**

know for (phrasal verb)

To know the whereabouts of: 'I know for the scissors – they're on the table in the kitchen.'

know (him/her) of old (phrasal verb)

To know what someone is like from extensive past experience of that person: ''E'd never do a thing like that – I know 'im of old!'

know the ins and outs (phrasal verb)

To know all the details. See also **wrinkles.**

know what for (phrasal verb)

A threat of future punishment: 'If he don't alter his stroke, he'll know what for!' Also **to give him what for,** which implies giving the punishment.

knowin(g) (adjective)

Precocious, advanced: ''E's only seven but 'e's very knowin' – ask 'im what the capital of Outer Mongolia is an' 'e'll tell you straight off!' Another word sometimes used in the same context is **forward** (q.v.).

knowin(g) (noun)

See **no knowin(g).**

kybosh (noun)

Ruining, spoiling: 'That'll put the kybosh on their plans!'. See also **moch / mockers / molochi and dampers**.

L

lambastin(g) / lampin(g) (noun)

A good hiding: 'If you carry on like that you'll get a good lambastin'!'

land (intransitive verb)

To arrive, to return home: 'When we landed back 'ome, there was no letric – must 'ave been that storm.'

landed (adjective)

(1) Very contented: 'When Dai saw the 'otel was right next to the cricket ground, 'e was landed!' See also **oils: in his oils**.

(2) Arrived. See **land**.

las' / la(a)ss (adjective and adverb)

Possible spellings and pronunciation of **last**: 'I seen 'im lass night down the club.'

last: not to last five minutes (phrasal verb)

To be very ephemeral, not to last a long time, to be flimsy: 'Them battries don't last five minutes – I'll afto go down the shop and get some new ones.'

last go off / last lap (adverbial phrase)

At/in the end, at the last moment: 'He turned up for the meetin' last lap as usual.'

lastic (noun)

Elastic: 'The lastic 'ave gone in these pants.'

lath: like a lath (phrase used predicatively with 'to be')

Very thin indeed: 'Look at 'er, like a lath she is, an' she still wants to go on a diet!'

laughin(g)

See **roarin(g) laughin(g)** and **crackin(g) laughin(g)**.

laundrette / launderette (noun)

Launderette.

lay down (intransitive verb)

To lie down. There is frequent confusion and interchangeability in Wenglish between the transitive and intransitive forms of Standard English verbs. See also **rise** and **raise**.

lay my/youer hand on (phrasal verb)

To locate, to find: 'I've had a good look for it but I can't lay my hand on it.'

lay off (phrasal verb)

(1) To desist, give up: 'Just lay off – I've 'ad a bellyful of youer nonsense!'

(2) To make redundant.

lead horse

See **ceffyl blaen**.

learn (transitive verb)

To teach as well as to learn. This follows Welsh usage of the verb 'dysgu', which means both 'to learn' and 'to teach'.

learn sense (phrasal verb)

To learn to improve, to apply one's common sense: 'Oh, 'e'll never learn sense – 'e'll always do as 'e pleases, that one.'

leave (transitive verb)

To let, allow: 'Leave me see it, will you!'

leave: to leave its mark

See **mark: to leave its mark**.

leave alone (prepositional phrase)

Let alone, besides, not to mention: 'I've got my 'ands full with the kids leave alone gettin' a dog.'

leave go (phrasal verb)

To let go, release. See also **loose go**.

leave it there (phrasal verb)

To let the matter rest: 'Leave it there, will you? I've just about had enough of you two bickerin' all the time.'

leave llonydd

See **llonydd: leave llonydd**.

le(c)tric (noun and adjective)

Electricity, electric, electrical.

lectrician / lectrishun (noun)

Electrician.

le(c)trics (noun, plural)

Electrical installations.

leg: not (to have) a leg under him (phrasal verb)

(To be) unable to walk properly due to excessive consumption of alcohol: "E din 'ave a leg under 'im when 'e came out from that weddin' reception.'

leg went

See **went**.

lemme (contraction of verb and pronoun)

Possible spelling and pronunciation of **let me**.

lend: to have a lend of (phrasal verb)

To borrow: 'Can I 'ave a lend of youer mower tomorro, please?'

lend (a) (h)and / lend an 'and (phrasal verb)

To lend a hand, to help.

length of his/her tongue (nominal phrase)

A reprimand, a telling-off: 'I was very polite with 'er but all I got was the length of 'er tongue – she's an 'ikey old cow!'

lenses

See **levenses**.

lerrem / lerrum (contraction of verb and pronoun)

Possible spellings and pronunciation of **let them**.

lerrer (contraction of verb and pronoun)

Possible spelling and pronunciation of **let her**.

lerrim (contraction of verb and pronoun)

Possible spelling and pronunciation of **let him**.

less (contraction of verb and pronoun)

Possible spelling and pronunciation of **let's**.

less / 'less (conjunction)

Unless.

let himself/herself go (phrasal verb)

To become indifferent to one's appearance/health, to take little care of one's appearance/health: 'She looked awful – she've reely let 'erself go – an' she was so pretty an' all when she was younger – all the boys were after 'er!'

let loose (phrasal verb)

To behave in such a way as to lead people to believe that one has been released

from an asylum, to behave wildly/without control: 'You can pack that in now
– people will think you've just been let loose!'

letric

See **le(c)tric**.

letrics

See **le(c)trics**.

lev / level: on the lev / on the level (adverbial phrase)

Honestly: 'You must be 'avin me on!' 'No, on the lev, now, 'e did find a gold
coin when 'e was diggin' the garden.' This is not a native Wenglish expression:
the influence of other dialect forms of English and the media is evident here.

leven (cardinal numeral)

Eleven.

levenses / levnses / levnziz / lenses (noun)

Possible spellings and pronunciation of **elevenses**, a mid morning drink of tea/
coffee, often served with biscuits.

liar

See **Tom Pepper**.

lick (noun)

Speed: 'We was goin' at a tidy lick so I atto slam on the brakes when that sheep
stepped onto the road.'

licket

See **lycet**.

lickrish / lickerish / lickorish (noun)

Liquorice. See also **spanish**.

lie on (nominal phrase)

A lie in: 'It was lovely to 'ave a lie on and not to 'ave to get up at aa pass six as
usual.'

life: to be for your life

See **be for your life**.

like (adverb)

An almost meaningless word, tagged on to the end of a sentence or phrase by
some speakers: I went down the club, like.' See also **like, see**.

like a shot (adverbial phrase)

Straight away: 'He was off like a shot as soon as the meetin' finished.'

like as if (conjunction)

As if: 'I can't 'elp it – iss like as if I lose my confidence when I gorrw do it for real.'

like, see (adverbial phrase)

An almost meaningless add-on phrase, often used when explaining something, perhaps to ensure that the speaker has the listener's attention: 'It was on the table, like, see.' See also **like**.

likely

See **most likely**.

line (noun)

Railway line, 'dramway' (q.v.) or the course of a former railway line after it has been closed and the tracks lifted and removed. Could also refer to the washing line. See **lineful**.

line: on the line (adverbial phrase)

On the railways: 'My uncle used to work on the line.'

lines

See **hard lines**.

lineful (noun)

A lot of washing on the clothes line: 'I had a lineful out when it started pickin' with rain.'

lineouts (noun, plural)

The plural of 'lineout' in rugby, generally 'lines out' in Standard English.

ling-di-long (adverb)

Unhurriedly, unconcerned, in a leisurely way: 'He's so half-soak – walking ling-di-long about the place. There's no shape on him.' (Welsh)

lissen (intransitive verb)

To listen. The spelling reflects the pronunciation.

liss(e)nin(g) (verb, present participle)

Listening. The spelling reflects the pronunciation.

live tally (phrasal verb)

To live together unmarried: 'They're not married – livin' tally they've been this years!'

live through and through

See **through and through**.

llaethdy (noun)

Dairy. Place where dairy products were stored. (Welsh – Western Wenglish)

llaw bwt (adjectival phrase)

Left-handed, often suggesting awkwardness. See also **cack handed / coggy handed**. (Welsh)

lle dda (adverbial and adjectival phrase)

Quite good, quite well (generally in answer to an enquiry about one's health). This is the colloquial South Wales Welsh form, the full form being 'lled dda'. 'How are you feelin after youer op, Dacu?' 'Lle dda, w! I can't complain. The doctors 'ave been marvellous with me!' See also **weddol**. (Western Wenglish)

llonydd (noun)

Peace and quiet, leisure: 'I haven't had llonydd to think about it yet.' (Welsh and pronounced as Welsh) (Western Wenglish)

llonydd: leave llonydd (phrasal verb)

To leave be, to leave in peace, to let alone. This is another English-Welsh hybrid, a direct translation of the Welsh idiom 'gadael llonydd'. 'Leave 'im llonydd now – 'e's got to swot for 'is exams!' (Western Wenglish)

Llungwyn (proper noun)

Whit Monday. (Welsh) (Western Wenglish)

llusi (noun, plural)

Whinberries: ''E's gone up the mountain to collect llusi.' (Welsh) See also **whimberries**. (Western Wenglish)

llwm (adjective)

Poor, penurious, shabby, of poor quality (Welsh for 'poor') (Western Wenglish)

llwyfan (noun)

Stage, especially the eisteddfod stage. 'Reaching the llwyfan' means getting to the final stage of an eisteddfod competition: 'You did very well to reach the llwyfan.' (Welsh and pronounced as in Welsh. Literally it means 'stage' as in the theatre etc.) (mostly Western Wenglish)

llwyth cart (nominal phrase)

A cartload, a lot of: 'They came 'ome with llwyth cart of tranglwns.' (Welsh) (Western Wenglish)

llyfyr ime (nominal phrase)

Hymn book, proudly taken to chapel, along with those other essential supplies, mint imperials. (Colloquial South Wales Welsh, from the Standard Welsh 'llyfr emynau') (Western Wenglish) See also **chapel losin**.

llywydd (noun)

President, chairperson, especially of a meeting, social club, religious fellowship etc. (Welsh – Western Wenglish)

loadsa (expression of quantity)

A lot of. Possible spelling and pronunciation of **loads of**.

long-winded (adjective)

Taking a long time to do something, slow: 'They should by rights 'ave finished the job by now but they've been awful long-winded with it.'

lonjery (noun)

Lingerie.

look (intransitive verb)

To appear, to have the appearance: 'It's lookin' good for the Swans now – six points clear and four games to go.' 'The bathroom's lookin' nice with you now Idris 'ave finished the tilin'.' See also **how's it looking?**

look (verb, imperative form)

An almost meaningless addition, conveying a measure of reassurance and intimacy/sympathy with the person addressed: 'Don't worry – you can give it to me agen, look!' 'Look, it's not a problem at all – I can pick you up from the surgery, no bother.'

look: by the look / by the looks of it (adverbial phrase)

By the appearance, it seems, it would appear: 'Jonathan Davies will be out of the Welsh team for three months now with that injury, by the look.' 'They've mowed the lawn agen by looks of it!'

look: don't look! (verb, negative imperative)

Please ignore, don't take any notice of: 'Don't look at the mess – I 'aven't 'ad a chance to put the things by.'

look and look (and look) (intransitive verb, repeated use)

To search thoroughly. 'Audrey looked and looked and looked for her ring and in the end she found it under the settee.' See also **hunt**. The repetition of a word for emphasis is a feature of Welsh.

look at you: as good as look at you

See **good**.

look daggers (phrasal verb)

To look disapprovingly.

look everywhere (phrasal verb)

To conduct a thorough search: 'I've looked everywhere for a pair of shoes to match my new suit but I can't find the right colour nowhere.' See also **hunt**.

look for someone (phrasal verb)

To look on behalf of someone: e.g. in a shop, 'Can I help you?' 'I'm looking for my mother.' It can also have its Standard English meaning.

look-in (noun)

A chance, an opportunity: 'Did you get picked for the first team?' 'No, I didn't get a look in – the coach 'ave got 'is favourites.'

look-out (noun)

(1) Prospect: 'It's a poor look-out for them now that the collery 'ave finished.'

(2) Responsibility: 'It's your look-out where you keep your tools.'

(3) **To be on the look-out for**, as in Standard English, means to keep an eye open for, to watch out for, but is used more frequently in Wenglish.

looks

See **by the looks of it**.

looks: to have no looks on (phrasal verb)

Not to like/favour any more: 'I've got no looks on them old shoes now I've got that new pair.'

loose go (phrasal verb)

(1) To let go, to release.

(2) (Of a toddler) To let go of his/her mother's hand and attempt to walk independently: 'She 'aven't loosed go yet, then?'

lorravue/lorravew: the lorravue/lorravew / lorravus: the lorravus / lorravem/lorravum: the lorravem/lorravum (definite article + contraction of noun + preposition + pronoun)

All of you/us/them. Possible spellings and pronunciation of **the lot of you, the lot of us, the lot of them** respectively, making use of extended contractions and a change of intervocalic 't' to 'rr'. These features are not used by all speakers: 'I'd give one to the lorrovew if I 'ad enuff.'

lose ground / losing ground (phrasal verb)

To get worse, to deteriorate, especially in health: 'I met old Dai Jones in the village. Losin ground 'e is, pooer dab.' See also **gain**.

lose on himself/herself (phrasal verb)

To get confused/forgetful, to become senile: 'She's beginnin' to lose on 'erself a bit but she can still shift for 'erself alright.' (Loan translation of Welsh 'colli ar ei hunan')

lose the bus (phrasal verb)

To miss the bus. A translation of the Welsh expression 'colli'r bws'.

losins / loshins (noun, plural)

Sweets. (Welsh) See also **chapel losin**.

lost

See **go lost**.

lot (noun)

(Partly in jest) Family, occasionally group of friends, team etc.: 'Her lot are coming round here on Satday.'

lot: a lot (adverbial phrase)

A goot deal, often: 'I like this new coat – I wear a lot of it!'

lotment (noun)

Allotment.

lottry (noun)

Lottery.

lovely (adjective and adverb)

Very nice, very well. Its use in Wenglish is much more common than in Standard English and its range of application also wider e.g. food, clothes, pretty much anything, really. See also **beautiful** and **lovely lovely**.

lovely boy / lovely girl (nominal phrases)

Terms of endearment.

lovely lovely (adjectival and adverbial phrase)

Very nice/good/well indeed. Repetition of the adjective to intensify its meaning has been carried over from Welsh. See also **beautiful beautiful**.

lump (noun)

A big one (usually a person): 'He's a real lump of a boy – he could do with losing a couple of stone easy.'

lush (adjective)

A colloquial adjective, in favour mostly with the younger generation, meaning 'luscious', 'very good', 'superb'.

lycet / licket (noun, plural)

Eyes. (Welsh) This is the colloquial South Wales pronunciation, the Standard Welsh form being *llygaid*. Found in the expression **moelyd your lycet** (q.v.) and in occasional use where Standard English would uses eyes, e.g. 'Watch youer lyced with that sheepdip.' (Western Wenglish).

lyer (noun)

Possible spelling and pronunciation of 'liar'.

M

macu gâm / magu gâm (phrasal verb)

To pluck up courage. (Welsh) (Western Wenglish)

mad on (adjective + preposition)

Mad about.

maes (noun)

Field, site, showground, especially of a major eisteddfod. (Welsh – literally 'field')

main

See **drag** and **thing**.

make (noun)

Brand, manufacturer: 'Dorma is a good make – should get good wear out of them sheets,' and, 'What make is your car?'

make for (phrasal verb)

To head to: 'Where you makin(g) for today, then?'

make (my/your/his etc) mind up (phrasal verb)

To decide: 'She took awful long to make 'er mind up which one to choose.'

make out to be (phrasal verb)

To pretend to be, to give the appearance of being: 'I made out I was 'appy about 'er getting' the job but reely I was gutted!'

make two of (phrasal verb)

To be much bigger than: 'Look at Steffan –'e's 'uge, mun – 'e'd make two of Nathan, poor dab!'

maldod / muldod (noun)

Indulgence, fuss and attention: 'He was givin' the dog a bit of maldod when the phone went.' (Welsh – 'maldod')

mam / mammy (noun)

Mother, mum, mummy.

Wenglish

mamgu / myngu / mungee (noun)

Grandmother. Often pronounced 'mungee', with the stress on the last syllable. (South Wales Welsh – 'mamgu')

mammy

See **mam**.

man

See **old man**.

man a man (adverbial phrase)

In the same position, there is no benefit, it's just the same, might as well: 'Man a man you are if you get a weekly ticket or buy a normal ticket on the days you go on the train.' 'Should I go on the trip to London?' 'Man a man – you 'aven't got nothin' else on, 'ave you?' (Welsh)

mandrel (noun)

A pick-axe/mattock.

manidge (transitive and intransitive verb)

To manage, to cope with. See also **shift**.

manylion (noun, plural)

Details: 'I had to give the receptionist my manylion.' (Welsh) (Western Wenglish)

Mari Winwns (nominal phrase)

The characteristic pinkish skinned onions sold by the itinerant Breton onion sellers and in markets in South Wales. See also **Sioni Winwns**. (Welsh for 'Mary Onions')

mark: to leave its mark (phrasal verb)

To affect: 'Movin' from the cottage to the 'ome 'ave definitely left its mark on 'im – 'e's not 'is old self some'ow.'

Martha and Mary

See **do a Martha and Mary**.

Mary Jane (nominal phrase)

An effeminate (male) person: 'He's a nice enough, but he's a bit of a Mary Jane.' See also **Bessie, Nancy** and **paish**.

match: like a match (adjectival phrase used predicatively with 'to 'be')

Fiery, quick tempered: 'Be careful what you say to 'im – like a match 'e is!'

matinay / matiny / matinee

Matinée (at the cinema).

matter

See **no matter**.

mawr

See **Arglwydd Mawr!**, **Iesu Mawr!**, **Duw Mawr!**, **peth mawr**, and **Cwrdd y Mawr**. It is the Welsh for 'big' or 'great'.

Mawredd (Mawr)! (interjection)

Goodness me! (Welsh, literally 'Greatness' / 'Great greatness!') (Western Wenglish)

mawve / morv (adjective)

Possible spelling of 'mauve', reflecting the pronunciation.

may have (modal verb, conditional perfect)

Might have: "E may 'ave been there, but I can't reely say coz the place was 'eavin'.'

meddw caib (adjectival phrase)

Very drunk. The Welsh expression literally means 'as drunk as a mattock/ pickaxe'. 'Meddw caib 'e was when 'e come 'ome from the rugby.' (Welsh) (Western Wenglish) See also **caib** and **ceibo: shwd mae'n ceibo?**

member: big member (nominal phrase)

A prominent, active member, especially in Welsh chapel circles. This expression was/is freely used in Welsh conversation in preference to the Standard Welsh form 'aelod mawr'. 'Elwyn's a big member in 'Epron.' (Hebron – the name of a Welsh chapel) (Western Wenglish)

mend (transitive verb)

To repair. More commonly used in Wenglish than 'to repair'.

menyn

See **bara menyn**.

menyw (noun)

Woman. Used as follows by an annoyed husband/man when addressing a woman: 'I don't know what you are tryin to do but I tell you, you better stop that nonsense now, menyw!' Could also be used ironically or humorously. (Welsh) (Western Wenglish)

Merched y Wawr (proper noun)

Welsh women's organisation, broadly similar to the Women's Institute. 'I can't come down on Thursday – I'm goin' on a trip with Merched y Wawr.' (Welsh, literally 'Women of the Dawn')

middlin(g) (adjective and adverb)

Average, so-so (e.g. in reply to an enquiry about one's health).

mile (noun, singular and sometimes plural)

Mile. This expression of distance sometimes remains unchanged in the plural as in other English dialects (e.g. Yorkshire) but the Standard English plural, 'miles', is more common.

miles (noun)

A long way: 'We travelled miles to get there and it wasn't so nice after.'

milgi (noun)

Greyhound (Welsh). The plural is **milgis**, not 'milgwn' as it would be in Standard Welsh.

mind (intransitive verb)

To mark, to listen. Often interpolated in conversation. It adds little to the meaning but acts as an intensifier or to ensure the listener's full attention: 'Mind you, I don't think he'll win the prize', or 'He's handy round the 'ouse, mind.'

mind: make (my/you/his etc.) mind up

See **make (my/you/his etc.) mind up**.

mind: not to mind a bit (phrasal verb)

To have no objection at all.

mind out (phrasal verb)

(1) To take care, to beware, to watch out: 'Mind out – you nearly hit that over!'

(2) To move, to shift: 'Mind that by there – move it can't you?' or 'Mind out of the way!'

mingy (adjective)

Mean, stingy, meagre: 'Don't be so mingy, mun – giss a lend of a fiver!' 'I wouldn't go to the new chip shop again – they only give you mingy little portions and it's pricey beyond!'

minute: in a minute (adverbial phrase)

(1) Shortly, presently, a little later on: 'Hang on – I'll be there in a minute!' 'She'll give it to you now in a minute.'

(2) Willingly, with no bother: 'Idris would do it for you in a minute!'

miss (transitive verb)

Not to recognise, to confuse with someone else. Generally used in the negative, introduced by **can't**: 'You can't miss 'er – she's got 'er arm in plaster.'

miss a chalk / miss a trick (phrasal verb)

To miss an opportunity: 'You missed a chalk there – could 'ave made a few bob if you'd played youer cards right.'

mitch (school) / mitch off school (transitive and intransitive verb/phrasal verb)

To play truant. See also **mootch** and **whipper-in**.

mitching (noun)

Playing truant.

moch / mockers / molochi (noun)

Ruining, spoiling: You've put the mockers on that fire proper with all that small coal!' See also **kybosh** and **dampers**.

mochyn (noun)

Pig: 'He's a dirty mochyn – I wouldn't trust 'im further than my nose.' (Welsh)

moelyd (transitive verb)

To fidget with, to play with: 'Don't moelyd youer lycet (eyes) like that – it's getting on my nerves!' (Colloquial South Wales Welsh) See also **lycet**. (Western Wenglish)

moither (transitive verb)

To confuse.

moithered (adjective)

Confused, flustered: 'I always get a bit moithered when I 'ave to talk in a roomful a people.'

molochi

See **moch**.

mootch (intransitive verb)

(1) To play truant. A variant of **to mitch** (q.v.).

(2) The colloquial Standard English meaning, 'to hang around', 'to loiter', 'to potter about'.

more fuss than the worth of it (nominal phrase)

Not worth the trouble; 'It's more fuss than the worth of it to take them bottles back to the Cop.'

morv

See **mawve**.

mosiwn

See **motion**.

mosiwns

See **motions**.

most likely (adverbial phrase)

In all probability: 'He went out about twoish. You'll most likely find 'im down the rugby club, love.' See also **most probably**.

most probably / most probly (adverbial phrase)

In all probability: 'He's most probly gone fishin' with 'is father.'

motion / motiwn / mosiwn (intransitive verb)

To gesture, make signs, to signal.

motions / motiwns / mosiwns (noun, plural)

Gestures, signs, signals: 'She made mosiwns to me to come over.'

mouth

See **finger: with your finger in your mouth** and **afraid to open my mouth**.

mouthful (noun)

A rude, impudent or stern utterance/reply: 'If she carries on like that much longer, I'll 'ave to give 'er a mouthful!'

much

See **up to much**.

muckle-dee-dun (adjective)

Strange, odd.

muffler (noun)

A warm scarf. Thought to have entered Wenglish via West Country/Forest of Dean dialects.

muldod

See **maldod**.

mun (noun)

(1) Used in address when speaking to a male (= man), or even to a female: 'Come on, mun! We 'aven't got time to 'ang around!' It sometimes indicates a mild annoyance or can be used jocularly.

(2) As an intensifying element, almost meaningless in itself, added on to the end of a statement. It is sometimes added when what is said should be obvious to the person being addressed: 'He've gone down Trecco, mun.' This could be said by or to a man or woman.

mungee

See **mamgu**.

munse / munce (noun, plural)

Months, the spellings reflecting the pronunciation. See also **twelmunth**.

murder: to half murder (phrasal verb)

To threaten with grievous punishment: 'I'll 'alf murder 'im if I catch 'im doin' that agen!' See also **cry blue murder**.

musheroom (noun)

Mushroom.

must afto / must (h)ave to (modal verb + modal verb)

It must be the case that it is necessary for one to, one probably has to: 'You must afto shut that door before you can open the other one.'

must be, praps (expression)

It must be, perhaps. This apparent contradictory utterance was/is quite commonly heard. It means 'as far as I'm aware it is, but I'm not 100% certain'. Maybe the doubt enters the speakers's mind mid-sentence...

'mychan i (nominal phrase)

My boy, my lad. The full form in Welsh is 'fy mychan i'. 'Now lissen 'ere 'mychan i, you can't go about the place sayin things like that about people!' (Welsh) (Western Wenglish) See also **bychan**.

myn jawl (i)! / myn diawl (i)! / myn jawch (i)! / myn diawch (i)! (interjections)

By the devil! By hell! These expletives are stronger than their English translations and would not be used in polite conversation. The forms with **jawch** and **diawch** are however milder than those with **jawl** and **diawl**. (Welsh) (Western Wenglish)

myn uffach (i)! / myn yffach (i)! (interjections)

By heck! A slightly toned down version of **myn uffarn i!** but still much stronger than the English translation and not used in polite conversation. (Welsh) (Western Wenglish)

myn uffarn (i)! / myn yffarn (i)! / myn uffern (i)! (interjections)

By hell! These Welsh expletives sre much stronger than their literal translation into English and they would definitely not be used in polite conversation. See also **uffarn!** (Welsh) (Western Wenglish)

mynew

Possible spelling and pronunciation of **mind you**. See **mind**.

N

'na peth od! / 'na beth od!

See **peth od**.

'na peth mawr! / 'na beth mawr!

See **peth mawr**.

Nancy / Nancy boy (noun/nominal phrase)

Homosexual, effeminate male. See also **Bessie**, **Mary Jane** and **paish**.

narf (contraction of conjunction + indefininite article + noun)

Possible spelling and pronunciation of **and a half**. See **boy narf**.

nash(y) (noun)

Nationalist. See also **Welsh nash(y)**.

nasty (adjective and adverb)

Severe(ly) (often of rain, weather): 'It's started to rain nasty now. I won't go down the village till later.'

National: the National (proper noun)

The National Eisteddfod (q.v.) or the Grand National (horseracing).

natur (noun)

Temper, especially in the Welsh expression **'na natur!** – 'what a temper!' (Welsh and pronounced as in Welsh) (Western Wenglish)

nawrte! (interjection)

Now then! Well then!: 'Nawrte! Let's get started!' (Welsh) (Western Wenglish)

ne' mind (adverb + verb)

Never mind. The spelling reflects a possible pronunciation.

neely (adverb)

Nearly.

neely (h)ad a fit (expression)

Was almost sent into apoplexy, was almost made to have a fit in reaction to something: 'I neely had a fit when she told me how much theyer holidays cost 'em.'

neither (adverb)

Either (following a negative statement): 'I don't blame you – I wouldn't go down there neither.' 'Either' could also be used here.

never (adverb)

(1) An expression of incredulity/shock: 'What do you think – Brenda Jones has won the lottery!' 'Never!'

(2) An emphatic negative: 'I never told 'im that!'

never all there (phrase used in predicate with 'to be')

Showing strange behavioural traits, of dubious sanity: 'Don't take no notice of 'im – 'e's never all there!'

never hear/year the end of it (phrasal verb)

To continue to be a topic of discussion/debate/reproach/boasting: 'You'll never hear the end of it if he manages to get into the darts final.'

never right (phrase used in predicate with 'to be')

Having a serious defect (generally in understanding): ''E's never right that one! Tell 'im one thing and 'e'll come out with somethin' completely diffrunt!' See also **not right in the (h)ead**.

never-never: on the never-never (adverbial phrase)

On hire purchase. See also **glad and sorry: on the glad and sorry**.

Newsy Landers (proper noun, plural)

Possible spelling and pronunciation of 'New Zealanders'.

niblo (noun)

A young male member of the family: 'How's Niblo feelin' after 'is fall?'

nice: it's nice to go and it's nice to come back (expression)

Often said after a holiday or trip, this expression suggests appreciation of the place visited but also of home: There's no place like home, after all.

niff (noun)

A smell, generally unpleasant: 'There's a bit of a niff in the shed – what is it?''

night school / night classes (nominal phrase)

Evening classes.

nip (noun)

Cigarette stub. Also **dog-end** and **tod-end**.

no age (nominal phrase)

Not at all old: 'Poor dab was no age when he died.'

no end (adverbial phrase)

(1) Extremely: 'That phone call from the council 'ave worried 'er no end!'

(2) Continually: ''E's nice enough, I spose, but he do talk no end. Drysu's me 'e do.'

no go at all (nominal phrase)

A lack of energy and enthusiasm: 'There's no go in 'im after 'is op!' See also **go** (noun).

no knowin(g) (nominal phrase)

No means of telling: 'There's no knowin' what Geraldine will get up to when she goes on 'er 'olidays to Spain!'

no looks on

See **looks: to have no looks on**.

no matter (nominal phrase)

It doesn't matter: 'No matter. I'll get another one down the market.' See also **dim ots**.

no more (adverbial phrase)

Any more, any longer (in double negatives): 'I don't like yoggut no more.'

no more (adjectival and nominal phrase)

No further, no additional. Often used, introduced by **there's**, in preference to 'there aren't any more'. 'There's no more apples on the tree now', rather than 'there aren't any more apples on the tree', as would be the norm in Standard English.

no perswâd

See **dim perswâd**.

nobody (pronoun)

Anybody (in double negatives): 'I 'an't seen nobody in the shop today.'

no-one (pronoun)

Anyone (in double negatives): 'I 'an't told nobody about it.'

noise: big noise (nominal phrase)

A person of significance, a VIP: 'He's a big noise with the rugby club – committee member or somethin'.'

nonsunse (noun)

Nonsense.

nor willin(g)

See **not willin(g)**.

normly (adverb)

Normally.

nose

See **sleep: I could sleep on my nose** and **joint: nose put your/his out of joint**.

nosso baad/bard (adverbial phrase)

Possible spelling and pronunciation of **not so bad**.

not all there

See **never all there**.

not fussed (adjectival phrase)

Not very keen: 'I wasn't fussed on them sofas in DFS.'

not in it (adverbial phrase)

Beyond that, inadequately describes it: 'Oh slightly overweight's not in it – she needs to lose at least two stone!'

not sorry a bit (adjectival phrase)

Not at all contrite, showing no regret: 'The cythrel's not sorry a bit for what 'e's done!'

not much money to play with (nominal phrase)

Not a great deal of disposable money: 'They 'aven't got much money to play with – she've got to be very careful with the pennies.'

not willin(g) / nor willin(g) / not a-willin(g) (adjectival phrase)

Not willing, not prepared to allow, unhappy about: ''E's not willin' for us to go on Saturday – I told you 'e'd be awkward, din I?' 'I'm not willing that you didn't get the job after they's promised it to you.' **not willin(g) a bit** means 'most unwilling', 'definitely not prepared to allow'. See also **a-willin(g)** and **quite willin(g)**.

nothing (pronoun)

Anything (in double negatives): 'I 'aven't got nothin' to wear to the weddin'.'

nothin(g) for (nominal phrase, used as predicate with 'to be')

Not very keen on: 'I love Joe's ice-cream but I'm nothing for Walls.'

'nough / 'nuff (adverb)

Enough.

now (adverb)

(1) At some (unspecified) future time, presently. It is rarely used to mean 'immediately'. 'I'll give it to you now'. Often, another indication of exactly when now may be, is added: 'I'll see to it now when I get home', or 'I'll do it now in a minute'. See also **minute: in a minute**.

(2) Only now: 'They were sposed to get there this mornin' but Freda phoned to say now they've arrived.' The **now** is emphasised in this type of sentence.

now after (adverbial phrase)

Shortly, presently, in a short space of time: 'I'll give you the money now after.' See also **now (1)**.

now jest, now just (adverbial phrase)

(1) In a little while, later on: 'I can't take them now, I'll come back to get them now jest.'

(2) A little while ago: 'What was she saying now jest – I didn't catch it all.'

cf **again / agen**.

nowhere (adverb)

Anywhere (in double negative): 'I can't go nowhere till the food's ready.'

'nuff

See **'nough**.

nuffsee-nuff (expression)

Possible spelling and pronunciation of **enough's enough**.

nugget (noun)

Nougat.

O

o / 'o (preposition)

Of. See also **a**.

-o (suffix)

The letter 'o' is often added to a name when calling to a friend: 'Billy-o!', 'Mary-o!'

o ddrwg i wâth (adverbial phrase)

From bad to worse: 'It's gone o ddrwg i wâth in work.' (Colloquial South Wales Welsh – Western Wenglish)

o with / o weeth (adverbial phrase)

Wrong, awry. The pronunciation is always 'o weeth': 'I dunno, it always seems to go o weeth when I do it.' (Colloquial South Wales Welsh, the standard being 'o chwith') (Western Wenglish)

oanee / oany (adverb)

Possible spelling and pronunciation of **only**.

obligin(g) (adjective)

Polite, courteous, attentive: 'Mr Harries in the lectrical shop is always very obligin'.'

obsorb (transitive verb)

To absorb.

obsorbant (adjective)

Absorbant.

obstropalous (adjective)

Obstreperous, troublesome, awkward (of person). See also **strobulous**.

odd (adverb)

Roughly, little more than: 'She solt it to 'im for fifty an' odd.'

oes oesoedd (adverbial phrase)

For ever and ever, for a very long time, for ages. This Welsh expression means 'for ever and ever' and occurs at the end of the Lord's Prayer in Welsh. 'You've had that sweater for oes oesoedd – about time you got a new one!'

of going (idiomatic construction)

Since I was already going, while I'm going, seeing as I'm going: 'Of going to Ponty, I thought I'd pick up some veg from the market.' This construction can be used with any verb and is very typical of Wenglish. It is a direct translation of the Welsh o + verb noun, e.g. 'o fynd', 'of going'.

off (adverb)

(1) Heading to: 'Where are you off to, then?' 'I'm off home now.'

(2) Angry, upset: 'She'll be off when she finds out what they've been up to!'

(3) On the go, having a disturbed time: ''E was off all night with diarrhoea.'

(4) On leave, off work, on holiday: 'I'll be off again next week. Going down Trecco for a couple a days.'

(5) Off-handed, rude: 'That woman in the shop was a bit off, wan she?'

off (preposition)

(1) From: 'I got that off Mam for my birthday.' ''Oo off did you 'ave them shoes?' See also **'oo off?**

(2) Having lost a liking for: 'I'm right off chicken since all this fuss with bird flu.'

off his head / off 'is 'ead (prepositional phrase, used adjectivally in predicate with 'to be')

Mad: 'Don't lissen to 'im –'e's off 'is 'ead!'

off non (adverbial phrase)

Possible spelling and pronunciation of **off and on**.

off sick (adverbial phrase)

Away from work due to ill health. See also **off** (adverb) (4).

ofnadw / ofnatw (adjective)

Awful. Tends to be used as a one-word comment in agreement with a statement made by the speaker or by somebody else: 'Those kids shouldn't be allowed to run about the place like that – ofnadw!' (Colloquial South Wales Welsh – Standard Welsh form is 'ofnadwy') (Western Wenglish)

ogowon! (interjection and contraction of interjection + verb, imperative)

Possible spelling and pronunciation of **oh go on!**

oil cloth (nominal phrase)

Linoleum.

oil works (nominal phrase)

Oil refinery.

oiled

See **well oiled**.

oils: in his oils (idiomatic expression)

In his element: 'John was in 'is oils when 'e seen 'ow near the 'otel was to the theatre.'

Derived from the Welsh 'yn ei hwyliau', 'hwyl' meaning 'good cheer', 'good spirits'. See also **hwyl** and **landed** (1).

ol' (adjective)

Old.

old (adjective and adverb)

The use of **old** in Wenglish mirrors the way 'hen' (old) can be used in Welsh. It is frequently used to imply faint or sometimes strong disapproval in statements like 'making a lot of old fuss about nothing!' or 'only old enjoying themselves they think about these days!' 'Funny old day, innit?' 'Funny old stick 'e is!'

old: as old as Adda

See **Adda: as old as Adda**.

old boy (nominal phrase)

An old man: 'The old boy 'as gottw be at least eighty now.'

old girl (nominal phrase)

Mother: 'My old girl's gorrw go into 'ospital agen on Wensday.'

old man (nominal phrase)

Father: 'I'm meetin' my old man down the club tonight.'

'old up

See **hold up**.

'olidays

See **holidays**.

'ollo

See **hollo**.

'ome (noun and adverb)

Home. See also **eat out of (h)ouse and (h)ome**.

on (preposition)

(1) Belonging to (often denoting a part of the body): 'There's some paws on that dog!', and 'He's got a good 'ead on him!' This is a literal translation from Welsh: the last example would be 'Mae pen da arno fe' in Welsh.

(2) See **call on** and **shout on**.

See also **always on**.

on a Sunday, Monday etc. (adverbial phrase)

On Sundays, every Sunday etc. This usage recalls the colloquial South Wales Welsh 'acha dy' Sul'.

on about (adverbial phrase)

Referring to, talking about. See also **what you on about?**

on fire (adverbial phrase)

Running a high temperature: 'Doctor, the baby's on fire!'

on (h)alf

See **half: on half**.

on (h)is own (phrase used predicatively with 'to be')

Singular in his behaviour, an amusing character: 'You never know what 'e's goin' to come out with next – 'e's on 'is own, 'e is!'

on my own self

See **self**.

on me (prepositional phrase)

On my person, with me right now: 'I'll afto pay you agen – I aven't got no money on me now.' **On** is stressed rather than **me**.

on pins (phrase used predicatively with 'to be')

Agitated, worried, preoccupied: 'I'm on pins waitin' for the results to come through.'

on stop (prepositional phrase, used adjectivally in predicate)

Stopped, not progressing: ''E've atto put the work on stop till 'is 'and gets better.'

on the bus (prepositional phrase, used adverbally)

By bus. **On the bus** follows the Welsh 'ar y bws'. See also **on the train** and **in the car**.

on the go (prepositional phrase)

(1) Current: 'I've got a couple of things on the go at the moment.'

(2) In motion, moving: 'He's like a hopping jinny (q.v.) – he's always on the go!'

(3) Being prepared/made: 'I coun come coz my tea was already on the go!'

on the lev / on the level

See **lev / level: on the lev / on the level**.

on the train (prepositional phrase, used adverbally

By train. **On the train** follows the Welsh 'ar y trên'. See also on the bus and **in the car**.

on the weekend (prepositional phrase, used adverbally)

At the weekend. The use of the preposition 'on' is common in American English, whereas 'at' is general in Standard British English. The phrase would also be 'ar y penwythnos' (literally 'on the weekend') in Welsh. See also **on times**.

on times (prepositional phrase, used adverbally)

On some occasions, sometimes. A direct translation of the Welsh 'ar brydiau'.

ondife (verb, question form or as interjection)

Isn't it? Sometimes said to agree with something that has just been said, in the sense of 'isn't it just!' See also **ife**. (Colloquial South Wales Welsh) (Western Wenglish)

one degree under

See **degree: one degree under**.

once over (nominal phrase)

A quick examination or inspection: 'She gave it the once over and it was fine.'

only for (preposition)

Except for: 'The 'otel was lovely, only for the tea – these forriners don't know 'ow to make a nice cup of tea, do they?'

'oo (relative pronoun) 'oo? (interrogative pronoun)

Who. Who?

'oo off? (interrogative pronoun)

From whom? 'Oo off did you 'ave that then?'

'ool

See **hool**.

'ool 'og

See **hool hog**.

'ool(h)(e)arted

See **hoolhearted**.

'oolmeal

See **hoolmeal**.

'oolsome

See **hoolsome**.

'ooze-pipe / 'ooze

See **hooze**.

op / opereshun (noun)

Operation.

'opes

See **hopes**.

'ope in 'ell

See **hope in hell**.

'opeluss (adjective)

Hopeless.

open

See **afraid to open my mouth**.

open tap (nominal phrase)

The time the pubs open: 'When's open tap down Swansea?' See also **stop tap**.

opening medicine (nominal phrase)

Laxative. See also **Ex Lax**.

operatta (noun)

Possible pronunciation of **operetta**.

opereshun / op (noun)

Operation.

opposight (preposition, adverb and noun)

Possible spelling and pronunciation of **opposite**.

or loze / all 'ose (contraction of adjective and demonstrative)

Possible spelling and pronunciation of **all those**.

or no (adverbial phrase)

Or not: 'I don't know for certain if 'e'll be coming or no!'

ordinry / ordinary (adjective)

Ordinary, standard, regular: 'Which one do you want? The ordinry ones or the best?'

'ose (demonstrative adjective and pronoun)

Those.

ots

See **dim ots**.

ouer (possessive adjective)

Possible spelling and pronunciation of **our**.

ouers (possessive pronoun)

Possible spelling and pronunciation of **ours**.

ouerselves / ouselves (reflexive pronoun)

Possible spellings and pronunciation of **ourselves**.

'ough (adverb)

Though: 'It was good, 'ough, you got to admit.'

'ouse (noun)

House. See also **eat out of (h)ouse and (h)ome**.

out (adverb)

(1) Outside: 'Is it raining out? 'What is it like out today?'

(2) Available, having been produced, to be had: 'What's the name of that film that's out now?' **New out** is a variant: 'Iris Gower's book is new out.'

out (preposition)

Out of: 'I chucked it out the window.'

out, out (adverb, repeated)

Note repetition for emphasis, following Welsh usage. Here it suggests that the action is repeated or continuous: e.g. 'She's out, out, all the time, chattin' to people', meaning 'She is always out and about, chatting to people.' The opposite **in, in** suggests that the person referred to is always indoors.

out of (phrase used predicatively with 'to be')

Having run out of: 'Daro, we're out of sugar agen!'

outings (noun, plural)

Problems: 'We've 'ad some outings with ouer neighbours, I can tell you!'

over (preposition)

(1) To, over to: 'I'm off over the Cop.'

(2) In preference to: 'When she 'eard that Freda 'ad 'ad the job over 'er, she was tampin'.'

It is also used with its Standard English meaning of 'above'.

over

See **all over**, and **place: all over the place / all over the shop**.

overcoat colder (adjectival phrase)

Much colder: 'It's an overcoat colder in Tredegar than down Newport and an overcoat and muffler (q.v.) colder in Brynmawr!'

ov(v)ious (adjective)

Obvious.

'ow (adverb and interrogative adverb)

How.

'owbe?

See **howbe?**

own: on (h)is own

See **on his own** and **self: on my own self**.

P

pabell (noun)

Tent, pavilion (in the Eisteddfod). Generally not the large main pavilion but smaller competition or display areas such as the **Pabell Lên** (Literary Pavilion) or **Pabell Gelf** (Art Pavilion). (Welsh and pronounced as in Welsh) (mostly Western Wenglish)

pack in (phrasal verb)

To stop (doing), to desist: 'Pack it in, now, will you? I've just about 'ad enuff of youer nonsense!'

packman (noun)

A door-to-door salesman.

packman's puzzle (nominal phrase)

A residential area where the house numbers are allocated in a confusing way, thus causing problems for visitors, tradesmen, postmen etc.

pafin / pavin (noun)

Pavement. (Welsh) (Western Wenglish)

paish (noun)

An overfussy, possibly somewhat effeminate, (male) person: 'He's nice enough but a bit of a paish.' (Welsh for 'petticoat') See also **Bessie, Nancy** and **Mary Jane**.

palaver (noun)

Inconvenience, fuss and bother: 'I'm not goin' through all that palaver agen!'

pantner (noun)

A partner, workmate or friend, generally male. Pronounced as in Welsh and also used in colloquial Welsh in the Western Wenglish area. (Western Wenglish)

See also **butty**.

pants: a pants (noun)

Note Wenglish use of singular where Standard English would say 'a pair of pants'.

paper

See **pin: like a pin in paper**.

pappish / paps / papsy (adjective)

Very easy: 'The spellin' test was papsy.' (Central and Eastern Wenglish)

parade (intransitive verb)

To walk back and forth repeatedly: 'There must be somethin' goin' on – she've been paradin' in front of 'er 'ouse all night.'

parafeen (noun)

Paraffin. The spelling reflects the way 'paraffin' is generally pronounced in Wenglish, with the stress on the last syllable.

paralatic / paraletic (adjective)

Drunk to the point of leglessness/incoherence: 'Paraletic 'e was comin' 'ome from the rugby club.'

parchus (adjective)

Respectable: 'You can't do that on the day of the funeral – it's not parchus.' (Welsh) (Western Wenglish)

parlour (noun)

Front room, reserved for best and ceremonial occasions.

particulars / particlars/ particklers / putickers (noun, plural)

Factual details: 'The policeman took down all the puticklers.' See also **manylion**.

particular / particlar / partickler / putickler (adjective)

(1) Fastidious, fussy: 'He's very particular about what time he eats.'

(2) The one in question: 'On that particular day, I din 'ave no money on me.'

partin(g) (noun)

A railway junction, points or sidings located at the junction. Sometimes used to mean a yard or depot situated at the junction. The word was also used in colloquial Welsh, the 'r' pronounced trilled. This pronunciation was often carried over into Wenglish. 'I'm taking a load of drams down to Parting Clai now.' ('Parting Clai' being the name of a depot/sidings located at the junction.)

partmunts / partments

See **apartments**.

pass

See **aa pass**.

pass the time of day (phrasal verb)

To make conversation, to exchange pleasantries: 'I stopped to pass the time of day with 'im.' See also **give the time of day**.

pass (very) (h)igh (phrasal verb)

To have done well in one's examinations: 'Ada was tellin' me that 'er grandson 'ave passed high.'

pass remarks (phrasal verb)

To make (usually unfavourable) comments: 'You know 'ow she is – always passin' remarks about somethin' or other.'

passage (noun)

(1) Corridor.

(2) See **front passage** and **back passage**.

pat: black pat (nominal phrase)

Cockroach.

patch: not a patch on (nominal phrase)

No comparison with, not as good as: 'He's not a patch on 'is brother!'

pavin

See **pafin**.

pay your way (phrasal verb)

To pay what one is committed to: 'By the time I've paid my way, there's nothing left gone these days.'

payshunt (noun and adjective).

Patient.

pechod

See **diflas**.

peeky (adjective)

(1) Not feeling/looking very well: 'She's still looking a bit peeky but she is feeling a bit better.'

(2) See **picky**.

pele (noun, plural)

A mixture of small coal and cement, made into squares or balls, or formed in moulds (e.g. old flowerpots etc), and used, when set, as coal. (Welsh for 'balls') (Western Wenglish)

pelt (transitive and intransitive verb)

(1) To rain heavily: 'It was pelting (down) when we landed back.'

(2) To throw: 'The boy was pelting stones at the greenhouse.'

See also **full pelt**.

pembleth / penbleth (noun)

A quandary: 'He's been in bit of a pembleth to know what to do with 'them apples he've got over (i.e. surplus).' See also **pickle / picil**. (Welsh) (Western Wenglish)

Pencwarter (noun)

(1) A special service in Welsh Baptist (and other Welsh non-conformist) chapels, occurring at the end of every quarter. Children were expected to take part by reciting a verse of scripture or perhaps singing a solo or duet.

(2) The end of the quarter for accounts purposes. See also **end of the quarter**.

penderfynol (adjective)

Determined, resolved. Also **sweet penderfynol**, meaning very determined, bordering on obstinate. (Welsh) (Western Wenglish)

penstiff (adjective)

Stubborn, obstinate: 'He won't change 'is mind now – he can be penstiff when he wants to be.' (Welsh)

perswâd

See **dim perswâd / no perswâd**.

peth mawr (nominal phrase)

(That's) a very grave/serious matter. This expression could be introduced by 'na' (short for 'dyna'), meaning 'there' in Welsh. Thus **'na peth mawr!** or **'na beth mawr!** literally means 'there's a big (i.e. serious) thing!' 'Dyna' and 'na' would normally require a soft mutation of the 'p' to 'b' in Welsh but this does not always occur in this usage in Wenglish. (Western Wenglish)

peth od! (nominal phrase and interjection)

How odd! Literally 'a strange thing!' This expression could be introduced by 'na' (short for 'dyna'), meaning 'there' in Welsh. Thus **'na peth od!** or **'na beth od!** literally meaning 'there's a strange thing!'

pewer (adjective)

Possible spelling and pronunciation of **pure**.

Phêbi (proper noun)

Possible spelling and pronunciation of Phoebe, the female name. This is the way it is generally pronounced in Welsh.

Philerstines (proper noun, plural)

Philistines.

pic(k)-chers

See **pictures**.

pic(k)-cher 'ouse

See **picture house**.

pick (with/to) rain (phrasal verb)

To begin to rain, to drizzle: 'It's picking to rain again – I'll take my mac in case it gets worse.' (From the Welsh word 'pigan' meaning 'to begin to rain')

pick up (phrasal verb)

To improve (e.g. of health): 'She's pickin up now after her pull.'

pick up on (phrasal verb)

To criticise: 'That old Mrs Jones is always picking up on the way the kids behave – an' they're good as gold reely.'

pick up with (phrasal verb)

To get into company with: 'They picked up with some nice people when they was on theyer 'olidays.'

pickies / piggies (noun, plural)

(1) Trouble: 'In the pickies again – 'e'll afto be more careful!'

(2) especially in the form **pickies**, brambles, thorns.

pickings (noun, plural)

Selection, choice: 'There were plenty of pickings to be 'ad in Howells's sale but, jew, it was like a rugby scrum down there – it was 'eavin'!'

pickle / picil (noun)

A spot of bother, a difficult situation: 'I'm in a bit of a picil: I don't know where I left my purse.' The form **picil** is used in Welsh in the same way. See also **pembleth/penbleth**.

picky (adjective)

Prickly, sharp. Sometimes pronounced **peeky**.

picky (with food) (adjective/adjectival phrase)

Fastidious about food and thus difficult to cater for: ''E's awful picky with 'is food gone – won't eat beef nor pork nor lamb; he will eat chicken but only if it 's in a sauce.'

pics (noun, plural)

(1) Welsh-cakes, from the Welsh 'piciau ar y maen' (literally 'pics on the bakestone').

(2) Pictures, films, cinema. See also **pictures**, **picture house** and **flicks**.

pictures / pic(k)-chers / pitchers (noun, plural)

The local film show or cinema of days gone by: 'She's off to the pic-chers – Saturday matinay.'

picture (h)ouse / pic(k)-cher (h)ouse / pitcher (h)ouse (nominal phrase)

Picture house, cinema.

piggies

See **pickies**.

pikelet / pikelut (noun)

A drop scone. Resembles a small, thickish pancake.

pilesa / pylesa / a pile of (expression of quantity)

Lots of. Possible spellings and pronunciation of **piles of / a pile of**. Similar to **'eapsa** for **heaps of** and **bagsa** for **bags of** and **loadṣa** for **loads of**.

pimp (intransitive verb)

To spy on courting couples.

pimper (noun)

Someone who spies on courting couples.

pimping (noun)

Spying on courting couples.

pin: like a pin in paper (prepositional phrase, used in predicate with 'to be', and idiom)

Meticulously clean: 'Like a pin in paper the 'ouse is with 'er.' (Direct translation of the Welsh 'fel pin mewn papur')

pins: on pins

See **on pins**.

pink up (phrasal verb)

To get oneslf ready, to do one's make-up. (From the Welsh 'pincio')

pishdy / pishty (noun)

Toilet, urinal. (Welsh – literally 'piss-house')

pishty / pishti (adjective)

Rather effeminate.

pisio cath / pisio crics (nominal phrase)

Very weak tea. (Welsh for 'cat's pee')

pisio lawr / pisho lawr / pish down (phrasal verb)

To rain heavily: 'Don't go out now – it's pisho lawr – wait till it eases off a bit.' (Welsh for 'to pee down')

pitch in (phrasal verb)

(1) To set to work with vigour and determination: 'You'll afto pitch in if you wasn't to pass that maths exam!'

(2) To begin to eat heartily: 'Pitch in – I bet you're starvin' after that long wait.'

pitch a tale (phrasal verb)

To tell an unlikely story: 'He tried to pitch me a tale about the bus breakin' down.'

pitchers

See **pictures**.

pitcher (h)ouse

See **picture house**.

pity (h)elp (noun + transitive verb, optative subjunctive)

It's a pity for: 'Pity 'elp them – they'll afto shift for themselves now.' The expression indicates sympathy with, or fear/concern for, the person(s) referred to. This is a rare example of the subjunctive mode in Wenglish, expressing a wish. **Duw (h)elp** and **God (h)elp** are also used in the same way.

place: about the place (adverbial phrase)

Everywhere, here and there. Translated from Welsh 'ar hyd y lle'. 'She's 'opeless, leaves 'er shoes about the place – anyone could trip over them and 'ave a nasty accident.'

place: all over the place / all over the shop (adverbial phrase)

Everywhere, strewn everywhere, at sixes and sevens. See also **place: about the place**.

plastrin(g) (noun)

Plastering.

play

See **Swansea play**.

play (h)ell (phrasal verb)

To object/react violently, to make a big fuss, to reprimand: 'He was playin' hell with her about spending the money Auntie Val give her for her birthday.'

play the game (phrasal verb)

To behave in a fair and honest way: 'Play the game, mun – you can't treat people like that!'

play the bear with (phrasal verb)

To cause pain/bother, to inconvenience: 'This 'eat do play the bear with me.'

pleess / p'lice (noun)

Possible spellings and pronunciation of **police**.

pleess car / p'lice car (nominal phrase)

Possible spellings and pronunciation of **police car**. The stress is sometimes placed on the word **car** rather than **police**.

pleessman / p'liceman (noun)

Possible spelling and pronunciation of **policeman**.

pleesswoman / p'licewoman (noun)

Possible spellings and pronunciation of **policewoman**.

plod (noun)

Wenglish pronunciation of 'plaid': 'She looks very smart in her Scotch plod rig-out.'

poin / poen (transitive verb)

To trouble, to cause pain: 'Go away, will you? Stop poinin' me, mun!' (From Welsh 'poeni', meaning 'to worry', 'to pain' or 'to tease')

poisnin(g) (noun)

Poisoning. See also **food poisnin(g)**.

ponjin (noun)

A mixture of mashed potato and swede, sometimes called **potch** (q.v.) or **stomp / stump** (q.v.).

poodi / poody

See **pwdi**.

pooer dab / poor dab (nominal phrase)

Unfortunate one: ''E got soaked in the rain, pooer dab!'

pooer look out / poor look out

See **look-out (1)**.

pooer one / poor one (nominal phrase)

Someone who is not very skilled: 'I'm a pooer one for plastrin' but I'm a dab 'and at bricklayin'.'

pop (noun)

Fizzy drink such as lemonade, dandelion and burdock, once sold in returnable glass bottles (with deposit), and produced by numerous small family businesses such as Lewis's in Pontardawe.

pop bottle (nominal phrase)

A bottle for pop.

pop works / pop factory (nominal phrase)

Place where pop was produced.

positive / poztiv (adjective)

Certain: 'I'm positive it was 'er I seen down Tesco's.'

pot of/a/o sêm/saim/saam/sâm (nominal phrase)

A mess, trouble: 'We'll be in a reel pot o saam if we don't finish in time!' 'Saim' is the Welsh word for 'grease'.

potatoes

See **fried potatoes**.

potch (noun)

(1) A mixture of mashed potato and swede. It is also called **ponjin** (q.v.) and **stomp / stump** (q.v.)

(2) Trouble: 'He's 'avin' a bit a potch with 'is green'ouse door.'

potch (around) (with) (phrasal verb)

To mess about with: ''E do love to potch around in the lotment.'

potch (transitive verb)

To botch, to make a mess of: 'He's potched that job agen!'

potchy (adjective)

Fiddly.

pound (noun, singular and plural)

As a measurement of weight and when referring to money, the plural is generally the same as the singular: 'Put me three pound of potatoes.' 'I owe you eight pound fifty, OK?'

pouring: it's raining pouring (expression)

It's raining heavily, it's pouring with rain.

poztiv

See **positive**.

praps (adverb)

Perhaps. ·

preesink (noun)

Precinct, shopping mall.

pregnant

See **go pregnant**.

price on (noun + preposition)

The price of. Follows the Welsh 'pris ar': 'There's a price on them apples!' See also **there's rain / there's a price on**.

pricey (adjective)

Expensive. See also **dear** and **salty**.

problems

See **women's problems**.

probly (adverb)

Probably. See also **most probably**.

promise (transitive verb)

To forecast, especially the weather: 'They're promising snow tonight.' See also **give (1)** and **lick and a promise**.

pronounciation (noun)

Pronunciation.

proper (adjective and adverb)

(as adjective) Real, true, serious: 'She was in a proper fix when I got there – the place was upside down.'

(as adverb) Properly, correctly.

provoke (transitive verb)

To annoy: ''E's provokin' me all the time – one of these days I'll be losin' my temper with 'im!'

provokin(g) (adjective)

Annoying, provocative.

prynhawn da! (interjection)

Good afternoon! (Welsh)

pudding rice / pwdin reis

Rice pudding. Note the word order, which follows the Welsh.

puff: out of puff (adverbial phrase)

Out of breath: 'He was out of puff after shiftin' the furniture.'

pug (adjective)

Dirty, grimy: 'There's pug you're looking – you could do with a good wash!' From the Welsh 'pyg', meaning 'pitch'.

pull (noun)

(1) A bout (of an illness etc): ''E've 'ad a nasty pull agen.' (Welsh 'pwl')

(2) A climb: 'It's a bit of a pull to the top of the 'ill.'

(3) Influence: 'He've got a bit of pull with the council.'

pull about (phrasal verb)

To untidy, to leave in disarray, to make a mess of: 'They atto pull the front room about when they fitted the central 'eatin'.'

pull jibs (phrasal verb)

To make faces. See **jibs**.

pull pictures (phrasal verb)

To take photographs. This is a direct translation of the Welsh expression 'tynnu lluniau'. Not so common these days.

pull to pieces (phrasal verb)

To criticise severely: 'The boss pulled 'im to pieces when 'e 'eard about 'is little caper.'

pull of colled (nominal phrase)

A fit of pique, a burst of anger or a moment of madness. 'Colled' is pronounced as in Welsh. It means 'loss'. See also **pull** (noun) (1) (Western Wenglish)

pushed for (adjectival phrase)

Short of: 'I'll see you agen, Glad – I'm a bit pushed for time now.'

put (transitive verb)

(1) To place: 'She didn't know where to put 'erself when he told 'er about Joan', or 'Put it over by there, will you, love?'

(2) To serve, to provide: 'I put dinner frum all but I din get no thanks frit.'

(3) To serve with: 'Put me a couple of them pears, please.' (Follows pattern of usage of the Welsh 'dodi', 'to put'.)

(4) To set/prepare a fire: 'She've put a fire in the parlour for the visitors.' (Direct translation of Welsh 'dodi')

put by (phrasal verb)

To put aside, to put away, to save money. See **by** (1) and (2).

put in for (phrasal verb)

To apply for: 'He've put in for a job with the council.'

put on (phrasal verb)

To impose on someone: 'Don't let them put on you!' The stress is on the word **put** in this expression.

put one over on (phrasal verb)

To get the better of someone, to teach someone a lesson: 'I'll put one over on him one of these days, you'll see!'

put safe (phrasal verb)

To put in a safe place: 'Put that safe now before Brian's kids land 'ere.'

put straight (phrasal verb)

To put oneself, or something, tidy: 'I put the kitchen straight before goin' down the bingo.'

put up

See **can't abear**.

put years on you: enough to put years on you (nominal phrase)

The cause of considerable vexation/frustration, the effect of which is to (metaphorically) age one.

putickler

See **particlular**.

pwdi / poodi / poody (intransitive verb)

To sulk, to pout: 'She pwdied coz we didn't bring 'er a present.' 'Pwdu' is the Welsh word for 'to sulk' or 'to pout'. Note also the formation of the past tense and past participle, **pwdied** from the Welsh root by adding English endings.

pwl

See **pull**.

pwylla / pwyllwch / cymer bwyll / cam bwyll / cym bwyll (verbs/phrasal verbs, imperative form)

Take care! Use your sense! Take your time! **cymer bwyll** and **cam/cym bwyll** are much more commonly heard. (Welsh) (Western Wenglish)

pyjamas: a pyjamas (noun)

Note Wenglsh use of singular where Standard English would say 'a pair of pyjamas'.

pylesa

See **pilesa**.

Q

quarter

See **end of the quarter** and **Pencwarter**.

quavers / quaavers / quarvers (noun, plural)

A trembling in the voice, affectations in speech: 'Ivor do think 'e've got a lovely voice but you ought to year all them quaavers in it!'

quid (noun, singular and plural)

A pound (money). Note that the plural is the same as the singular, except in the phrase **quids in** (q.v.): 'Lend me ten quid, will you?'

quids in (nominal phrase)

Well off, standing to benefit (usually financially): 'We're quids in there – good job I told you about it, innit?'

quick (adjective and adverb)

Quick(ly).

quite a few (adjectival and pronominal phrase)

A fair number: 'There was quite a few down the club on Sunday.' **Quite a few** and **a tidy few** are both in common use in Wenglish.

quite willin(g) / quite a-willin(g) (adjectival phrase)

Perfectly willing, prepared to allow.

quizzy (adjective)

Inquisitive, curious.

R

racks (jibidaires) / rhacs (jibidêrs): in racks (jibidaires) / in rhacs (jibidêrs) (prepositional phrase used predicatively with 'to be')

In tatters, in chaos, in a mess. The form **rhacs jibidêrs** is used in colloquial Welsh. 'That shirt of his is in racks now, no use at all it is.' (Welsh for 'rags' or 'tatters') (Western Wenglish)

radically wrong (adjectival phrase)

As in Standard English, 'very wrong' but used more frequently in Wenglish: 'There's somethin' radically wrong with this kettle – it's not the fuse – must be the element.'

rag

See **wash like a rag**.

rage: all the rage (nominal phrase)

The height of fashion.

rain

See **right as rain**.

rain nasty (phrasal verb)

To rain very heavily: 'It's coming on to rain nasty.'

raining pouring

See **pouring**.

raise / rise (transitive verb)

To lift: 'Rise youer arm up, will you!?' The form **rise** is probably more common, though its use would be wrong in Standard English. The colloquial Welsh verb 'cwnnu / cwni' and its Standard Welsh equivalent 'codi', can mean both 'to raise' (the transitive verb) and 'to rise' (the intransitive verb). See also entries listed under **rise**.

raisley (noun)

A powdery raisng agent for baking, sometimes known as **golden raisley**.

rampin(g) (adjective)

Rampant, Very painful: 'I got rampin' toothache – I'll afto go to the dentist.'

rant and rave (phrasal verb)

To remonstrate vociferously, to shout unreasonably: 'There she was agen – rantin' an' ravin' about 'ow she should 'ave got that job.'

rarcol (y byd)!

See **ryrcol (y byd)!**

rare (transitive verb)

To rear, to bring up: ''E was rared by 'is Auntie Sal up in Nanty.'

rasper

See **jasper**.

rather (transitive verb)

To prefer. 'I like the green one but I rather the brown.' Also used as in Standard English: 'I'd much rather...'

ravel (intransitive verb)

To tangle, to run (thread of garment): 'Youer sweater 'ave ravelled – I'll afto darn it for you.'

really speaking / reely speaking (adverbial phrase)

In actual fact: 'They all say it was made in France but reely speakin' it was made in Belgium.'

read / red (transitive verb, past tense and past participle)

Read. Can also mean 'examined' in the expression 'You should get your 'ead read!' (You are crazy).

reeal (adjective and adverb)

Real.

reeal baad/bard (adverbial phrase)

Seriously wrong or ill: 'They say 'e's reeal baad – might not see the week out.'

reely / reelly (adverb)

Really.

regular / reglar (noun)

A regular customer: 'Brian's a reglar in the 'King's Arms'.'

regular / reglar (adjective)

Regular, usual: 'She was 'ere at the reglar time agen today.'

regular / reglar (adverb)

Regularly: 'They come in 'ere evry day at three reglar, like.'

reindeers (noun, plural)

The generally heard plural of **reindeer**, as opposed to 'reindeer', the plural in Standard English.

relations (noun, plural)

Relatives: 'We atto go and see my relations in Devon.' See also **belonging** and **tylwth**.

repertoier (noun)

Possible pronunciation of 'repertoire', rhyming with **choier**, the possible pronunciation of 'choir': 'The choier 'ave got a good repertoier now.'

reumatic / reumatics (noun, singular and plural)

Rheumatism. The singular is more commonly heard.

rewbob

See **ruebob**.

Rewby (noun and proper noun)

Ruby, the gem and female name.

ribbler / riddler / riddle (noun)

The sieve used to separate small coal from lumps.

ribblin(g)s / riddlin(g)s (noun, plural)

Cinders, ashes sieved through a **riddler** (q.v.). The form **ribblings** is probably more common.

riddle / riddler

See **ribbler**.

riddlin(g)s

See **ribblin(g)s**.

right (adverb)

Completely: 'I've gone right off sausage now!'

right: never right

See **never right** and **not right in the (h)ead**.

right enough (adverbial phrase)

Definitely right, quite so.

right as rain (adjectival phrase)

Fit, fully recovered: "E's right as rain agen after that pull 'e 'ad last week.'

right-o (adverb)

Yes indeed, yes, fine: 'Right-o, I'll be there in a minute, now.' An alternative to this is **right you are then**.

right off

Straight away: 'I'll do it right off so I don't forget.'

See also **off** (6) and **straight off**.

right through (adverbial phrase)

Everywhere, completely: 'It takes a good few hours to clean right through the 'ouse.'

rights

See **by rights**.

rig-out (noun)

Suit of clothes, outfit: "Er new rig-out for the weddin' was lovely lovely.'

ripe (adjective)

Worn very thin: 'I'll afto chuck them sheets out – they're proper ripe gone.' (Central Wenglish)

rise (transitive verb)

(1) To lift, to raise: 'When he meets someone on the road, he do genrally rise 'is 'at', and, 'Rise up the latch and peep in!'. 'Go up the garden and rise some potatoes!' and 'I'll 'afto rise the ashes before I go down the village.' This last example is a direct translation from the colloquial South Wales Welsh 'cwnnu'r llutu', meaning to clear the dead ashes from the grate after a fire has burnt out. See also **raise**.

(2) To collect (money), to cash a cheque: 'I'm goin' down the Post Office to rise my pension.' 'I'll 'afto go down the bank to rise some more money'. Note that this does not mean the same as 'to raise money' (e.g. for charity).

(3) To purchase: 'I'm goin' to rise ouer tickets for the train to London tomorrow.' (Direct translation of the Welsh verb 'cwnnu / cwni')

(4) To commence (of a funeral): 'The funeral will rise from the house at two o'clock.' (Direct translation of the usage of the Welsh verb 'cwnnu / cwni')

The verbs 'cwnnu / cwni' and 'codi', are both transitive and intransitive in

Welsh, and so when their meaning is carried over into Wenglish, the form 'to rise' is often used where 'raise' would correctly be called for in Standard English. See also **raise**.

rise up (h)is/(h)er sleeve (phrasal verb)

To encourage, to urge on: 'Why din you try to stop 'im? All you done was rise up 'is sleeve for 'im.'

rise: not to rise to (phrasal verb)

Not to be sufficient for: "Is pay don't rise to gettin' one like that, I can tell you now!'

road: always on the road (adverbial phrase)

Always out and about: 'She's always on the road'. Used in particular to describe someone who is often seen out and about.

road: like the road (phrase used predicatively with 'to be')

Very dirty: 'Look at 'im – like the road after playin' up the back!'

road: on the road (prepositional phrase, used adverbally)

Outside, out and about: 'I see 'er now an' agen on the road.'

roarin(g) laughin(g) (verbs, present participles)

Laughing heartily. An alternative is **crackin(g) laughin(g)**.

roaster (noun)

A roast potato.

roastin(g) (adjective)

(Feeling) very hot: 'Dew, It's roastin in 'ere – better open the window quick!' See also **boiling**.

rob (noun)

Something which takes your money, a constant expense: 'A house is a rob, innit?'

Rodney (noun)

A disreputable person. The last train up the valleys from Cardiff and Newport was once called 'The Rodneys'. It is derived from the name given to itinerant navvies.

rolling in it (adjectival phrase)

Having it (especially money) in abundance: 'They don't want for nothin' even though they're not rollin' in it.'

ronk (adjective and adverb)

Staunch: 'It's Tory ronk up in Surrey – jest like it's Labour ronk in the Rhondda!'

'He's a ronk Communist, you know.' (Welsh 'rhonc')

rotten (adjective and adverb)

Bad(ly): 'They let me down rotten last time so I've got to be careful, like.' 'I'm feeling rotten after that old operation.' See also **call someone rotten**.

rough (adverb)

Not very well: 'Feelin' a bit rough this mornin'?!'

ructions (noun, plural)

Fuss and bother, remonstrations, arguments.

ruebob / rewbob (noun)

Typical Wenglish pronunciation of 'rhubarb'.

rush (transitive verb)

To charge (money) for: 'They rushed me two quid for them spuds – daylight robbery I call it!' (Central Wenglish)

ryrcol (y byd)! / yrcol (y byd)! / rarcol (y byd)! (interjection)

Good grief! Bloody hell! Welsh expletive, mild to moderate in tone.

S

's (suffix at the end of shop names)

See **Howells's**.

sâm / saam

See **saim**.

sack: in the same sack (prepositional phrase used in predicate with 'to be')

In the same category: 'One's as twp as the other – you could put 'em in the same sack, you could!'

saim / sâm / saam / sêm (noun)

Grease, oil, fat. **All saam** means 'greasy, oily'. In Western Wenglish, **like saam trucks** means 'full of grease, like the grease on colliery/railway wagons'. This was sometimes used to describe the hair of someone who used excessive Brylcreem. (Welsh) See also **pot of saim** and **bara sâm**.

salong

See **slong**.

salty (adjective)

Expensive: 'That new baker's is awful salty.' See also **pricey** and **dear**.

same

See **always the same, just the same** and **sack: in the same sack**.

samwidge (noun)

Wenglish pronunciation of 'sandwich'.

san ferian (expression)

The way the French 'ça ne fait rien' is generally pronounced in Wenglish. Its meaning in French – 'it doesn't matter', 'It is not important' – is sometimes what is intended when it is used in Wenglish but it can also mean 'we can't do anything about it'. It is occasionally used adjectivally, meaning 'careless' or 'indifferent': 'He did it it a san ferian sort of way.'

Satday / Sat'day (proper noun)

Saturday.

sausage (noun, singular and plural)

Sausage, used for the singular and plural, though 'sausages' is also possible for the plural.

savin(g) (adjective)

Thrifty: 'Very savin' she is – 'Take care of the pennies and the pounds will take care of themselves', she do say.'

say stories (phrasal verb)

To tell lies: 'Don't say stories!'

scatty (adjective)

(1) Mad: 'Driving me scatty, 'er singin' is!'

(2) Very fond of: 'Scatty for sultanas she is but 'er brother can't stand 'em!'

scavenger (noun)

Refuse collector. Now more or less obsolete. See also **ashman**.

scent / sent (noun)

Perfume.

scet

See **sket**.

scholar

See **good scholar**.

scholarship (noun)

The name by which the 11-plus selective exam was once known.

school

See **night school**.

schoolteacher (noun)

Teacher. A generation or so ago **schoolteacher** was the more usual expression.

scissors: a scissors (noun, singular)

Note Wenglish use of singular where Standard English uses the plural: a 'pair of scissors'.

sclein

See **sglein**.

scoot / scwt (noun)

A boost, a help forward: 'That hundred pound will give them a good scwt on.' The 'oo'/'w' is generally pronounced short.

scoot! / scwt! (interjection)

Be off! Clear off! Shoo! 'Scoot, will you – that's enough!'

scrage (transitive verb)

To scratch, to scrape.

scram (transitive verb)

To scratch.

scramcat (noun)

A girl who 'scrams' (scratches) when quarrelling/fighting.

screch / sgrech (noun)

Screech, yell. It can also mean 'an unpleasant person'. The spelling with 'c' reflects the colloquial South Wales Welsh pronunciation, the 'e' is long and pure, while the 'ch' is also pronounced as in Welsh. (Welsh)

screw (noun)

(1) Payment, wages: ''E's on a good screw by there in Thyssen's, I bet.'

(2) A sharp-tongued woman, a shrew: 'Real old screw she is – always moanin' about something or other.' The pronunciation of the word with this meaning is usually as in Welsh, with a long, open 'e'.

screws: the screws

Rheumatism. 'E do get the screws awful when the weather's damp.' See also **reumatic / reumatics**.

screwed

See **head screwed on**.

script (noun)

Doctor's prescription: 'I'm goin down the surgery to pick up my script.'

scrudge / scrooge (noun)

Sweet and often sticky cake or dessert.

scrump (transitive verb)

To pinch, to take.

scrumps / scrumpies (noun, plural)

Pieces of broken off batter in the chip shop.

scullery (noun)

Kitchen. See also **back kitchen**.

scuse (transitive verb)

To excuse: 'Scuse me! 'Ave you got the right time, please?'

scwt!

See **scoot!**

scwt

See **scoot**.

see is she in (expression)

To see if she is at home: 'Knock the door and see is she in?' Note how the word order differs from Standard English.

self: on my own self (prepositional phrase, used adverbally)

On my own, alone. This echoes the Welsh 'ar ben fy hunan'.

sell

See **how do you sell?**

sêm

See **saim**.

send (transitive verb)

To see off, to accompany while bidding farewell to: 'Three o'clock it was before I could send them.'

sent

See **scent**.

serchus / syrchus (adjective)

Miserable, moody, unpleasant in manner. In Wenglish this word is not generally used with its Standard Welsh meaning of 'pleasant' or 'agreeable', rather in an ironic or sarcastic manner to describe a miserable person: 'He's syrchus today, in' 'e?' **Syrchus** reflects the colloquial South Wales Welsh pronunciation. It can occasionally mean 'pleasant'/'agreeable' as in Welsh: 'She was syrchus enough to me today, mind.'

serviceable (adjective)

Suiting the purpose, hard-wearing: 'That jacket's very serviceable and smart an' all!'

set (transitive verb)

(Of a fire) To prepare ready for lighting: 'I'll set the fire now so we don't have to do it when we come back after.' See also **put** (4).

sexy (adjective)

Having sexual content: 'I didn't like that old film – it was too sexy.'

sget

See **sket**.

sglein / sclein (noun)

Shine, sparkle: 'There's a lovely sglein on 'er things.' (Welsh)

sgrech

See **screch**.

shake

See **shook rigid**.

shame: for shame on you! (interjection)

Shame on you! The expression is generally introduced by the preposition **for** in Wenglish: 'For shame on you, you ought to know better by now!'

shammy (noun)

Chamois (leather/suede cloth for cleaning).

shandivang / shandibang (adverb)

In a terrible mess: 'That place is all shandivang with 'er!' **Shandivang** is the more common form.

shape (noun)

Efficiency, system/manner (of working/doing), ability to do, condition: 'There's no shape on 'im in the garden.' 'We done it some shape in the end.' 'Same shape it was in as last week.' The word 'siàp' is used colloquially in Welsh in the same way. See also **di-siâp**.

shape (transitive verb)

To move (oneself), to shift, to hurry up: 'You better shape youerself or we'll be late.' This mirrors the use of the colloquial Welsh verb 'siapo'.

shape (intransitive verb)

To take shape, to be making good progress: "Ow's the bathroom shapin' with you, then?'

sharang

See **head sharang**.

shark (transitive verb)

To cheat: 'Don't shark the gwt – we been waitin' 'ere a good 'alf hour before you come!' (i.e. 'Don't cheat the queue – we'd been waiting at least half an hour before you arrived!'). (Central Wenglish)

sharp (adjective and adverb)

(1) Stern(ly): 'She's a bit sharp but she's aright once you get to know 'er.'

(2) Cold: 'It's a bit sharp today, innit?'

(3) Astute: 'He's a sharp kid – 'e'll go far.'

sharpish (adverb)

Quickly, in a hurry: 'Let's get out of 'ere sharpish!'

shencyn / shenkin

See **shinkin**.

shewer

See **shuer**.

shibbwns / shibwns / gibbons (noun, plural)

Spring onions.

shift (intransitive verb)

(1) To cope, to manage: 'How are you shiftin' round the 'ouse after youer fall, love?' The colloquial Welsh 'siffto' is used in the same way. See also **di-shift**.

(2) To move/run very quickly: 'That new winger for Ponty – he can shift!'

To shift as a transitive verb is used as in Standard English to mean 'to move (something)'.

shift your stumps! (transitive verb, imperative)

Move yourself!

shiggle (transitive and intransitive verb)

To shake: 'I was shigglin' the tablecloth outside when Anty Edith came.' 'Don't shiggle that too much for fear it breaks.' (From Welsh 'siglo')

shinkin / shincyn / shenkin / shencyn (noun)

A rather sloppy mixture of tea (usually with sugar) with bread in it. Sometimes cheese is/was added. This drink/snack is, strangely, not so popular these days...

shoes full of my feet (nominal phrase)

Swollen feet (after walking/standing).

shook rigid (adjectival phrase)

Shocked: 'I was shook rigid when I 'eard someone breakin' a window downstairs last night.'

shoots

See **chutes**.

shop

See **place: all over the place / all over the shop**.

short: too short to cut cabbage (adjectival phrase)

Very short in stature.

shout an(d) bawl (phrasal verb)

To shout unreasonably, to make a fuss vociferously: 'You know 'oe 'e is – always shoutin' and bawlin' about somethin' or other.'

shout on (phrasal verb)

To shout (aloud) to, to call (aloud) to. This is a direct translation of the Welsh 'gwaeddu ar' or 'galw ar'. See also **call on**.

show

See **all show**.

shuer / shewer (adjective and adverb)

Sure.

shutes

See **chutes**.

shw(d) mae? / shw(d) ma'r (h)wyl?/ shw mai? (adverb + verb/ interjection)

How are you? (South Wales Welsh)

shwd mae'n ceibo?

See **ceibo: shwd mae'n ceibo?**

sick

See **hit him sick** and **off sick**.

sick: on the sick (adverbial phrase)

Off work, generally receiving benefit money.

sick and baad (adverbial phrase)

Very ill.

sick(e)ner: to have a sick(e)ner (phrasal verb)

To have enough of something to make one sick, 'I've 'ad a proper sickner of football with this World Cup!'

sicknuss (noun)

Sickness.

siop popeth / shop popeth (nominal phrase)

A shop that sells everything. (Welsh – literally 'shop of everything')

sink

See **enough … to sink a battleship**.

sinking fast: to be sinkin(g) fast (phrasal verb)

To be rapidly reaching a point where recovery from illness is unlikely: "E's sinkin' fast – there's not much 'ope for 'im now.' See also **verge: on the verge**.

sinking for: to be sinkin(g) for (phrasal verb)

To be longing for: 'I was sinking for a cup of tea when we landed back 'ome.'

Sioni / Sioni Oy / Shwni Dai (nominal phrase)

A badly dressed person: 'Haven't you got something better to wear to the meetin'? You look a proper Sioni Oy in them trousers.'

Sioni bob och(o)r / Siwni bob och(o)r (nominal phrase)

Someone·who 'runs with the hare and hunts with the hounds'. Literally 'Johnny all sides'. (Welsh)

Sioni Winwns / Sioni / Siwni Winwns / Siwni / Johnny Onions (proper noun)

An itinerant Breton onion seller. Their wares – the characteristic pinkish skinned onions – were – and still are – a popular addition to the gastronomy of the Valleys. The onions themselves were sometimes referred to as **Mari Winwns** (Mary Onions).

sisno (on) / sizno (on) (intransitive verb)

To insist on, to take a special liking to, to seize upon: 'I don't know why, but she's sizno'd on that one.' This is another example of English verb endings being added to a Welsh verbal root. The Welsh equivalent of the past pasticiple – **wedi sisno** – can also be used in Wenglish: "E's wedi sisno on 'avin the red one.' Note that the final 'o' of 'sisno' is pronounced short, as in Welsh. (Colloquial South Wales Welsh) (Western Wenglish)

Sisterood / Sister'ood (noun)

In Welsh Baptist (and other nonconformist) circles, a women's afternoon fellowship, partly religious and partly social. The expression **Sisterood** was also used in Welsh even though there is a perfectly good Welsh word 'Chwaeroliaeth'.

sit: is there anybody sitting there? (expression)

Is that seat free?

sizno (on)

See **sisno (on)**.

sketch (noun)

A person with an untidy or unusual appearance: 'Doesn't she look a sketch in that dress!'

sket / sget / scet (with rain) (phrasal verb)

An expression used especially in Western Wenglish for 'drizzle', 'spitting with rain', 'intermittent rain'. 'When we landed in Ponty it was sketting with rain.'

skew-whiff / skew-wiff (adverb)

Not straight, not in the correct way: 'Them tiles are all skew-wiff gone – must be the deesive.'

skimp (intransitive verb)

To be mean with, to economise on, not to use the best quality/full quantity: 'She's always skimpin' on 'er ingredients when she's cookin'.'

skinful (noun)

A large amount (of beer etc) to drink: ''E atto be carried 'ome from the Colliers last Saturday and 'e's 'ad another skinful tonight an' all.'

skulk (intransitive verb)

To sneak, to lurk, to make surreptitious/illicit visits to, e.g. the pantry. 'Tom was skulkin' for food cos 'e din eat 'is dinner.'

slac

See **dal(a) slac yn dynn**.

slap it off (phrasal verb)

To spoil by wearing too often: 'Change youer sweater now – you musn't slap it off or you won't 'ave nothin' tidy to wear.' (Central and Eastern Wenglish)

sledge (noun)

(1) A stupid person, the expression providing an indication of extreme stupidity: 'Twp as a sledge 'e is sometimes!' The meaning is probably from (2).

(2) A sledge-hammer.

sleep: I could sleep on my nose (expression)

I am extremely tired and could sleep just about anywhere. An expression to emphasise just how tired one is.

sleish / slysh (noun)

A small shovel used for coal, cinders etc.

slip (intransitive verb)

Not to be as competent/efficient as formerly: 'You're slippin', 'mychan i! You normly finish the hool lot in under an hour.'

slip up (phrasal verb)

To make a mistake, to miss an opportunity: 'You slipped up there – you should ask him before he changes 'is mind about payin' overtime.'

sloch (noun)

A slovenly person. Pronounced as in Welsh.

slong / salong (interjection)

So long, good-bye.

slong 'en (interjection)

Commonly used inWenglish for **so long, then**.

slouch hat (nominal phrase)

Trilby (hat).

slowly / slow fach (adverb/adverbial phrase)

Gradually: 'He's comin slow fach' means 'He is gradually getting better (especially after an illness)'. The hybrid form **slow fach** is an example of an English adjective being qualified by a Welsh adverb. (Western Wenglish)

slummocky (adjective)

Slovenly, untidy, though not as bad as **didoreth** (q.v.): 'She've always been a bit slummocky – there's norra lorra shape on 'er!' 'Ler 'erself go, she 'ave – gone to look proper slummocky, she 'ave!' (mostly Central and Eastern Wenglish)

slysh

See **sleish**.

smack (noun)

An accident, particularly in the pit.

smack in front / smack be(h)ind (prepositional and adberbial phrases)

Directly in front/behind: 'When you come out of the station, It's smack in front of you.'

smack in the chops (nominal phrase)

A setback, a disappointment, a blow to one's hopes: 'When she found out that Diana 'ad 'ad the job over 'er, it was a reeal smack in the chops for 'er.'

smala (adjective)

Funny, odd, queer, with a hint of being awkward and contrary: 'Smala 'e can be – you got to be careful how you handle 'im.' (Colloquial South Wales Welsh, the Standard Welsh form being 'ysmala')

small small (adjectival phrase)

Very small. The Welsh use of a double adjective for emphasis is echoed in Wenglish so that one hears: 'Oh it was small small – you could 'ardly see it!'. One also hears of 'a small little man', or a 'big 'uge factory'.

small beer (nominal phrase)

A home made drink, made out of herbs, – especially nettles – water, sugar and yeast. See also **jovain**.

small coal

See **glo mân**.

smash (noun)

Car crash, accident: 'There was a big smash on the main road – there were loadsa plice cars and fyer engines!'

smasher (noun)

An excellent one.

sment (noun)

Cement.

smoothe (transitive verb)

To iron (clothes).

smoothing (noun)

Ironing (clothes): 'It aa pass leven an I an't done the smoothin yet!'

so there for you! (interjection)

That's it!: 'I've finished my work, so there for you!'

soak / soaked

See **half soak**.

sobor o gomwn/gomon

See **common**.

soc / swc: in a soc / in a swc (prepositional phrase)

In a soporific state, sleepy (literally or metaphorically): 'The baby's in a nice swc now!' 'That girl they got be'ind the counter must be in a soc or somethin' – she give me more change than what I spent in the first place!'

soft (adjective)

Stupid, foolish, mad: 'He's soft in the 'ead gone!' 'Don't be so soft, gul! The post don't come till ten.'

soft-soap (transitive verb)

To try to persuade by flattery: ''E tried to soft-soap me but I wasn't 'avin' none of that nonsense.'

solt (transitive verb, past tense and past participle)

Sold. A common form of the past tense and past participle of 'to sell'. 'I solt my car for five 'undred quid.'

some

See **there's some weather we're having**.

sore: bear with a sore head

See **bear with a sore head**.

sorry in (h)is/(h)er (h)eart (adjectival phrase)

Extremely sorry for, very sympathetic towards: 'When 'e told 'is mother about the way the'd treated 'im, she was sorry in 'er 'eart for 'im.'

so(a)sh: on the so(a)sh (prepositional phrase)

Receiving benefit payments, on the Social Security. Pronounced 'soash', with a long 'o'.

sospan (noun)

Saucepan. This is also the spelling used in Welsh.

spanish (noun)

Liquorice.

spark (noun)

Electrician. See also **lectrician**.

spark (with) (intransitive verb)

To court, to be courting, to be going out (with).

sparkin(g) (present participle and noun)

Courting. **To be sparkin(g) with** means 'to be courting', 'to be going out with'.

spec: on spec (adverbial phrase)

Speculatively, without pre-arranging: 'Only went there on spec, we did!'

specs (noun, plural)

Spectacles, glasses.

spect / 'xpect (transitive verb)

To expect.

spell (noun)

(1) A period of time: ''E lived in Bridgend for a spell before movin' back to Port Talbot.'

(2) A rest: I'm going to have a little spell before finishin the job'. See also **whiff**.

spiteful (adjective)

Unwilling, uncooperative: 'The fire's awful slow comin' – being spiteful it is today!'

sponar / sponer (noun)

Girlfriend. (Welsh)

spose (transitive verb)

To suppose: 'I sposed 'e'll be 'ere now in a minute.'

sposed: to be sposed to (phrasal verb)

To be supposed to. Used frequently in Wenglish to express what 'ought' to happen. ''E was sposed to be 'ere by now but 'e's late agen!'

spout (intransitive verb)

To talk, generally loquaciously: 'What was she spoutin' about agen?'

sprachus (adjective)

Presentable, of acceptable standard. (Colloquial South Wales Welsh) (Western Wenglish)

sprag (noun)

A bar inserted into **dram** (q.v.) wheels to stop them running backwards. This gives rise to the following two entries.

sprag (transitive verb)

To trip: ''E spragged 'imself on that step out the back.'

sprag: to put a sprag (in) (phrasal verb)

To put a stop (to).

sprateus (noun)

A sharp-tongued person. (Central Wenglish)

sprats (noun, plural)

Whitebait, small fish eaten whole.

sprottin(g) / sprwtin(g) (present participle used adjectivally)

Prying, interfering.

spread (noun)

A generous meal: 'There was a lovely spread waiting for us when we got back.'

spreathed (adjective)

Chapped by cold weather

sprwtin(g)

See **sprottin(g)**.

spuds (noun, plural)

(1) Holes in stockings.

(2) Potatoes.

square (transitive verb)

To deal with: 'I'll square 'im when I get back!'

square up (phrasal verb)

(1) To settle up, to settle one's debts: 'I'll square up with you tomorrow, Dai.'

(2) To make tidy: 'I'll have to square up the bedrooms before startin' downstairs.'

squeeze chwps

See **chwps**.

squint (noun)

A quick look: 'I 'ad a squint at the Echo but I 'aven't 'ad a chance to read it tidy.'

stais / stays (noun, plural)

Corset. **Stais** is pronounced as in Welsh, **stays** as in Standard English.

stamp (noun)

Build, appearance: ''E's the same stamp as 'is granfather exactly.' See also **dap** (2).

stand on the door (phrasal verb)

To stand at the door, on the doorstep.

stange (adjective)

Decent, respectable, a good example of something: ' Nice suit you got – looks very stange.' (Western Wenglish)

star turn (nominal phrase)

An amusing person: ''E was a star turn, mun – you ought to 'ave 'eard 'im singin' in the karaoke!'

state (noun)

Condition: 'Look at the state on that fryin' pan – disgustin' it is!'

stays

See **stais**.

stecks

See **stex**.

'steddfod

See **eisteddfod**.

steek (noun)

Older pronunciation for **steak** (meat).

steppin (noun)

Step(s), generally outside a house: 'I seen 'er when I was comin' up the steppin.'

Used also in colloquial South Wales Welsh. It is the word 'stepping' taken over onto Welsh, then loaned back to Wenglish with slight modification. (Western Wenglish)

stex / stecks / sticks (noun, plural)

A (generally sticky and unpleasant) mess: 'The baby's bib is all sticks and stecks – I'll get 'im a clean one now.'

stick: funny (old) stick (nominal phrase)

Strange person: 'Funny old stick that Tom White – I never know 'ow to take 'im.'

sticks (noun, plural)

Firewood. See also **stex**, **cut sticks** and **chop sticks**.

sticky (noun)

The adhesive (of an envelope etc.) 'The sticky's gone on this envelope – we'll 've to put some Sellotape on it.' See also **deesive**.

stillions (noun, plural)

A hand-held balance.

stir your stumps

See **shift your stumps**.

stitch: every whip stitch (adverbial phrase)

Constantly, all the time: 'She's down the shops every whip stitch.'

stomach

See **can't abear**.

stomp / stump (noun)

A mixture of mashed potato and swede, otherwise called **potch** or **ponjin**.

stoppage (noun)

Constipation.

stumps

See **shift your stumps**.

stone the flags/doorstep (phrasal verb)

To clean the stone floor/ doorstep.

stop: on stop

See **on stop**.

stop tap (nominal phrase)

The time when the pubs and clubs stop serving. See also **open tap**.

stories (noun, plural)

Lies. See also **say stories**.

straight (adverb)

(1) In a direct manner: 'I told 'im straight that 'e'd afto go.'

(2) Immediately: ''E went straight then.' (He left immediately at that juncture.)

straight off (adverbial phrase)

Straight away, immediately. See also **right off**.

strip off to (h)alf (phrasal verb)

To take off one's upper clothing: 'Stripped off to 'alf 'e was workin' in the garden.'

stoary (noun)

Story. The spelling reflects the pronunciation, with a long 'o' sound.

stone (noun, singular and plural)

As a unit of weight, the plural is the same as the singular: 'She weighs leven stone three – she could lose two stone easy.'

strobulous / obstropolous (adjective)

Argumentative, awkward (of person); awful, difficult (of situation). The form **obstropolous** is used mostly to describe people. Derived from 'obstreperous'.

stroke (noun)

A stroke of work, any work at all: "E don't do a stroke round the 'ouse never!'

stroke: to alter your stroke (phrasal verb)

To change and improve your method/attitude: 'I wonder if 'e'll ever alter 'is stroke.'

struck (by/with) (adjective)

Fond (of), impressed (by): 'I wasn't struck with that new suit of 'is.'

stump (noun)

(1) See **stomp**.

(2) The core of an apple.

stummuck (noun)

Stomach.

stute / 'stute (noun)

Institute, often the Miners' Institute, venue of social activities, snooker/billiards etc.

suck-in (noun)

Disappointment, especially when a good outcome or result was expected: 'Newport 'ad a real suck-in – Ebbw came back from be'ind and won easy in the end.'

sudden (adjective and adverb)

Sudden(ly): 'Harriet Jones 'ave died sudden.'

Sul y Blodau / Sul y Blode / Sul y Blote (proper noun)

Palm Sunday. Flowers were/are traditionally put on family graves at this time. (Welsh) (Western Wenglish)

Sul y Pasg / Sul y Pasc (proper noun)

Easter Sunday (Welsh). (Western Wenglish)

Sulgwyn (proper noun)

Whitsun. (Welsh) (Western Wenglish)

summons (transitive verb)

To summon to appear in court: 'He've been summonsed again for speeding.'
See also **have up**.

supper (noun)

(1) A moderately light later evening meal, eaten around 8 to 9 in the evening, separate from and later than tea (q.v.).

(2) The main evening meal.

sure to be (adverbial phrase)

Probably, almost certainly: 'They'll be off on theyer 'olidays next week now, sure to be.' This is a direct translation of the Welsh 'siwr o fod'. See also **bound to be**.

sustificate (noun)

An occasionally heard variant of **certificate**.

swank (noun)

A posh person or someone possessing/wearing something swanky. See **swanky** and **all swank**.

swank (intransitive verb)

To show off.

swanky (adjective)

Posh, grand elegant, showy, impressive: 'They've just bought a swanky new car.' Not just Wenglish, of course, but characteristic of 'Classical' Wenglish.

Swansea (noun)

A Swansea loaf, an elongated, roughly oval-shaped loaf of bread.

Swansea play (nominal phrase)

(In sport, especially bowls and tactical sports) Safety play or playing by the rules in order to secure the desired result.

swc: in a swc (prepositional phrase)

In a sleepy, docile mood (of a baby). See also **soc: in a soc**.

swci (adjective)

Given over to attention, spoiling etc., especially a baby or small child, sleepy and docile: 'Aw look at 'er, she's all swci b'there!'

sweet penderfynol

See **penderfynol**.

swell

See **swole**.

swill (transitive verb)

(1) To rinse, to wash quickly.

(2) To have a quick wash: 'You better swill youer hands before you eat youer dinner.'

(3) To empty and rinse the teapot.

swill (noun)

A quick wash.

swill through (phrasal verb)

To wash out by hand: 'It'll be alright once you give it a quick swill through.'

swindle (noun)

A sweepstake, prize draw or raffle.

swllt

See **dwy 'wech am swllt**.

swmpo (intransitive verb)

To shift, to budge: 'Swmp up a bit – I 'an't got enuff room by 'ere.' (Colloquial South Wales Welsh) (Western Wenglish)

swmpus (adjective)

Substantial, solid, thick: 'Them curtains are nice and swmpus – there's plenty of gafael on them.' (Welsh) (Western Wenglish)

swole (intransitive verb, past tense and past participle)

Swelled, become swollen: ''Is foot swole up nasty after he fell.'

swot (transitive and intransitive verb)

To revise, to study.

swot (noun)

A studious person, usually a **good scholar** (q.v.) and likely to **pass 'igh** (q.v.).

swottin(g) (noun)

Revising, revision, studying for exams.

swotty (adjective)

Studious.

syrchus

See **serchus**.

T

ta (interjection)

Thanks.

ta / tuh (preposition)

To. These spellings reflect a pronunciation sometimes encountered in Wenglish, especially when speakers do not want to sound too 'Welshy'. The traditional pronunciation of **to** in Wenglish involves a pure 'w' sound: in this modified pronunciation, the vowel is short and rather indistinct, like the 'e' at the end of 'the' in 'the books'.

ta ra / tah rah (interjection)

Goodbye. Probably introduced from other English dialects (e.g. Scouse). It is the childish/familiar 'ta ta' (meaning 'goodbye'), with the intervocalic 't' pronounced as a trilled 'r'.

tablets / tabluts: on a course of tablets / tabluts (prepositional phrase)

Taking tablets prescribed by the doctor. Use of this expression (rather than just saying 'I'm taking tablets') serves to add to the seriousness of the treatment (and by implication the illness).

tadcu

See **dadcu**.

tack (noun)

Merchandise, produce. See also **cheap tack**.

taffy (noun)

Toffee.

tafod teg (nominal phrase)

A smooth talker. (Welsh for 'fair tongue')

tah rah

See **ta ra**.

take: don't know how to take him / her

See **know**.

take away: to have it all taken away (phrasal verb)

To have a hysterectomy: 'Dora 'ave 'ad it all taken away, poor dab – I'll afto take 'er some grapes in 'ospital.' Often whispered or uttered in hushed tones.

talk (transitive verb)

(1) To speak: 'He can talk a bit o' French – he've been goin to night school.'

''E carn talk proper!' 'Talk tidy, will you!'

(2) See **don't talk!**

talk: might as well talk to the wall (expression)

It is no use talking to him/her – he/she won't listen/respond.

talk nineteen to the dozen (phrasal verb)

To talk a great deal and very quickly, to talk in a garbled manner.

talu 'fory (verb + adverb used as adverbial phrase)

On hire purchase. (Welsh for 'pay tomorrow')

tamp (noun)

The bounce, the way the ball bounces, as found in the following expressions: 'The tamp of the pitch', 'The tamp of the ball'.

tamp (intransitive verb)

To bounce (of ball).

tampin(g) (adjective)

(1) Bouncing (of ball): 'He done well to 'it a tampin' ball in from that distance.'

(2) Very angry: ''E was tampin' when 'e 'eard what they'd been up to while 'is back was turned.' **Tampin(g) mad** is a variant of this expression.

tanner to raise/rise the latch (nominal phrase)

Formerly sixpence (or a small amount) to pay for drinks at the beginning of an evening's drinking session in the hope that others would pay later.

tan(t) telyn: like tan(t) telyn (prepositional phrase, used in predicate with 'to be')

Tight, like a corset: 'You don't want it like tant telyn – you've got to be comftable in it.' (Welsh, literally 'harp strings') (Western Wenglish)

tap / tip (noun)

Metal pieces, tapped onto the soles of shoes for extra durability.

tap (transitive verb)

(1) To repair (of shoes): 'I'll 'ave to go and 'ave my shoes tapped.' This could involve the application of **taps** (q.v.).

(2) To tap the wheels of railways wagons and carriages with a hammer to ensure, from the sound, they are sound and not cracked. The men who undertook this work were called **wheeltappers**.

tapped (adjective).

Mad, demented: 'You can't believe 'alf of what 'e comes out with – I think 'e's a bit tapped.'

taste on (noun + preposition)

The use of **taste on** in Wenglish is a direct translation of the Welsh 'blas ar': 'There was a lovely taste on that dinner.'

tatws

See **blodyn**.

taw (noun)

One's best marble.

tawch (noun)

An unpleasant taste: 'Ach y fi! There's a bit of a funny tawch on this cheese!' The Welsh word 'tawch' literally means a haze or fog.

tea (noun)

(1) Lightish meal consisting typically of bread and butter, cake etc, washed down with tea.

(2) The main evening meal, generally served fairly early (around 5 to 6 in the evening), high tea. See also **supper**.

(3) See **cup of tea in the hand**.

tea fight / bun fight (nominal phrase)

A free tea or meal, often in the chapel vestry or hall.

tea: for all the tea in China and all the coal in Wales (expression)

At no price.

teisen lap / teeshun lap (nominal phrase)

A simple fruit cake, a local speciality. (Welsh)

tell by him/her (phrasal verb)

To be able to tell by his/her appearance/manner: 'You could tell by 'im that 'e was upset about somethin'.'

tell lies like talking Welsh (phrasal verb)

To tell lies habitually and/or convincingly.

tell straight (phrasal verb)

To tell directly, unambiguously or immediately: 'I told 'em straight that they atto go.'

telyn

See **tant telyn**.

terrible / terruble (adjective and adverb)

Awful(ly), terrible/terribly: (as adjective) 'er youngest 'ave 'ad this terrible chest frages – could be asma.' (as adverb) 'My leg is 'urtin' me terrible.'

testamunt (noun)

Testament.

thank you: I wouldn't give thank you (expression)

I would not give thanks for it because I don't like it: 'I wouldn't give thank you for an 'oliday in Spain.'

thank you fawr (nominal phrase)

An English–Welsh hybrid meaning 'thank you very much'. Also used in colloquial Welsh.

thar way (demonstrative adjective + noun)

Possible spelling and pronunciation of **that way**.

thar wun (demonstrative adjective + pronoun)

Possible spelling and pronunciation of **that one**.

thass (contraction of demonstrative pronoun + verb)

Possible spelling and pronunciation of **that's / that is**.

thasserfack / that's a fac(t) (contraction of demonstrative pronoun + verb + indefinite article + noun)

Possible spelling and pronunciation of **that's a fact**.

thasser good 'un / that's a good one (expression)

Don't tell me lies! Pull the other one! You must be joking!': 'You mow the lawn and do the garden! That's a good one!'

thass go(w)in(g) / that's goin(g) / goin(g) (relative pronoun + verb)

That's going, that exists: 'You must be the biggest fool goin' if you believe that rubbish!' In the case of **goin(g)**, the relative pronoun and verb are dropped but their meaning understood.

thass typical / that's typical (expression)

That's just like: 'Thass typical of you – never turn up when you say you will!' See also **all over**.

the lorrovew/lorrovue / the lorravus / the lorravem/lorravum

See **lorrovew: the lorrovew**.

theeáter (noun)

Theatre. Often pronounced with the stress on the penultimate syllable.

them (demonstrative adjective and pronoun)

Those.

there

See **all there**, **by there** and **never all there**.

there's (adverb + verb, intransitive, present tense)

There is, there are. **There's** is used with both singular and plural nouns. 'There's six or seven envelopes on the table.' 'There's neely forty in Angharad's class.'

there's rain / there's a price on (adverb + verb, functioning as adjectival phrase, + noun/article + noun)

What awful rain / How expensive: 'There's rain we've been 'avin'!' 'There's a price on beef gone!' (How expensive beef has become.) See also **here's**. (From the Welsh construction 'dyna' + noun)

there's nice/lovely/posh etc. (for you) (adverb + verb, functioning as adverbial phrase, + adjective)

How nice/lovely/posh etc.: 'There's lovely youer new dress is!' Such expressions are a direct translation from the Welsh construction 'dyna' + adjective. The optional addition of **for you / for them** etc. also follows Welsh usage.

there's...there! (expression)

An emphatic way of drawing someone's attention to someone (who might be passing) or something of interest (which might be visible): 'There's Janine there!' means 'Look! Janine's over there!'.

there's times (adverbial phrase)

There are occasions: 'There's times I could 'it 'im, 'e's so twp!'

there you/we are then (expression)

That's it, there we have it: In conversation, a conclusion of some sort is often signalled by this expresson: 'Well there you are then – you can't go any further with the job till you can afford to pay for it!' It is a loan translation of the Welsh construction 'dyna chi/ni 'te'.

these days (adverbial phrase)

Nowadays, currently: 'I'm gone I can't get a good night's sleep these days.'

theyer (possessive adjective and pronoun; occasionally contraction of pronoun + verb)

Possible spelling and pronunciation of **their** and occasionally **they're / they are** too.

theyselves (reflexive pronoun)

Possible variation of **themselves**.

thick (adjective)

Stupid: 'She's a bit thick that Anthea – you gorrw tell 'er at least three times before the understands.'

thick: a bit thick (adjectival phrase)

A bit much: 'It's a bit thick to expect me to drop evrythin' and go down to Bridgend to pick 'em up!' In colloquial Standard English, 'rich' is used in this sense.

thing: first thing

See **first thing**.

thing: the main thing (nominal phrase)

The most important thing: 'The main thing is that everybody got their presents.'

think

See **thought sure**.

think: and there was me thinking (expression)

And I assumed all along: 'They're off on a world crewse and there was me thinking they was llwm llwm.'

this ages / 'issages / frages (adverbial phrase/adverb)

For a long time, for ages.

this long time (adverbial phrase)

For a long time: 'Where have you been this long time?' (said to an acquaintance one has not seen for a long time.). It translates as the Welsh 'ers lawer dydd' or 'ers amser hir'. Can also be used as an alternative to **this ages / frages**.

this years (adverbial phrase)

For many years, for a long time. **This years, this long time**, and **this ages / 'issages** can all be used more or less interchangeably.

thought sure (expression consisting of verb + adverb)

Was convinced, sure: 'I thought sure he'd 'ave turned up by now.' Only used in the past tense.

three-piece (suite) (noun/nominal phrase)

A three piece suite of furniture, consisting of a sofa/settee and two armchairs. See also **two-piece**.

throat

See **jump down my throat**.

throw it up

To remind about something by way of reproach: 'She jest can't let go of it – she threw it up to me again when I seen 'er down the Post Office.'

throwed (transitive verb, past tense and past participle)

Possible past tense and past participle of **to throw**: 'They 'ad it all goin for them an' then they throwed it away.' **Threw** is just as commonly used.

through

See **go through me**.

through and through (nominal phrase)

Lumps of coal and small coal mixed together, unsieved.

through and through (adverbial phrase)

Thoroughly, as in Standard English.

through and through: to live through and through (phrasal verb)

To share accommodation in a house without having any specific private rooms other than a bedroom.

tickle (transitive verb)

To amuse, to give cause for amusement/wonder: 'That's tickled me now! I can't get over it!'

tiddly bit (nominal phrase)

An old silver threepenny coin.

tidy (adjective and adverb)

A significant and very commonly used word in Wenglish. As an adjective, it generally means 'good', 'splendid', 'decent' and also corresponds to the Standard English 'quite a' . Thus **a tidy spell** (quite a long time), **a tidy few** (quite a number), **a tidy feller** (a decent man), **a tidy step (back and fore)** (quite a long way (there and back)), **a tidy bit in the bank** (being well-off) and **tidy!** (excellent! splendid!).

As an adverb it means 'well', 'properly, 'competently', thus **talk tidy!** (speak properly!) and **he can do that tidy now, ware teg!** (he can do that competently now, fair play!)

See also **half tidy**.

tight (adjective)

(1) (slightly) drunk.

(2) mean.

(3) in short supply, especially money.

tight-fisted (adjective)

Mean.

time (noun)

Occasion. See also **there's times**.

time

See **all the time**, **pass the time of day** and **give the time of day**.

time: in no time (adverbial phrase)

Swiftly: 'He done the job in no time!'

times: on times (prepositional phrase, used adverbally)

At times, sometimes, on some occasions. A direct translation of the Welsh 'ar brydiau'.

tin cream (nominal phrase)

Tinned, sterilised cream, once popularly eaten with tinned fruit.

tin fruete / tin ffriwt / tin fruit (nominal phrase)

Tinned fruit. See also **fruete** and **heavily fruited**.

tin peaches (nominal phrase)

Tinned peaches, generally in syrup. These, were 'traditionally' served with tinned cream or **Ideal Milk** (q.v.). Often bread and butter was served with them. This was a popular treat for afternoon tea on Sundays.

tin pears (nominal phrase)

Tinned pears, generally halved and in syrup. These, were 'traditionally' served with tinned cream or **Ideal Milk** (q.v.). Often bread and butter was served with them. This was a popular treat for afternoon tea on Sundays.

tin tacks (nominal phrase)

Small nails or drawing-pins.

tip

See **tap**.

tip down (phrasal verb)

To rain very heavily.

tired: too tired to get out of (h)is own way: (adjectival phrase and expression)

Very lazy and/or tired: ''E's a lazy old bugger – too tired to get out of 'is own way 'e is!'

titchy (adjective)

Very small: 'They've got a titchy little dog – not much bigger than 'amster it is!'

to: where's it to?

See **where's it to?**

to be (verb infinitive, used as adverbial phrase)

In existence, in being, to be had: 'I got three pairs but here's another pair to be somewhere – praps iss fallen be'ind the settee.'

tod-end (noun)

Cigarette end. Also **dog-end** or **nip**.

toe the line (phrasal verb)

To conform to the rules: 'You'll have to toe the line if you want to get on in that firm.'

tomorro (adverb and noun)

Tomorrow, the spelling reflecting the 'Classical' Wenglish pronunciation.

Tom Pepper: a bigger liar than Tom Pepper (expression)

An outrageous liar. Not exclusively Wenglish but commonly used in Wenglish.

tommy-box (noun)

A miner's food container.

tongue

See **length of his/her tongue**.

ton (noun, singular and plural)

Ton. This expression of quantity generally remains unchanged in the plural: 'I've ordered two ton of sand.'

tons (noun, plural, expressing quantity)

Very many: 'There were tons of people there.'

tools ar y bar (expression)

Time to down tools and have a rest. A hybrid English and Welsh expression, functioning equally in Wenglish. and colloquial South Wales Welsh. It was probably restricted to the Western Wenglish area. The 'bar' referred to was a bar or trestle on which tools were put when not in use so that each worker could find them easily. (Western Wenglish)

toot: on my toot

On my nerves: 'Them kids do get on my toot, with all theyer shoutin'!'

tooth (noun)

As in Standard English but the 'oo' is pronounced short.

tooth : bell on/in every tooth

See **bell**.

toothless (adjective)

As in Standard English but the 'oo' is pronounced short.

toothpaste (noun)

As in Standard English but the 'oo' is pronounced short.

toothpick (noun)

As in Standard English but the 'oo' is pronounced short.

toothy (adjective)

As in Standard English but the 'oo' is pronounced short.

torri: wedi torri (verbal adjective, equivalent of past particple)

Having lost his/her marbles, become senile. The Welsh expression literally means 'broken'. ''Er uncle Dai 'as wedi torri – can't shift for 'imself these days.' The Welsh verb 'torri' does not take English endings. **Wedi torri** is only encountered in the perfect tense, with present meaning – 'Idris has wedi torri' means 'Idris is senile/has become senile'. (Western Wenglish)

tossel (noun)

The usual pronunciation of 'tassel'.

touch and go (adverbial phrase)

In the balance. See also **verge: on the verge**.

toy (noun)

An amusing character: 'That Gary's a reeal toy – you never know what 'e's goin' to say next!'

trachwantus (adjective)

Greedy, excessive: 'Now that's trachwantus – you don't need to eat all that – keep a bit for tea!' (Welsh, and pronounced as in Welsh) (Western Wenglish)

trade

See **roaring trade**.

trafó (noun)

Fuss and bother, difficulty, goings-on. The **f** of this loan from colloquial South Wales Welsh is pronounced as a **v**, and the stress is on the second syllable – **o**. (Western Wenglish)

trailer (noun)

Caravan: 'They gorra lovely trailer down the Mumbles.' See also **'van**.

train

See **on the train**.

tramway / tramroad

See **dramway**.

tranglwns (noun, plural)

Bits and pieces, odds and ends. (Colloquial South Wales Welsh) (Western Wenglish)

trash

See **drash**.

travel the side/back (phrasal verb)

To use the side/back entry to a house. (Central Wenglish)

tread

See **trood**.

trewth / trueth / truth (noun)

Truth.

trick

See **miss a chalk / miss a trick**.

tricks: how's tricks? (interjection)

How are things?: 'Hiya, Ron! How's tricks then?'

trim up (phrasal verb)

To decorate for Christmas.

trimmings (noun, plural)

Christmas decorations.

trip (noun)

(1) An outing, an excursion.

(2) A hill, or rise: 'Theyer 'ouse is on top of the trip.'

trood (intransitive verb, past tense and past participle)

A possible form of the past tense and past participle of **to tread**: 'I trood in some dog muck on the pavement agen – it's awful gone these days, filthy!'

trot: on the trot (prepositional phrase, used adverbally)

Consecutively: 'They've won six games on the trot now.'

trouble

See **water trouble**.

troughing (noun)

Roof guttering. See also **chutes**.

trouser: a trouser / trousers: a trousers (noun)

Note use of singular where Standard English would say 'a pair of trousers'.

trucks

See **saim**.

trust you to... (expression)

It's typical of you to...: 'Trust you to find something wrong – you are too putickler for youer own good.'

truth

See **trewth**.

tub

See **brought up under a tub**.

tuh

See **ta**.

tump (noun)

A hillock, mound or small hill.

turn (intransitive verb)

To proceed: 'I din know which way to turn!'

turn (noun)

(1) Time, occasion: 'This will do another turn at least.'

(2) A shift at work.

(3) See **hand's turn**.

turn it over (phrasal verb)

To change TV channels: "There was nothin' on BBC, so I turned it over to the other side.'

turn round (phrasal verb)

To follow up with: 'After all that cryin', she turned round and told us she was leavin' 'er 'usbunt!'

turn spiteful (phrasal verb)

To become difficult/unhelpful: 'She turned spiteful on me when I told 'er she couldn't come with us.'

twang (noun)

An unusual or affected accent: 'She talks with a bit of a twang – fancies 'erslf a bit, I think!'

twelvemonth / twelmonth / twelmunth (noun)

A year: 'Dad will have been dead a hool twelmunth in April.'

twig (intransitive verb)

To guess, to deduce, to realise fully, to understand: 'Took me a while before I twigged.'

twndish (noun)

A funnel. (Welsh)

two

See **make two of**.

two-piece (noun)

A two-piece ladies' suit, consisting of a jacket and skirt: 'That's a lovely two-piece you got, Glad. Bought it down Howells's?' See also **three-piece**.

twp (adjective)

Slow on the uptake, stupid: 'He's a nice enough old boy but 'e is a bit twp, if you ask me!' See also **twpsyn**, **twpsen** and **sledge**.

twpsan / twpsen (noun)

A female who is **twp**, i.e. a bit slow on the uptake. A very stupid female person would be called a **twpsen (d)dwl** or **twpsen (h)urt**. (Welsh: 'dwl' means 'dull' and 'hurt' – pronounced 'hirt' – means 'stupid')

twpsyn (noun)

A male who is **twp** (q.v.), a stupid person. A very stupid person would be called a **twpsyn dwl** or **twpsyn (h)urt**. (Welsh: 'dwl' means 'dull' and 'hurt' – pronounced 'hirt' – means 'stupid'.)

twt / dwt (noun)

A little child or a small/short person: 'We used to come here a lot when you was a little dwt.' (Welsh)

twti down (phrasal verb)

To crouch, to squat. See **coopy down**, **cwat**.

twll (of a place) (noun)

(1) A hole, an unpleasant place: 'I wouldn't give thank you to live in a twll of a place like that.' 'Abercynon's a bit of a twll, so they say.'

(2) A hole, e.g. in clothing: ''E's got a twll in 'is best trousers!'

'Twll' is the Welsh word for 'hole'.

twsh (noun)

A small moustache.

tŷ bach (nominal phrase)

Toilet. (Welsh – literally means 'little house')

tych (intransitive verb)

To grunt (e.g. when making a physical effort): 'He was tychin' a lot but 'e didn't do a lot a work reelly.' Pronounced as in Welsh. Also **to ach and tych.** (Colloquial South Wales Welsh 'tychan') (Western Wenglish)

tylwth / tylwyth (noun)

Family, clan, blood relations: 'Her hool tylwth will be 'ere now in 'alf an hour.'

U

uffach! / yffach! (interjection)

Heck! Much stronger expletive than English translation suggests. A variant is **yffach wyllt!**, literally 'wild hell!'. See also **myn uffach i!** (Welsh) (Western Wenglish)

uffarn! / uffern! / yffarn! (interjection)

Hell! A much stronger expletive than the English translation suggests. A variant is **yffarn dàn!**, literally 'hell fire!' but again a much stronger expletive in Welsh and Wenglish than the Standard English translation would suggest. See also **myn uffern i!** (Welsh) (Western Wenglish)

ugly big (adjectival phrase)

(Of garments etc) Too big and with an overall effect that is ugly and unflattering: 'That dress is ugly big on 'er.'

under

See **degree: one degree under.**

under my feet (prepositional phrase)

In the way: 'I can't get on with my work tidy with them kids under my feet!'

under the doctor (prepositional phrase)

Under the doctor's care, receiving medical treatment: 'There's not much shape on 'im – 'e've been under the doctor neely a hool twelmunth.'

up (preposition)

The preposition is used to mean 'up in' or 'up towards': e.g. 'He's going up his

Gran's tonight to stay.'

See also **all up** and **down**.

up and downer (nominal phrase)

A violent argument: 'We 'ad a bit of an up and downer about 'er tylwth stayin' 'ere for Crissmuss.'

up England way (adverbial phrase)

Somewhere in England. It is used without any sense of geographical precision: 'They're livin' up England way somewhere these days, I think.'

up for the cup (prepositional phrase)

Willing to have a go at anything, in a positive frame of mind. (mostly Central and Eastern Wenglish)

up together (phrase used adjectivally in predicate with 'to be')

Well organised: 'She's so up together – that 'ouse of 'ers is like a pin in paper!'

upside down (phrase used in predicate with 'to be')

In a real mess, very untidy. It also has its Standard English meaning as an adverbial phrase.

'urdy-gurdy

See **(h)urdy-gurdy**.

'urt

See **hurt**.

'usbunt (noun)

Husband.

V

'van

Caravan. See also **trailer**.

verge: on the verge (prepositional phrase)

Nothing to do with the side of the roadway, this expression signifies 'on the border between life and death'. It is said of someone who is dying and about to pass to the 'other side'.

Velouty (noun)

A proprietory brand of skin cream (Velouté).

venter (transitive verb)

(1) To guess, to bet, to assume: 'You can venter it was him who put them up to it!'

(2) Ought to, ought to make an effort to, you had better: 'You can venter tidy the parlour before the Minister do come.'

'Mentro', the soft mutated form of which is 'fentro' (pronounced 'ventro'), is the Welsh for 'to venture'.

vidjio (noun and transitive verb)

Video, VCR, video cassette and, as a verb, 'to video'. The combination 'di' often becomes 'j' in colloquial South Wales Welsh (e.g. 'diawl' > 'jawl').

viewing (noun)

The selection of programmes on television: 'What's the viewing tonight, then?'

vinnygar (noun)

Vinegar.

W

w! / oo! (interjection)

Difficult to translate precisely, this expression/sound is often tagged on to an answer or statement, especially by older, Welsh-speaking Wenglish speakers: 'How are you feeling after youer op. Dacu? 'Lle dda, w!' It serves to emphasise a statement.

wait on someone (phrasal verb)

To wait for someone: 'He's waitin on me to come.'

Wales

See **tea: for all the tea in China and all the coal in Wales**.

wall

See **talk: might as well talk to the wall**.

wanc (noun)

A desire: 'He had a wanc for some shibbwns with his tomatoes.' **Wanc** is the soft mutated form of the Welsh 'gwanc'. It is heard much less these days because of the meaning of its colloquial Standard English homophone. (Western Wenglish)

wanged / wanged out (adjective/adjectival phrase)

Exhausted, tired out: 'She was wanged out after all that washin' and scrubbin'.' See also **fagged out**. (Central and Eastern Wenglish)

wanopeth (adjective)

Hopeless, useless: 'I know I'm not much cop but 'e's wanopeth!' (from Welsh 'anobeithiol') (Western Wenglish)

ware teg / chware teg / wara teg (nominal phrase and interjection)

Fair play. Adaptations of the Welsh 'chwarae teg' based on its pronunciation in colloquial South Wales Welsh.

warm

See **wrap up warm**.

warn

See **won**.

wash like a rag (phrasal verb)

To wash well, to come up a treat after washing.

wash my head (phrasal verb)

To wash one's hair (from Welsh 'golchi'r pen', literally 'to wash one's head')

wass / wuss

Lad, man. It can also mean 'my lad', 'man', 'mate' etc, when calling someone. It does not suggest particular respect towards the person thus addressed, though could also be used ironically/humorously to show affection. (Welsh 'gwas', meaning 'man or 'manservant'.)

wassname

See **wossname**.

waste (noun)

Possible spelling of **waist**, reflecting the usual pronunciation in Wenglish – the vowel is a simple long 'e', not a diphthong.

watch points (phrasal verb)

To observe carefully: 'Watch points an' you'll soon be able to do it grand!'

water trouble (nominal phrase)

Urinary problems.

Wawr

See **Merched y Wawr**.

way

See **tired: too tired to get out of his own way**.

weather

See **there's some weather we're having**.

'wech

See **dwy 'wech am swllt**.

weddol / gweddol (adverb)

Fair, average, so-so, alright, not so bad: 'How are you feelin', Mr Jones?' 'Oh, weddol, thanks.' **Weddol**, the soft mutated form, is in general use in both Wenglish and colloquial South Wales Welsh. (Welsh 'gweddol', meaning 'fair') (Western Wenglish)

wedi heneiddio

See **heneiddio: wedi heneiddio**.

wedi torri

See **torri: wedi torri**.

wedjan / wodjen (noun)

Girlfiend. (Welsh)

weeth

See **o with**.

weekend

See **on the weekend**.

wel i jew jew! / wel i jiw jiw!

See **jew jew!**

well away (adjectival phrase, used predicatively with 'to be')

(1) Well-to-do, prosperous: ''E's well away – gorra good job and 'e 'ad a win on the lottry by all account.'

(2) In an advantageous position, in a good position to avail oneself of: 'You'll be well away for the shops when you start workin' in Cardiff!'

(3) Somewhat inebriated: ''E was well away when I seen 'im at about 'alf ten.'

well oiled (adjectival phrase)

Having drunk a fair amount of alcoholic drink.

Welsh conchy

See **conchy**.

Welsh fashion (adverbial phrase)

Manner of nursing an infant with the shawl wrapped round the child and the person nursing it: 'The baby do love a cwtch Welsh fashion.'

Welsh nash(y) (nominal and adjectival phrase)

Welsh nationalist.

Welshy (adjective)

Having a marked Welsh accent. Some Wenglish speakers, even though their own accent is to an outsider's ear very 'Welshy' indeed, use this term, sometimes in a slightly derogatory way, to describe other people whose accents – in their estimation – are even stronger still, particularly in respect of purity of vowel sounds and sing-song Welsh intonation.

Welshy (noun)

A Welsh-speaking person; a pupil at a Welsh-medium school. Used by some monoglot Wenglish speakers sometimes in a slightly derogatory way.

Wensday (proper noun)

Wednesday.

went: arm / back / knee / leg went. (expression)

My arm / back / knee / leg has given out/become incapacitated: 'I was walkin' down the village when my leg went.'

went (intransitive verb, past tense)

Came/developed to a point that: 'She went, she wouldn't talk to me no more.' Echoes colloquial Welsh usage.

See also **go** (verb).

went flying

See **go flying**.

went in for

See **go in for**.

wfft! (interjection)

Fie! For shame! (the original meaning in Welsh). It is also used as an expression of disgust/exasperation to mean something on the lines of 'Sucks to them!'

wfflon / yfflon (adjective)

In bits, in pieces, in a mess: 'That sweater's gone all wfflon with you!' (Welsh) (Western Wenglish)

wha' (interrogative adjective and pronoun)

Possible pronunciation of **what**.

what's/what are the onions/carrots/apples/oranges? (expression)

How much do the onions/carrots/apples/oranges cost? See also **how do you sell?**

what-do-you call / what-you-call (interrogative pronoun + verb, present tense + pronoun + verb)

Something or someone whose name one has temporarily forgotten.

what's the onions? (expression)

What are the prospects? What is the situation?

what (are) you on about? (expression)

What are you talking about?

what's up? / wossup? (expression)

What is the matter?

what you call (nominal phrase)

Used when one cannot quite remember the name of someone or something, e.g. 'What time is what you call comin over?' or 'Pass me the what you call, will you?' See also **hurdy-gurdy**.

wheeltapper (noun)

A man who tapped the wheels of railways wagons and carriages with a hammer to test, from the sound made, that they were sound and not cracked.

when it came to (expression)

When it came about, when it happened: ''E said 'e'd be there but when it came to, 'e din show up.'

where by? (interrogative adverbial phrase)

Where?

whereabouts? (interrogative adverb)

Where? Where exactly?

where's it to? (expression consisting of interrogative adverb + verb + pronoun + preposition)

Where is it? Note that there is no idea of motion towards here, simply position. (Eastern/Central Wenglish)

whiff / wiff (noun)

A short rest: 'We'll work on till aa pass then we'll 'ave a whiff.' See also **spell**. Could also denote a smoke or cigarette during this rest, or generally.

whimberries / wimberries (noun, plural)

Whinberries. A local delicacy, Whinberries belong to the blueberry family, and grow wild on the mountain sides in the Valleys area. See also **llusi**.

whip

See **stitch: every whip stitch**.

whipper-in (noun)

The schools attendance officer.

whool

See **hool**.

whool (hog)

See **hool hog**.

whoolhearted

See **hoolhearted**.

whoolmeal

See **hoolmeal**.

whoolsome

See **hoolsome**.

whose coat is that jacket? (expression)

This type of sentence, in which the second noun is a particular type of the category stated in the first noun, is quite common.

wieldy (adjective)

Unwieldy.

willin(g) (adjective)

Willing, prepared to allow: 'She's willing for us to go to town.' See also **a-willing** and **not willin(g)**.

wilmuntin / wilmuntan / wilmentin / wilmentan / chwilmentan (intransitive verb)

To rummage about, to pry into: ''E was wilmetin' in the drawers and left it all in 'ell of a mess.' Note the present participle takes the same form as the verb itself. (From Welsh 'chwilmentan')

windo (noun)

Window, the spelling reflecting the 'Classical' Wenglish pronunciation, without any hint of diphthongisation of the final vowel.

winks: forty winks

See **forty winks**.

winky: in a winky / like a winky (adverbial phrase)

Very quickly: ''E was out of bed like a winky.'

wise: awake before he's wise (adjectival phrase)

Rising very early, and thus not being 100% efficient: ''E's awake before he's wise most mornings!' This echoes the Welsh 'ar ddihun cyn bod e'n yn gall/ ar ddihun cyn ei fod yn gall' – 'awake before he's aware/capable/ in his full senses'.

wisp (noun)

A stye. (Central Wenglish)

witch (transitive verb)

To bewitch

witched (adjective)

Bewitched.

with

See **o with**.

with his/her leg/chest etc. (preposition + possessive adjective + noun)

Because of/on account of his/her leg/chest etc.: 'I atto go up the surgery with my leg.'

with you (preposition + pronoun)

At your house/home: 'It always looks lovely with you.' A little reminiscent of the French 'chez' and German 'bei'.

wit–wat (adjective)

Undependable, unreliable, flighty: 'Oh, you can't rely on 'er to turn up – she's so wit-wat.' (From the Welsh 'chit-chwat', meaning 'fickle', 'undependable')

wodjen

See **wedjan**.

women's problems (nominal phrase)

Unspecified gynaecological ailments. Often uttered confidentially, in hushed tones. See also **front passage** and **down below**.

won / warn (extended contraction of verb, past tense, negative)

Possible spelling and pronunciation of **wasn't**.

wondrin(g) (transitive verb, present participle)

Wondering: 'I was wondrin' if you could come with me.'

wonky (adjective)

Defective, not straight: 'That new bike of 'is is wonky, I reckon – I've seen 'im push it more than ride it.'

woods (noun, plural)

Note Wenglish use of plural where Standard English would generally say 'wood'.

work (transitive verb)

(1) To operate, to make function (transitive) as well as to function (intransitive): 'I don't know 'ow to work that new washing machine.' See also **act**

(2) To have a laxative effect: 'Them bananas work you.'

work: a good day's work would kill him (expression)

He is very lazy.

worse / worst: to go on its worse/worst (phrasal verb and idiom)

To deteriorate, to worsen in condition or quality: 'That sofa's going on its worse – we'll have to think of getting a new one.' (Literal translation of Welsh idiom 'mynd ar ei waethaf'.)

worth: more fuss than the worth of it

See **fuss: more fuss than the worth of it**.

woss (contraction of interrogative pronoun and verb, present tense)

Possible spelling and pronunciation of **what's**.

wossa marra? (contraction of interrogative pronoun + verb, present tense + definite article + noun)

Possible spelling and pronunciation of **what's the matter?**, showing use of extended contractions.

wossname / wassname / wossisname (contraction of interrogative pronoun + verb, present tense + possessive adjective verb + noun)

Possible spelling and Wenglish pronunciation of **what's-his-name**.

wossup?

See **what's up?**

wotchermacall / wotchewcall / wotchuecall (contraction of interrogative pronoun + verb, present tense + pronoun + verb)

Something or someone whose name one has temporarily forgotten.

wrap up warm (phrasal verb)

To wear warn clothing: 'Wrap up warm – it's cold out!'

wrgi (noun)

A Lothario, a lecher. (From Welsh)

wrinkles: to know all the wrinkles (phrasal verb)

To know all the ins and outs.

wrong

See **radically wrong**.

wun (numeral and pronoun)

Possible spelling and pronunciation of **one**.

wunt (noun and transitive verb)

Possible spelling and pronunciation of **want**: 'What did Dai wunt? A lend of money agen, no doubt!'

wuss

See **wass**.

wyer (noun)

Possible spelling and pronunciation of **wire**, consisting of two distinct syllables. Similarly **fyer, lyer** etc.

wyless / wyluss (noun)

Radio, wireless: 'I caught the news on the wyluss this mornin'.'

'wyl

See **hwyl**.

'wylus

See **hwylus**.

winwns

See **Mari Winwns** and **Sioni Winwns**.

X

'xpect

See **spect**.

Y

yap (intransitive verb)

To chatter.

yappin(g) (noun)

Chattering: 'I'd 'ad a gutsful of 'er yappin' in the end.'

yarn (noun)

An amusing story or joke: 'Dai come out with some yarns agen – we was crackin' laugin', aye!'

year (transitive verb)

Possible spelling and pronunciation of **to hear**. See also **never hear the end of it**.

year (noun)

Ear. The spelling reflects the usual pronunciation.

yearache / yurrick (noun)

Earache. The spellings reflect the usual pronunciation.

yearin(g) / yurrin(g) (noun)

Hearing. The spellings reflect the usual pronunciation.

yearin(g)s / yurrin(g)s (noun, plural)

Earrings. The spellings reflect the usual pronunciation.

years on you: enough to put years on you

See **put**.

years: this years (adverbial phrase)

For a long time, for years: 'I bumped into Mary Jones in the village – I 'adn't seen 'er this years.' See also **this ages, this long time, this years, donkey's years** and **yonks**.

yell blue murder

See **cry blue murder**.

yello (adjective)

Yellow, the spelling reflecting the 'Classical' Wenglish pronunciation.

yew

See **yue**.

yffach!

See **uffach!** and **myn uffach i!**

yffarn!

See **uffarn!** and **myn uffarn i!**

yfflon

See **wfflon**.

yoggut (noun)

Yoghurt.

yonk (noun)

An amusing (if rather uninhibited and unconventional) person, the life and soul of the party.

yonks (noun)

Many years, a long time: I haven't seen him for yonks'. See also **years: this years** and other entries mentioned there.

yorks (noun, plural)

Ties in trousers above the ankles to keep out dust/dirt.

yrcol (y byd)!

See **ryrcol (y byd)!**

youer (possessive adjective or contraction of pronoun + verb, present tense)

Possible spelling and pronunciation of **your** and occasionally **you're**.

yue / yew (pronoun)

Possible spellings of **you**, reflecting the pronunciation.

yurrick

See **yearache**.

yurring

See **yearing**.

yurrings

See **yearrings**.

Z

zoomy (adjective)

Fast, surging, powerful: 'I don't like using fifth gear coz it's too zoomy.'

zonked (adjective)

Very tired. See also **fagged out, wanged out, bished** and **buggered up**.

PART FOUR

THE GRAMMAR OF WENGLISH

Note: The answers to the Exercises in this section may be found at 4.17 at the end of the book.

4.1 VERBS – THE PRESENT TENSE

4.1.1 Affirmative Statements

In Wenglish, there are **three forms** of the **present tense** (used to describe what is going on now, or generally goes on). They are: the simple form, the form with and the verb 'to do', and the form with and the verb 'to be'.

The simple form

This corresponds to the normal statement form in Standard English, and is regular except for three of the most important and commonly occurring verbs, **to have**, **to do**, and **to be**, which we will deal with separately below. The simple form of the present tense is used to describe what is generally or usually the case.

A typical simple form present tense, is given below:

I eat	we eat
you eat (sg)	you eat (pl)
he, she, it eats	they eat

It will be noted that the form of the verb in the third person singular (he, she, it) ends in **s**, while the form of the verb for all other persons does not. This is exactly as in Standard English.

Note: You might hear a few Wenglish speakers, possibly in Swansea or in the central and eastern parts of the core area under the influence of Cardiff and Newport, using verb forms ending with **s** for all persons (e.g. **I eats, you eats, he eats etc.**). This should be avoided as it is untypical of Wenglish usage and was unknown in 'Classical' Wenglish.

to have

This is one of the most important verbs in Wenglish (as in most languages) as it is used (in Wenglish almost exclusively) as an auxiliary (helping) verb to form other tenses (e.g. the perfect tense, used to describe what has gone on in the past).

In Wenglish, the simple present tense of **to have** runs:

I have	we have
you have (sg)	you have (pl)
he, she, it have	they have

This differs from the Standard English form in the third person singular (he, she, it). In Standard English, this form of the verb is *he (she, it) has*, but the characteristic and recommended form in Wenglish is **he (she, it) have**.

Note: The **h** is not pronounced.

As in Standard English, the basic forms are very often contracted (shortened) as below:

I've	we've
you've (sg)	you've (pl)
he've, she've, it have	they've

Note 1: You might hear some Wenglish speakers using the Standard English form *he (she, it) has*. While permissible, this usage is not recommended.

Note 2: In Wenglish, the verb **to have** is generally used only to form other tenses (e.g. perfect and pluperfect). It is only very occasionally used to mean *to possess* or *to own*. In this sense of the Standard English *to have*, Wenglish uses the perfect tense of **to get**, which runs:

I have got	we have got
you have got (sg)	you have got (pl)
he, she, it have got	they have got

The usual contractions apply:

I've got	we've got
you've got (sg)	you've got (pl)
he've got, she've got, it have got	they've got

When statements are made in the perfect tense, the **have** part can be dropped, leaving just the personal pronoun (or noun) and **got**, the past participle of **to get**. Thus:

I got	we got
you got (sg)	you got (pl)
he, she, it got	they got

to do

The verb **to do** is very important in Wenglish, not only in its own right but also because it is used to form the second form of the present tense, which we will deal with below.

The simple present tense of **to do** in Wenglish runs thus:

I do	we do
you do (sg)	you do (pl)
he, she, it do	they do

Note 1: As with **to have**, the third person singular form, **he (she, it) do**, differs from that of Standard English, which is *he (she, it) does*.

Note 2: You might hear the Standard English form *does* (pronounced **duz**) being used by some Wenglish speakers but its use is not recommended, except in questions.

to be

The verb **to be** follows the same pattern as in Standard English.

I am	we are
you are (sg)	you are (pl)
he, she, it is	they are

As in Standard English, contracted (shortened) forms are generally used, other than when something is stressed. Thus:

I'm	we're
you're (sg)	you're (pl)
he's, she's, it's	they're

Note: In these contractions, the **r** in **we're** and **they're** is generally trilled. It tends not to be pronounced in **you're**, which thus rhymes with **law**.

The second form of the present tense, with *to do*

This is a characteristic feature of Wenglish as spoken in the Central and Eastern parts of the core area but it is much less common in the Western area, where the simple forms are in general use. However, the use of this second form of the present tense is recommended as a norm as it is so typical of Wenglish and is one of the features which sets it apart from Standard English. Using it is an immediate sign of good Wenglish! It is used to describe action which is habitual in nature – that which 'usually happens'.

The second form combines the present tense of the verb **to do** (see above) with the relevant verb. For example:

I do run	we do run
you do run (sg)	you do run (pl)
he, she, it do run	they do run

There is no real difference in meaning between this form of the present tense and the simple form. They are both used to describe what is generally or usually the case. Thus **I do run** has the same meaning as **I run**, and so on.

Forms like **I do do**, **you do do**, **he do go**, and others like them, may appear and sound a little strange to those who are not accustomed to them but they are quite characteristic of Wenglish, and as such, their use is recommended.

Note 1: In this form of the present tense, the word **do** often tends to be unstressed, and so the vowel tends to be shortened. The pronunciation can sometimes sound like **I d'do**, though this is not generally reflected in the spelling. If however the word **do** is stressed (as in the Standard English method of emphasising, e.g. *I do understand*), then, the vowel length is maintained, as in Standard English.

Note 2: This second form of the present tense does exist in Standard English – the *does* earlier in this sentence is an example of it – but it is restricted to emphasising something or to questions (e.g. *do you understand?*).

The third form, with *to be*

This is the same as in Standard English and is formed from the present tense of the verb **to be** (see above) and the present participle of the relevant verb (ending -**ing**). For example:

I am running	we are running
you are running (sg)	you are running (pl)
he, she, it is running	they are running

This form is used as in Standard English to describe action that is going on right now.

The contracted forms of the verb to be are generally used, except when emphasis is required (e.g. **I am going to town whether you like it or no**):

I'm running	we're running
you're running (sg)	you're running (pl)
he, she, it's running	they're running

Note: The **-ing** of the present participle is **always** pronounced **-in**. Thus **I am running** is pronounced as **I am runnin'**. This pronunciation is however not always reflected in the spelling.

EXERCISE 1: Present Tense – Affirmative Statements

Give the 3 forms of the present tense for each of the following:

Example:	
I eat	**a) I eat** **b) I do eat** **c) I'm eatin(g)**
1. we run	
2. she goes	
3. you walk	
4. he drinks	
5. they work	
6. I leave	
7. she plays	
8. we read	
9. they sing	
10. you write	

EXERCISE 2: Present Tense – To have

Give the 3 forms of the present tense of 'To have' for each of the following persons:

Example:

Example:	
You	**a) you have** **b) you do have** **c) you're havin(g)**
1. she	
2. they	
3. we	
4. it	
5. he	
6. I	

EXERCISE 3: Present Tense – To do

Give the 3 forms of the present tense of 'To do' for each of the following persons:

Example:	
We	a) we do b) we do do c) we're doin(g)
1. it	
2. you	
3. I	
4. he	
5. she	
6. they	

4.1.2 Negatives

The negative of the simple form and the second form, with *to do*

The negative of both these forms is the same. As in Standard English, the negative form of **to do** is used, followed by the relevant verb.

to do

The full forms **I do not**, **you do not** etc are only used in cases of emphasis. Otherwise contracted (shortened) forms are used instead. The basic contracted forms are similar to those in colloquial Standard English but the third person singular form is generally **he (she, it) don't**, not *he (she, it) doesn't*:

I don't	**we don't**
you don't (sg)	**you don't (pl)**
he, she, it don't	**they don't**

In combination with a verb to be made negative, we have the following pattern:

I don't run	**we don't run**
you don't run (sg)	**you don't run (pl)**
he, she, it don't run	**they don't run**

> **Important general rule concerning the pronunciation of the letter t in contracted negatives**
>
> In all contracted negative forms (like **don't, won't, haven't, didn't** etc.), the **t** is generally not pronounced if something else immediately follows it. Thus:
>
> **I don't run** and **I don't eat** are generally pronounced **I don' run** and **I don' eat**, as the words **run** and **eat** immediately follow the contracted negative **don't**. However, in this book the normal spelling is retained except in cases where particular attention is drawn to the non-pronunciation of **t**. The non-pronunciation of **t** in these circumstances is a fairly general feature but it is not found among all speakers.
>
> If, however, a question such as **do you smoke?** is asked, to which the answer is **I don't**, then the **t** is generally pronounced, as there is nothing immediately following it.

Assimilation of the exposed n of *don'* in contracted negatives

Having lost the final **t**, the **n** of **don'** can then be subject to a process of assimilation which affects its pronunciation, if the next word begins with any of the following consonants: **c, g, k, q, p, b, m, l, r, w, th, sh,**

c, g, k, q

If the next word begins with any of these four consonants, the **n** is pronounced **ng**. For example: **I don' care** is pronounced **I dohng care; I don' grow** is pronounced **I dohng grow.**

Note that the **h** in **dohng** serves only as an indication that the **o** is long.

This does not apply to words starting with a silent **g** or **k**: e.g. in **I don' know**, the **n** of **don'** is regularly pronounced.

p, b, m

If the next word begins with one of these three consonants, the **n** of **don'** is pronounced as an **m**. Thus **he don' preach** is pronounced 'e **dom preach** and **they don' bother** as **they dom bother**. The **o** is to pronounced long, just as in **don't**.

l, r, w, th, sh

If the next word begins with one of these five consonants or consonant sounds, there is a tendency for the **n** not to be pronounced at all. This is generally the case with **w** but only sometimes occurs with **l, r, th** and **sh**. It is however general with the verb **like**. For example, **I don' like** is normally pronounced **I doh like**. Thus, **they don' want** is generally pronounced

they doh want, while **he don' run** is sometimes pronounced **he doh run.** The **h** in **doh** is merely to show that the **o** is pronounced long.

Note 1: The pronunciation of the exposed **n** is not affected by a following word beginning with a vowel or any other consonant.

Note 2: This assimilation of the exposed **n** is not to be found among all speakers, and though quite widespread, is therefore not an obligatory part of Wenglish pronunciation.

to have

The negative of **to have** when used as an auxiliary verb to form the perfect tense is similar to Standard English. The full forms (**I have not, you have not** etc.) are only used in cases of emphasis (e.g. **I have not been**). Otherwise, contracted (shortened) forms are used. The basic contractions follow a similar pattern to those in Standard English, except that the third person singular is **he, she, it haven't** rather than Standard English's *he, she, it hasn't*. Thus:

I haven't	we haven't
you haven't (sg)	you haven't (pl)
he, she, it haven't	they haven't

Note 1: The general rules concerning the pronunciation of **t** in contracted negatives apply.

Note 2: The initial **h** is not pronounced.

Note 3: Extended forms of contraction may be heard, especially in the City of Swansea and in some parts of the central and eastern core areas. Thus:

I ain't / an't	we ain't / an't
you ain't / an't (sg)	you ain't / an't (pl)
he, she, it ain't / an't	they ain't / an't

The general rules concerning the pronunciation of the **t** also apply to these extended contractions.

The negative forms of **to have got** (i.e. the perfect tense of **to get**), the Wenglish for *to possess* or *to own*, run:

I haven't got	we haven't got
you haven't got (sg)	you haven't got (pl)
he, she, it haven't got	they haven't got

The extended contracted forms may also be used, thus:

I ain't got	we ain't got
you ain't got (sg)	you ain't got (pl)
he, she, it ain't got	they ain't got

Or:

I an't / in't got	we an't / in't got
you an't / in't got (sg)	you an't / in't got (pl)
he, she, it an't / in't got	they an't / in't got

Note 1: The general rules apply concerning the pronunciation of the final **t** in contracted negatives. It follows that the final **t** is often lost in pronunciation when another word follows immediately. In the Exercises, the use of any of the contracted forms, with or without the **t** is permissible. It follows that **haven't** is quite often pronounced **an** or **in**.

Note 2: I haven't been is often pronounced **I am been**, where the initial **h** of **haven't** is not pronounced at all, the final **t** of **haven't** is lost and the exposed **n**, by the rules of assimilation of consonants (see above) is pronounced as an **m** before the **b** of **been**.

On those few occasions where **to have** is used to mean *to possess* or *to own*, the negative forms are regularly formed, thus:

I don't have	we don't have
you don't have (sg)	you don't have (pl)
he, she, it don't have	they don't have

to be

The negative forms of **to be** are as in Standard English:

I am not	we are not
you are not (sg)	you are not (pl)
he, she, it is not	they are not

However, these full forms are generally only used for emphasis. More usually contracted forms are used. The basic contracted forms are like those of colloquial Standard English:

I'm not	we're not
you're not (sg)	you're not (pl)
he's not, she's not, it's not	they're not

However, Wenglish also has extended contracted forms. These are not used by all speakers and were not a feature of Wenglish of the 'Classical' period. Like the extended contractions of **to have**, they are most likely to be heard in the City of Swansea and in parts of the Central and Eastern core area. Their use is optional rather than recommended.

Extended contracted forms are thus:

I ain't / in't	we ain't / in't / an't
you ain't / in't / an't (sg)	you ain't/ in't / an't (pl)
he, she, it ain't / in't	they ain't / in't / an't

Note 1: The form **ain't** can be the extended contracted negative of **to have** or **to be**. The alternatives, **in't** and **an't** can belong to **to have** or **to be**. However, when making statements, **an't** is not used with the first person singular (I) and third person singular (he, she, it) in the case of **to be**.

Note 2: The general rules concerning the pronunciation of the final **t** in contracted negatives apply. It follows that the final **t** is often lost in pronunciation when another word follows immediately. In the Exercises, the use of any of the contracted forms, with or without the **t** is permissible.

The negative of the third form of the present tense, with to be

This is formed as in Standard English by combining the negative form of the verb to be (see above) with the present participle of the relevant verb (ending in –**ing**). Thus:

I'm not going	we're not going
you're not going (sg)	you're not going (pl)
he, she, it's not going	they're not going

The extended contracted forms may also be used:

I ain't going	we ain't going
you ain't going (sg)	you ain't going (pl)
he, she, it ain't going	they ain't going

or alternatively:

I in't going	we in't / an't going
you in't / an't going (sg)	you in't / an't going (pl)
he, she, it in't going	they in't / an't going

Note 1: The general rules concerning the pronunciation of the final **t** in contracted negatives apply.

Note 2: The –**ing** of the present participle is always pronounced –**in**, thus **going** is pronounced **goin'**. This is not always indicated in the spelling.

EXERCISE 4: Present Tense – Negatives

Give the 2 forms of the negative of the present tense of each of the following:

Example:	
He washes	a) he don'(t) wash b) he's not/he isn't washin(g) / he ain't/in't washin(g)
1. I run	
2. you walk	
3. they lissen	
4. I work	
5. she sits	
6. it flies	
7. he reads	
8. they play	
9. she writes	
10. we cook	

4.1.3. QUESTIONS

The simple form and second form, with *to do*

Basically this is similar to Standard English. The form of **to do** is inverted, followed by the relevant verb. For example:

do I like?	do we like?
do you like? (sg)	do you like? (pl)
do he, she, it like?	do they like?

There are no contractions.

to have

This is also as in Standard English. It involves the inversion of the verb **to have**. It is used to form the question form of the perfect tense.

have I?	have we?
have you? (sg)	have you? (pl)
have he, she, it?	have they?

There are no contractions but, as always, the **h** is not pronounced.

When used to ask questions in the perfect tense, the pattern is the same as in Standard English. Note however that the Wenglish form of the third person singular is **have** (not *has* as in Standard English).

As previously mentioned, the Standard English **to have**, meaning **to possess** or *to own* is expressed by the perfect tense of **to get** in Wenglish. In the question form this runs:

have I got?	have we got
have you got? (sg)	have you got? (pl)
have he, she, it got?	have they got?

All questions in the perfect tense are formed in a similar way.

to be

This is formed by inversion, as in Standard English. Thus:

am I?	are we?
are you? (sg)	are you? (pl)
is he, she, it?	are they?

There are no contractions.

The third form of the present tense, with *to be*

This is formed in exactly the same way as in Standard English, by inverting the relevant part of the verb **to be** (see above) and adding the present participle (ending in **–ing** but always pronounced **–in**). Thus:

am I running?	are we running?
are you running? (sg)	are you running? (pl)
is he, she, it running?	are they running?

4.1.4 NEGATIVE QUESTIONS

Simple form and second form of the present tense, with to do

These are formed in a similar way to Standard English. However, only the basic contracted forms of **to do** are used. The contracted negative forms of **to do** are inverted, followed by the relevant verb. Thus:

don't I know?	don't we know?
don't you know? (sg)	don't you know? (pl)
don't he, she, it know?	don't they know?

Note 1: The usual rules apply concerning the pronunciation of the **t** in **don't**.

Note 2: The third person singular form is **don't**, not *doesn't* as in Standard English.

to have

The negative question form of **to have** is formed in a similar way to Standard English. However, the full forms are never used, only the basic contracted and extended contracted forms (see above).

The basic or extended contracted negative forms of **to have** are inverted, thus:

Basic contracted forms

haven't I?	haven't we?
haven't you? (sg)	haven't you? (pl)
haven't he, she, it?	haven't they?

Extended contracted forms

ain't I?	ain't we?
ain't you? (sg)	ain't you? (pl)
ain't he, she, it?	ain't they?

or

an't I?	an't we?
an't you? (sg)	an't you? (pl)
an't he, she, it?	an't they?

Any of these forms may be used to make negative questions in the perfect tense. Using the example of **to have got**, the Wenglish for *to possess* or *to own*, we have:

haven't you got? or **ain't you got?** or **an't you got?**

The basic second extended contracted forms (**an't**) are most commonly used in negative questions.

to be

The negative question form of **to be** is formed, as in Standard English, by inversion of the relevant part of the verb in the negative. However, only the basic or extended contracted forms are used, as follows:

Basic contracted form

aren't I?	aren't we?
aren't you? (sg)	aren't you? (pl)
isn't he, she, it?	aren't they?

Extended contracted forms

ain't I?	ain't we?

ain't you? (sg)	ain't you? (pl)
ain't he, she, it?	ain't they?

or

in't / an't I?	in't /an't we?
in't / an't you? (sg)	in't / an't you? (pl)
in't he, she, it?	in't/ an't they?

The basic and second extended contracted forms (**in't**) are most commonly used to form negative questions with **to be**. Note that the form **an't** is not used in the third person singular (he, she, it) when asking questions.

The third form of the present tense, with *to be*

Negative questions in the third form of the present tense, with **to be**, are formed in a similar way to Standard English, with the inverted negative form of **to be** (see above) and the present participle (ending in **–ing** but always pronounced **–in**). Only the basic and extended negative forms are used, as follows:

Basic contracted forms

aren't I running?	aren't we running?
aren't you running? (sg)	aren't you running? (pl)
isn't he, she, it running?	aren't they running?

Extended contracted forms

ain't I running?	ain't we running?
ain't you running? (sg)	ain't you running? (pl)
ain't he, she, it running?	ain't they running?

or

in't / an't I running?	in't / an't we running?
in't / an't you running? (sg)	in't / an't you running? (pl)
in't he, she, it running?	in't / an't they running?

The basic and second extended contracted forms are most commonly with negative questions of this kind.

EXERCISE 5: Present Tense – Negative Questions

Make negative questions in the present tense. Use both forms.

Example:	
He washes	a) don'(t) he wash?

	b) isn't he washin(g)? / ain'(t)/in'(t) he washin(g)?
1. you throw	
2. we tie	
3. they water	
4. she polishes	
5. it shuts	
6. I walk	
7. you read	
8. they swim	
9. we cook	
10. I run	

EXERCISE 6: Present Tense of 'to have' and 'to be' – Extended contractions in the negative

Give the extended contracted forms of the following:

Example:	
He isn't going.	he ain'(t) goin(g) / he in'(t) goin(g)
1. Aren't you well?	
2. I haven't done it.	
3. They aren't lissnin(g).	
4. We're not runnin(g)	
5. She is not goin(g)	
6. He is not havin(g) it.	
7. They are not on holidays.	
8. You haven't got it.	
9. It is not happenin(g).	
10. Haven't you done that yet?	

4.2 VERBS – THE PAST TENSES

The past tenses in Wenglish are much the same as in Standard English, though there are several variations in the form of the simple past tense and in the past participles.

4.2.1 The Perfect Tense

This is used to describe what has happened in the past. As in Standard English, it is formed by combining the simple present tense of the verb **to have** with the past participle of the relevant verb. For example:

I have been	we have been
you have been (sg)	you have been (pl)
he, she, it have been	they have been

The basic contractions of the verb **to have** are normally used, thus:

Basic contractions

I've been	we've been
you've been (sg)	you've been (pl)
he've, she've, it have been	they've been

However, in the perfect tense of four very common verbs**, to be, to get, to come** and **to do**, the form of the verb **to have** may be dropped in ordinary statements in the perfect tense, with no change in meaning. Thus:

I been	we been
you been (sg)	you been (pl)
he, she, it been	they been

I got	we got
you got (sg)	you got (pl)
he, she, it got	they got

I done	we done
you done	you done (pl)
he done	they done

Note: **To have been** means much the same as **to have gone**. For example, **I've been** or **I been to town** means much the same as **I went to town**.

EXERCISE 7: Perfect Tense – Regular Verbs

Give the perfect tense of the following:

Example:	
I close	I've closed
1. I act	
2. you walk	
3. they warn	
4. she opens	
5. we look	
6. it arrives	
7. they close	
8. he parades	
9. they operate	
10. we support	

NEGATIVES, QUESTIONS AND NEGATIVE QUESTIONS IN THE PERFECT TENSE

These all follow the same patterns as in Standard English. The **negative form** combines the basic contracted or extended contracted negative forms of the verb **to have**, and the past participle of the relevant verb, as follows:

Basic contractions

I haven't been	we haven't been
you haven't been (sg)	you haven't been (pl)
he, she, it haven't been	they haven't been

Extended contractions

I ain't/an't been	we ain't/an't been
you ain't/an't been (sg)	you ain't/an't been (pl)
he, she, it ain't/an't been	they ain't/an't been

The **question form** involves an inversion of the verb to have plus the past participle of the relevant verb, as follows:

have I been?	have we been?
have you been (sg)	have you been? (pl)
have he, she, it been?	have they been?

There are no contractions. In questions, the part of the verb **to have** cannot be omitted.

The **negative question form** involves an inversion of the contracted negative forms of **to have** in combination with the past participle of the relevant verb, as follows:

Basic contractions

haven't I been?	haven't we been?
haven't you been? (sg)	haven't you been? (pl)
haven't he, she, it been?	haven't they been?

Extended contractions

ain't/an't I been?	ain't /an't we been?
ain't/an't you been? (sg)	ain't/an't you been? (pl)
ain't/an't he, she, it been?	ain't/an't they been ?

The basic and second form of extended contractions (**an't**) are more commonly used.

Irregular past participles

While most past participles are the same as in Standard English, there are some which differ. These are listed below:

Infinitive	Past participle	Standard English
to boil	boilt	*boiled*
to break	broke or broken	*broken*
to bring	brought or brung	*brought*
to bust	bust or busted	*busted*
to catch	catched or caught	*caught*
to commit	commit or committed	*committed*
to creep	crept or creeped	*crept*
to cross	crosst	*crossed*
to draw	drawn or drawed	*drawn*
to drink	drank or drunk	*drunk*
to drown	drowned or drownded	*drowned*
to earn	earnt	*earned*
to eat	eaten or ate or et	*eaten*
to forget	forgot or forgotten	*forgotten*

to ketch	ketched or caught	caught
to kill	kilt	killed
to lay / to lie (= to recline)	laid or lied	lain
to lay / to lie (= to place)	laid or lied	laid
to leap	leapt or leaped	leapt
to read	read or red	read
to ring	rang or rung	rung
to rise (= to lift)	raised, rised or risen	raised
to sell	solt or sold	sold
to show	showed or shown	shown
to sing	sung or sang	sung
to swear	sworn or sweared	sworn
to swim	swum or swam	swum
to take	taken or took	taken
to tear	torn or teared	torn
to throw	throwed or thrown	thrown
to tread	trood, trod or trodden	trodden
to wear	worn or weared	worn
to write	written or wrote	written
drysu	drysu'd or drysu-ed	n/a
heneiddio	wedi heneiddio or wedi hedeiddio'd	n/a
torri	wedi torri	n/a
(to) sisno / (to) sizno	sisno'd / sizno'd or wedi sisno'd / wedi sizno'd or wedi sisno / wedi sizno	n/a

Note: With the Welsh verb-nouns **heneiddio, torri** and **(to) sisno / sizno,** the past participle may follow the regular pattern in Welsh (using **wedi**), and add the English past participle ending **-d**. However, **torri**

follows the Welsh pattern only. See these words listed in the Glossary for further details.

There is a general tendency for the **–ed** in all regular past participles to be pronounced as **t**.

EXERCISE 8: Perfect Tense – Irregular Past Participles

Give the perfect tense of the following:

Example:	
I come	**I've come**
1. I am	
2. you see	
3. she boils	
4. they tread	
5. we sell	
6. it rises	
7. I write	
8. he reads	
9. they put	
10. you understand	

EXERCISE 9: Perfect Tense – Questions

Form questions in the perfect tense:

Example:	
I sing	**Have I sung?**
1. you bust	
2. she breaks	
3. they kill	
4. we earn	
5. he throws	
6. I do	
7. we support	
8. she operates	
9. they read	
10. you write	

EXERCISE 10: Perfect tense – Negative questions

Form negative questions in the perfect tense. Use either a standard or extended contraction:

Example:	
We show	**Haven'(t) you shown/shwed? /** **Ain' (t) you shown/showed? /** **In'(t) you shown/showed? /** **An'(t) you shown/shwed?**
1. we go	
2. they throw	
3. I understand	
4. she cooks	
5. he builds	
6. they dig	
7. you understand	
8. they write	
9. she walked	
10. they get	

4.2.3 THE SIMPLE PAST TENSE

This is the one-word past tense, used to describe action in the past which is over and done, e.g. **he went, we found, they understood**. The form of the verb is the same in all persons and is generally the same as in Standard English. Its usage is also as in Standard English. Past tense normal statement forms which differ from their Standard English equivalents are listed below:

Irregular past tense forms

Infinitive	Past tense	Standard English form
to be	**was, were or been**	*was, were*
to boil	**boilt**	*boiled*
to bring	**brought or brung**	*brought*
to bust	**bust or busted**	*busted*
to catch	**catched or caught**	*caught*
to come	**came or come**	*came*
to commit	**commit or committed**	*committed*

to creep	crept or creeped	*crept*
to do	done or did	*did*
to draw	drew or drawed	*drew*
to drown	drowned or drownded	*drown*
to drink	drunk or drank	*drank*
drysu	drysu'd or drysu-ed	*n/a*
to earn	earnt	*earned*
to eat	et or ate	*ate*
to give	gave or give	*gave*
to ketch	ketched, caught	*caught*
to kill	kilt or killed	*killed*
to lay / to lie (=to recline)	laid or lied	*lay*
to lay / to lie (=to place)	laid or lied	*laid*
to leap	leapt or leaped	*leapt*
to read	read or red	*read*
to ring	rung or rang	*rang*
to rise/ to raise(=to lift)	rose, raised or rised	*raised*
to see	seen or saw	*saw*
to sell	solt or sold	*sold*
to sing	sung or sang	*sang*
(to) sisno / (to) sizno	sisno'd / sizno'd	*n/a*
to swear	swore or sweared	*swore*
to swim	swam or swum	*swam*
to tear	tore or teared	*tore*
to tread	trood or trod	*trod*
to throw	throwed or threw	*threw*
to wear	wore or weared	*wore*
to write	wrote or writ	*wrote*

As with the past participles, there is a tendency to pronounce the **-ed** at the end of regular past tense forms as a **t**.

EXERCISE 11: Past Tense

Give the simple past tense of the following:

Example:	
He goes	He went
1. they do	
2. we understand	
3. you sit	
4. she scrams	
5. they chuck	
6. we tread	
7. we write	
8. they read	
9. he plays	
10. we congratulate	

Negatives

As in Standard English, this is formed by using the negative of the past tense of **to do** with the relevant verb. The contracted form **didn't** is used rather than the full form **did not**, except in cases of emphasis. Thus:

I didn't know	we didn't know
you didn't know (sg)	you didn't know (pl)
he, she, it didn't know	they didn't know

Note: The usual rules concerning the pronunciation of the **t** in contracted negatives apply. An **extended contraction** of **didn't** to **din** is possible. Thus:

I din go	we din go
you din go (sg)	you din go (pl)
he, she, it din go	they din go

EXERCISE 12: Past Tense – Negatives

Give the negative of the following in the simple past tense. Use simple or extended contractions.

Example:	
I sell	I didn'(t) sell / I din sell
1. I cross	
2. you know	
3. he throws	
4. they rise	
5. she argues	
6. we go	
7. you congratulate	
8. we support	
9. he reads	
10. she writes	

Questions

As in Standard English, **did**, the past tense of **to do**, is used with subject inverted, plus the relevant verb, as follows:

did I go?	did we go?
did you go? (sg)	did you go? (pl)
did he, she, it go?	did they go?

Note 1: The statement form **done** is not used in questions.

Note 2: There are no contractions.

EXERCISE 13: Past Tense – Questions

Form questions in the past tense.

Example:	
We went	**Did we go?**
1. you knew	
2. they crosst	
3. he kilt	
4. we ketched	
5. they rang	
6. she rised	
7. we sang	
8. he showed	
9. you eat	
10. she drank	

Negative Questions

As in Standard English, the inverted negative form of the verb **to do** is combined with the relevant verb. Only the contracted forms are used, as follows:

Basic contractions

didn't I go?	didn't we go?
didn't you go? (sg)	didn't you go? (pl)
didn't he, she, it go?	didn't they go?

Note: the usual rules concerning the pronunciation of **t** in contracted negatives apply.

Extended contractions

din I go?	din we go?
din you go? (sg)	din you go? (pl)
din he, she, it go?	din they go?

to be

The verb to be has two forms in the past tense, **was** and **were**, as in Standard English. However, their usage is less fixed in Wenglish.

I was	we was or were
you was or were (sg)	you was or were (pl)
he, she, it was	they was or were

In Wenglish it is possible to use the form **was** for all persons, even where Standard English requires *were*.

The past tense of **to be** is used to form the standard **imperfect tense** of all verbs.

Negatives with *to be*

These are formed as in Standard English, by adding **not** (e.g. **I was not**). However, the contracted forms are generally used except in cases of emphasis.

I wasn't	we wasn't/weren't
you wasn't/weren't (sg)	you wasn't/weren't (pl)
he, she, it wasn't	they wasn't/weren't

Note: The usual rules apply concerning the pronunciation of the final **t**.

There is also a tendency not to pronounce the **s** in **wasn't**. When combined with the non-pronunciation of the **t**, an extended contracted form arises:

I wan	we wan
you wan (sg)	you wan (pl)
he, she, it wan	they wan

Questions with to be

As in Standard English, these involve the inversion of the past tense forms of **to be**.

was I?	was/were we?
was/were you? (sg)	was/were you? (pl)
was he, she, it?	was/were they?

No contractions are used.

The **negative question** form of **to be** uses an inversion of the negative contracted forms (see above).

Basic contractions

wasn't I?	wasn't we/weren't we?
wasn't you/weren't you? (sg)	wasn't you/weren't you? (pl)
wasn't he, she, it?	wasn't they/weren't they?

Extended contractions

wan I?	wan we?
wan you? (sg)	wan you? (pl)
wan he, she, it?	wan they?

to have

As in Standard English, the basic past tense of **to have** is **had** in all persons.

Note: The past tense of **to have** can express possession or ownership. It is also used to form the pluperfect tense (see below).

The **negative form** of the past tense of **to have** is **hadn't** in all persons.

The negative form is not used to denote non-possession or non-ownership, rather only to form the negative of the pluperfect tense. The form **didn't have** or the extended contacted form **din have**, is used to express non-ownership.

The **question form** of the past tense of **to have** involves a simple inversion of verb and subject, thus: **had I? had he?**

The question form, like the negative form, is not used to denote non-ownership or non-possession, rather only in the formation of the pluperfect tense. Questions regarding ownership are formed regularly with the question form of **to do**, thus **did I have?**.

The **negative question form** is formed regularly and involves an inversion of the verb and subject of the negative form of the past tense of **to have**. This, too, is only used in the formation of the pluperfect tense. Negative questions regarding ownership use the inverted negative form of **to do**, thus **didn't you have? din he have?**

EXERCISE 14: Past tense – Negative questions

Form negative questions in the past tense. Use simple or extended contractions.

Example:	
I went	**Didn'(t) I go? / Din I go?**
1. they boilt	
2. we earnt	
3. she scrammed	
4. he planted	
5. you lived	
6. it showed	
7. you supported	
8. they done	
9. he examined	
10. you shut	

4.2.4 The Imperfect Tense

There are two forms of the imperfect tense in Wenglish, the **progressive form** with the verb **to be**, which describes action which **was going on**, and the **habitual form**, with **used to**, which describes what **used to be** the case.

The progressive form, with the past tense of to be

As in Standard English, this is formed from the past tense of **to be** and the present participle of the relevant verb, ending **–ing**. It is similar in structure to the present progressive form. Thus:

I was walking	we was/were walking
you was/were walking (sg)	you was/were walking (pl)
he, she, it was walking	they was/were walking

EXERCISE 15: The Imperfect Tense – Statements

Turn to the imperfect tense, progressive form with **to be**:

Example:	
I ran	**I was running**
1. you watched	
2. they looked	
3. she drove	
4. we turned	
5. she polished	
6. it grew	
7. I congratulated	
8. he played	
9. she wrote	
10. it opened	

Negative

The negative forms of the past tense of the verb **to be** are used (see above), with the present participle of the relevant verb, e.g. **he wasn't running, I wan going, they wasn't lissning.**

EXERCISE 16: The Imperfect Tense – Negatives

Turn to the negative in imperfect tense, progressive form with 'To be'. Use standard or contracted negative forms:

Example:	
They shoved	**We wasn'(t)/weren'(t) shovin(g) / We wan shoving**
1. I laughed	
2. you coughed	
3. he sneezed	
4. she bit	
5. it closed	
6. you done it	
7. it opened	
8. she played	

9. we read
10. I talked

Questions

The inverted forms of **was** and **were** are used, with the present participle of the relevant verb, e.g. **was I walking? were you lissning?**

EXERCISE 17: The Imperfect Tense – Questions

Turn into questions in the imperfect tense, progressive form with 'To be'.

Example:	
I ran	Was I running?
1. he walked	
2. you drove	
3. we cheered	
4. it worked	
5. they lissened	
6. we shoved	
7. you supported	
8. he talked	
9. she played	
10. I sang	

Negative Questions

The inverted negative forms of **was** and **were** are used, with the present participle of the relevant verb, e.g. **wan he going? weren't you running? wan she eating?**

EXERCISE 18: The Imperfect Tense – Negative questions

Turn the following into negative questions in the imperfect tense, progressive form with 'To be'.

Example:	
we went	Wasn'(t)/Weren'(t) we goin(g)? / Wan we goin(g)?
1. they lost	
2. he smoked	
3. she ate	
4. you drank	
5. they hunted	
6. we yapped	
7. I congratulated	
8. it went	
9. they came	
10. I looked	

The imperfect with 'used to'

The formation is as in Standard English, with the past tense of **to use** followed by the infinitive of the relevant verb. However, the **d** of **used** is always unvoiced and thus pronounced as a **t** before the preposition **to**. Used is therefore normally pronounced **youst** or **iwst**. Thus:

I used to run	we used to run
you used to run (sg)	you used to run (pl)
he, she, it used to run	they used to run

EXERCISE 19: The Imperfect Tense – Forms with Used to:

Put the following into the imperfect tense, using forms with **used to**:

Example:	
they played	they used to play
1. you wanted	
2. you were having a good time	
3. they ran	

4. we marched	
5. it worked	
6. she tried	
7. he supported	
8. you read	
9. she wrote	
10. they typed	

Negative

The negative is formed using the negative past tense of **to do**, either in the contracted or extended contracted form. Thus, **I didn't used to run, he din used to go, they didn't used to say** etc.

EXERCISE 20: The Imperfect Tense – Forms with used to – Negatives

Put the following into the imperfect tense, using negative forms with **used to**:

Example:	
I do	I didn'(t) used to do / I din used to do
1. you run	
2. he drinks	
3. they lay	
4. we chops	
5. they hunt	
6. he smells	
7. he manages	
8. she helps	
9. they write	
10. we watch	

Questions

The questions form uses the question form of the past tense of **to do**, thus **did I used to go? did she used to run?**

EXERCISE 21: The Imperfect Tense – Forms with 'used to' – Questions

Put the following into the imperfect tense, using question forms with **used to**:

Example:	
I go	**Did you used to go?**
1. he runs	
2. we feel	
3. you love	
4. she waters	
5. they cry	
6. I make	
7. we read	
8. they travel	
9. you work	
10. he cuts	

Negative Questions

The negative question form of the past tense of **to do** is used, with the contracted or extended contracted forms. Thus, **din I used to go? didn't he used to sing?** etc.

EXERCISE 22: The Imperfect Tense – Forms with 'used to' – Negative questions

Put the following into the imperfect tense, using negative question forms with **used to**. Use standard or extended contractions:

Example:	
We love	**Didn'(t) we used to love? / Din we used to love?**
1. they buy	
2. they sell	
3. he answers	
4. she shiggles	
5. we burn	
6. you sit	
7. I read	

8. she writes
9. he plays
10. she boasts

4.2.5 PLUPERFECT TENSE

As in Standard English this is used to describe action which has taken place further back in the past. As in Standard English it is formed using the past tense of **to have**, i.e. **had**, and the past participle of the relevant verb. Thus:

I had been	we had been
you had been (sg)	you had been (pl)
he, she, it had been	they had been

Contracted forms are generally used.

I'd been	we'd been
you'd been (sg)	you'd been (pl)
he'd, she'd, it'd been	they'd been

EXERCISE 23: The Pluperfect Tense – Statements

Turn the following into the pluperfect:

Example:	
you do	you'd done / you had done
1. they make	
2. we mend	
3. she knits	
4. he drives	
5. you find	
6. it goes	
7. they play	
8. she reads	
9. he worked	
10. I am	

Negative

The negative forms of the past tense of **to have** are used, with the past participle of the relevant verb, e.g. **he hadn't seen, they hadn't been?**

Note: The usual rules regarding the pronunciation of the **t** in the contracted negative apply.

An extended contracted form, **han**, may be used in the negative, e.g. **he han gone**

EXERCISE 24: The Pluperfect Tense – Negatives

Turn the following into the pluperfect tense, negative form:

Example:	
you rush	you hadn'(t)/han rushed
1. We own	
2. she rows	
3. you buy	
4. we ketch	
5. you go in	
6. I vanish	
7. she writes	
8. they play	
9. we have	
10. I realise	

Questions

The question form involves a simple inversion verb and subject of the past tense of **to have**, plus the past participle of the relevant verb. Thus, **had I been? had he seen?**

EXERCISE 25: The Pluperfect Tense – Questions

Turn the following into the pluperfect tense, question form:

Example:	
I was	Had I been?
1. you give	
2. we crossed	
3. she cooked	
4. he worked	
5. it happened	
6. they fell	

7. I had
8. he played
9. they lit
10. we froze

Negative Questions

The negative forms of the past tense of **to have** are used, with the past participle of the relevant verb. For example, **hadn't you seen? hadn't he been?** The contracted negative forms are **han you seen? han he been?**

EXERCISE 26: The Pluperfect Tense – Negative Questions

Turn the following into the pluperfect tense, negative question form. Use standard or extended contractions:

Example:	
You was	**Hadn'(t) you been? / Han you been?**
1. we had	
2. she turned	
3. they cheated	
4. we wiped	
5. he goes	
6. you do	
7. you played	
8. we wore	
9. they wrote	
10. he noticed	

4.3 VERBS –THE FUTURE TENSES

The standard future tense is formed much as in Standard English, using the modal auxiliary verb **will**. **Shall** is occasionally used to form the future but **will** is normally used in Wenglish.

I will go	we will go
you will go (sg)	you will go (pl)
he, she, it will go	they will go

The same contractions occur as in Standard English.

I'll go	we'll go
you'll go (sg)	you'll go (pl)
he'll, she'll, it'll go	they'll go

EXERCISE 27: Future Tense

Turn the following into the Future:

Example:	
I was	I'll be / I will be
1. you see	
2. they walk	
3. he lectured	
4. we talked	
5. she realised	
6. he clicks	
7. you did	
8. they introduce	
9. we manage	
10. you print	

Negative

In negation, will changes to won't in all persons.

I won't go	we won't go
you won't go (sg)	you won't go (pl)
he, she it won't go	they won't go

Note: The usual rules concerning the pronunciation of the final t in contracted negatives apply.

EXERCISE 28: Future Tense – Negatives

Turn the following into negatives in the Future:

Example:	
we like	we won'(t) like / we will not like
1. he understands	
2. there are	
3. she croshos	

4. they knit
5. we burn
6. they do
7. we play
8. she writes
9. he hears
10. I go

Questions

Questions in the future are formed by simple inversion of verb and subject, as in Standard English, thus **will I go? will he speak?**

EXERCISE 29: Future Tense – Questions

Turn the following into questions in the Future:

Example:	
He goes	**Will he go?**
1. they hurry	
2. you run	
3. we see	
4. it shakes	
5. she was writing	
6. we walk	
7. he understands	
8. he races	
9. she blames	
10. we put	

Negative Questions

Negative questions in the future involve a simple inversion of the subject and the negative form **won't**, thus **won't he see? won't they eat?**

EXERCISE 30: Future Tense – Negative Questions

Turn the following into negative questions in the Future:

Example:	
We show	**Won'(t) we show?**
1. they run	
2. he aggravates	
3. she puts	
4. we finish	
5. he boxes	
6. John writes	
7. I like	
8. you play	
9. he reads	
10. she writes	

4.3.1 Use of the Present to Express the Future

The present tense, either simple form or more commonly the progressive form with **to be**, is quite often used to express action in the future. For example:

> I go next week, I am going tomorrow, he's arriving next Tuesday

As in Standard English, the construction **going to + verb** is commonly used to express future action. For example:

> he is going to eat, we're going to sing

The present tense with **to do** is not used to express future action.

EXERCISE 31: Use of the Present tense to express the future

Use the present tense as alternatives to the following, written in the Future Tense:

Example:	
I will go tomorrow	**I'm goin(g) tomorrow / I go tomorrow**
1. He will arrive on Thursday.	
2. John will leave on Monday.	

268

3. The castle will be open tomorrow.	
4. I will come again tomorrow.	
5. You will go.	
6. We will dock at 3 tomorrow.	
7. He'll arrive next week.	
8. They will call tonight.	
9. She will go in an hour.	
10. The ship will sail at midnight.	

4.3.2 Progressive Future Tense

The formation and use of this are as in Standard English. It involves **will** plus **be** plus the present participle of the relevant verb. For example, **I will be running, she will be eating.**

Negatives, questions and negative questions use the forms **will** or **won't** as in the standard future tense, followed by **be** and the past participle of the relevant verb, e.g. **he won't be running, will he be running? won't she be singing?** The contracted forms with will are commonly used.

EXERCISE 32: Future Tense – Progressive (Continuous) Form

Put the following into the Future Tense, Progressive (Continuous) Form:

Example:	
We run	we'll be runnin(g)
1. they don't run	
2. I'm not worryin(g)	
3. Are you comin(g)?	
4. they dig	
5. she drinks	
6. Does he eat?	
7. he was playin(g)	
8. they was arguin(g)	
9. I was competin(g)	
10. she collects	

4.3.3 Future Perfect Tense

This is used to denote what will have happened. It is not commonly used and follows the same pattern as in Standard English, namely **will** or **won't** as in the standard future tense plus **have** plus the past participle of the relevant verb. Negatives, questions and negative questions use inversions of verb and subject with **will** or **won't** as in the standard future tense, plus **have** plus the past participle of the relevant verb. The contracted forms with **will** are commonly used.

Thus, **I will have done, he will have eaten, will she have eaten? he won't have found, won't he have eaten?**

EXERCISE 33: The Future Perfect Tense

Put the following into the future perfect tense:

Example:	
we put	we'll have put / we will have put
1. you have not grown	
2. we catch	
3. they don't learn	
4. have you gone?	
5. we go	
6. she knits	
7. we showed	
8. they tried	
9. they lit	
10. I play	

4.4 THE CONDITIONAL, THE CONDITIONAL PERFECT AND MODAL VERBS

4.4.1 The Conditional

The conditional is formed with the modal verb **would** as in Standard English. It is the same in all persons.

I would go	we would go
you would go (sg)	you would go (pl)
he, she, it would go	they would go

The contracted forms are more commonly used, except in cases of emphasis.

I'd go	we'd go
you'd go (sg)	you'd go (pl)
he'd, she'd, it'd go	they'd go

The negative uses **wouldn't** in all persons as in Standard English, though an extended contracted form **woun** also exists in Wenglish. For example, **he wouldn't go** or **he woun go.**

The formation of the **negative, question** and **negative question** forms follows the same pattern as the standard future tense, with **would** and **wouldn't/woun** replacing **will** and **won't.**

The usual rules concerning the pronunciation of the final **t** in contracted negatives apply.

EXERCISE 34: The Conditional

Put the following into the Conditional:

Example:	
I go	I'd go / I would go
1. she don't go	
2. they arrive	
3. we send	
4. Annie eats	
5. Doesn't she like that?	
6. he works	
7. I have	
8. they congratulate	
9. you freeze	
10. he lose	

4.4.2 The Conditional Perfect

This is formed much as in Standard English, and consists of the conditional **would** + **have** + the past participle of the verb in question. Thus:

I would have gone	we would have gone
you would have gone (sg)	you would have gone (pl)
he, she, it would have gone	they would have gone

The contracted forms of the conditional are generally used. Thus:

I'd have gone	we'd have gone
you'd have gone (sg)	you'd have gone (pl)
he'd, she'd, it'd have gone	they'd have gone

The **h** of **have** is not generally pronounced.

Negatives, questions and negative questions are formed from the relevant part of the Conditional – **would** – with **have** + the past participle of the relevant verb added. The extended contracted forms of the conditional may be used. Thus:

I wouldn't have gone
you woun have gone
would she have gone?
wouldn't they have gone?
woun he have gone?

The conditional perfect of the modal verbs **could** and **should** is formed by substituting **could** or **should** for **would**. Thus:

I could have come
you shouldn't have done it
could they have come?
couldn't she have come?

The extended contracted forms (see Modal Verbs) may also be used, thus:

she coun have done it
coun we go?
shoun they be there now?

EXERCISE 35: The Conditional Perfect

Put the following into the Conditional Perfect:

Example:	
We go	we'd have gone / we would have gone
1. she reads	
2. it finishes	
3. does he eat?	
4. they cook	
5. they never eat	

6. it opens	
7. he plays	
8. we write	
9. she sees	
10. they close	

4.4.3 Modal Verbs

We have already encountered the modal verbs **will** and **would**, used to form the future, conditional and conditional perfect tenses. Modal verbs are very frequently used in Wenglish as in Standard English. The following are in common use in Wenglish.

can	could
will	would
shall	should
must	
to have to	
to have got to	
(to have) got to/gorrw	
ought	
may	might

The use of these verbs in Wenglish is much as in Standard English but the contractions and extended contractions of the negative forms should be noted. In all cases, the usual rules regarding the pronunciation of the **t** in contracted negatives apply.

can't	couldn't, extended contraction coun
won't	wouldn't, extended contraction woun
shan't	shouldn't, extended contraction shoun
musn't	extended contraction musn
oughtn't	
mightn'	extended contraction mighn

EXERCISE 36: Modal Verbs

Translate the following to Wenglish using suitable modal verbs:

Example:	
It is essential that I go.	I have to go / I gorrw go
1. I am able to lift the box.	
2. I am allowed to go out now.	
3. It is not good for you to go out after washing your hair.	
4. It is possible that he will come soon.	
5. Are you able to speak Chinese?	
6. It is certain that it comes from their house.	
7. Would you be able to come?	
8. It will possibly work.	
9. It is possible that she will come.	
10. I would not be able to say that with certainty	

All these modal verbs can be used with **have** and the past participle of the relevant verb to form conditional perfect expressions, as follows:

I can't have done
he ought to have seen
we couldn't/coun have seen
they might have been

Another point to note is that with the expression **to have to**, the **v** of **have** is unvoiced and pronounced as **ff** before **to**. For example, **I have to go** is pronounced **I haff to go**.

To have got to can itself be contracted to **to have gorrw**, an example of an intervocalic **t** being pronounced as **rr**. Furthermore, the **have** can be dropped. Thus:

I haff to go, I have got to go, I got to go and **I gorrw go**, are all acceptable alternative ways of expressing **I must go**.

4.5 THE REMAINING VERB FORMS

4.5.1 The Passive Voice

Use of the passive voice is not particularly common in Wenglish, which
tends to prefer active, concrete expressions. The passive is formed in all
cases as in Standard English, using the appropriate tense and form of the
verb **to be** plus the past participle of the relevant verb. For example:

it's done
it's being seen to
they were made
it will be eaten
it's been eaten
it will have been cooked
it might be cooked
it coun have been eaten

4.5.2 Gerunds

The gerund is a verbal noun, identical in form to the present participle of
the verb, ending in **-ing** but always pronounced **-in**. It is in fairly common
use in Wenglish but is not in all cases used as in Standard English.

One use of the gerund is a direct translation of the Welsh construction
o + verb-noun. For example, the Welsh *o fynd* is translated literally into
Wenglish as **of going**. This means *as I was going anyway* or *if you are going*,
as the following examples demonstrate:

Of going, you might as well go in style. (*If you are going, you had
might as well go in style.*)

Of making a dress, you might as well make a good one. (*If you
are making a dress, you had might as well make a good one.*)

Of going to Ponty, I'll pick one up in the market. (*As I'm going
to Ponty anyway, I'll pick one up in the market*).

This use of the gerund is unknown in Standard English.

The gerund can also be used to avoid using a full subordinate clause, as
shown in the following examples:

I didn't mind him going. (*I didn't mind his going* or *I didn't mind that
he went*).

He liked me singing. (*He liked my singing* or *he liked the fact that I was
singing.*)

With them coming, I didn't have time to make dinner. (*Because
they were coming, I didn't have time to make lunch*).

Note that in this type of construction, the pronouns **me, you, him, her, it, us, you, them** are used in conjunction with the gerund, and not possessive adjectives *my, you, his, her, its, our, your, their* as is usually the case in Standard English.

As in Standard English, the gerund is sometimes used to form absolute constructions, such as the following:

> **Seeing that she was going to Cardiff, I asked him to go to Howells's for me.**

> **Considring she've been baad, she do seem quite cheerful in herself.**

4.5.3 The Subjunctive

The subjunctive mood is very little used in Wenglish – even less so than in Standard English. It is effectively limited to set expressions such as **Duw help!**, **pity help!**, **long live the king!** and **thy kingdom come!** Modal verbs are always preferred to express possibility or doubt. Thus:

> **he might come**

> **he would come if he could**

> **I told him that he shouldn't have done it**

Otherwise the indicative is used:

> **If I was you, I'd go now while you can**

> **I suggest that he goes straight away**

4.6 GENERAL OBSERVATIONS ON VERB USAGE

Verb formation and usage has already been covered in some detail in the previous sections but there are some general points which should be noted.

4.6.1 Plural Noun Subject, Singular Verb

It is possible to use a verb in the third person singular with a plural noun subject. This mirrors the construction in Welsh, thus:

> **Them two boxes is still in the hall**

> **John and Gladys is coming to see us today**

Standard English usage is also possible.

4.6.2 Multiple Negatives

Double negatives are in common use in Wenglish. For example:

I never told him nothing

I don't need no more pencils

There are instances of triple or even quadruple negatives, though these are of course much less common. Some examples:

They never do nothing no more

I never done nothing nowhere, I never.

4.6.3 Verb + Noun constructions

Another widespread feature is the use of **verb + noun constructions** where Standard English would use a verb only. For example:

to have a lend of	to borrow
to have a look at	to look at
to have a swim	to swim, to bathe
to have a bath	to bathe, to bath
to have a go	to try
to have a smell of	to smell
to have an anch of	to bite

EXERCISE 37: The remaining Verb Forms / Verb Usage

Translate the following into Wenglish:

1. He liked my piano-playing.
2. Since you are going to Pontardawe, can you get some potatoes for me?
3. If you are building a wall, it's just as well to build a high one.
4. If I were you, I would depart immediately.
5. Billy and George are still receiving treatment from the doctor.
6. I don't want anything.
7. I was unable to locate it anywhere.
8. They never go anywhere.
9. Give me a bite of your apple!
10. I don't want any more gravy.

4.7 ARTICLES AND DEMONSTRATIVES

The **definite article, the**, is usually pronounced **thee** before a vowel.
The **demonstratives** are:

Singular	Plural
this	these
that	those or them

Note 1: The initial **th** of all the above, including the definite article **the**, is quite often not pronounced by some speakers, more often in unstressed positions but sometimes in stressed positions too. Thus:

'Is man I saw
I never seen 'e news on 'e box las' night
'Ose books are still on 'e table
He've come to help me with 'em jobs I tol' you about

Note 2: The final **t** of **that** is not pronounced by some speakers. **That** can sometimes be contracted to **'a'** in pronunciation, though the stress which would have been given to **that** is retained. Thus:

'A' bloke was down 'e club again las' night

The contractions noted above are not used by all speakers, though the dropping of the initial **th** of the definite article and of demonstratives is fairly commonly heard in unstressed positions. The use of these contractions in stressed positions tends to give the language a rather downmarket feel.

These contractions are not generally reflected in the spelling, unless particular attention is to be drawn to the contracted pronunciation.

The **indefinite article** is **a**, or **an** before a vowel and **h**. It is however sometimes omitted altogether, as in Welsh. For example:

give me an orange! or give me orange!
he haven't got hope in hell of winning

Note that because **h** is not pronounced, the following vowel is 'exposed', and so the form **an** can be used.

the farmer got a cow and an horse

EXERCISE 38: Articles and Demonstratives

Translate to Wenglish. Use standard or contracted forms.

1. Those two letters are in my handbag.
2. That fellow was in the pub again.
3. In her model collection, the little girl has a horse and two deer.
4. They can assist me with those little tasks.
5. A man whom I saw entered the turf accountant's shop.
6. She never understands those things.
7. Those knives are in the drawer.
8. The spoons are on that small table over there.
9. I'll give you those papers after lunch.
10. Get those dirty shoes off that chair!

4.8 NUMBERS AND TIME

4.8.1 Numbers

The cardinal numbers are similar to their equivalents in Standard English but note the following:

Two, three, four	These have a pure long simple vowel sound. There is no hint of diphthongisation.
seven	Sometimes the pronunciation approximates to **sem**.
leven	The initial **e** is generally dropped in pronunciation.
twenty (and 21-29)	The second **t** is not pronounced by some speakers (thus **twenny**), as in American English. This is however not general to all speakers.
thirty (and 31-39)	The second **t** is voiced by some speakers as **d** (thus **thirdy**). Other speakers have a tendency to pronounce this second **t** as **rr** (thus **thirry**). However, neither of these pronunciations is general to all speakers.
hundred	Generally without **a** to prefix it.
thousand	The final **d** is not pronounced.

The ordinal numbers are much as in Standard English, with the following variations:

first	The final **t** is not generally pronounced if another word follows directly.
second	The final **d** is not generally pronounced if another word follows directly.

fifth	Both f's are always pronounced, not as in Standard English, where there is a tendency for the second f not to be pronounced.
seventh	Pronounced **senth** by some speakers.
leventh	As with the ordinal number, the initial **e** is generally not pronounced.
twentieth	As with the ordinal number, some speakers have a tendency not to pronounce the second **t**, resulting in the pronunciation **twenieth**.
thirtieth	As with the ordinal number, some speakers have a tendency to pronounce the second **t** as **d** or **rr**, giving rise to the pronunciations **thirdieth** and **thurrieth**. These pronunciations are not standard and need not be emulated.

The **fractions** are expressed in a similar way to Standard English but with **half**, the indefinite article, **a**, is often left out, thus **half**, rather than **a half**.

However, in combination with other numbers, the **a** (or **an**, as the **h** of **half** is not pronounced) is generally used, thus **one and a half, two and an half**.

In shoe sizes, an **s** is added to the cardinal number: **fives, sixes, fours**. For half sizes, **and-a-half** is generally added, thus: **threes- and-a-half, fours-and-a half**.

4.8.2 Time

Expressions of time are similar to Standard English, though the following points should be noted:

half past	This is usually subject to severe contraction, with the initial **h** and final **f** of **half** and the final **t** of **past**, not being pronounced. The resultant pronunciation is therefore **aapass** or **aapaass**
past	The final **t** is not usually pronounced.
to	This has a clear, pure long vowel with no diphthongisation.
quarter	Certain speakers have a tendency not to pronounce the **t**, though this is not general.
five past	The **–ve** of **five** is sometimes not pronounced.

| five to | Older speakers may use the form **five and twenty to** rather than **twenty five to**. For example: **What's the time? Five and twenty to five.** |

Wenglish has many **adverbs of time**, which do not have the same meaning as their Standard English equivalents:

now	Can mean *now, in a little while, presently, at some indefinite time in the future*. In fact it is a designator for any future action and as such is often qualified by a more specific indicator of when the action is to take place. Thus: **now in ten minutes, now next year**
now jest	Can either mean *in a little while* or *a little while ago*
in a minute now in a minute	*shortly*
this ages for ages frages this ages issages	*for a long time* For example, *I haven't seen her frages*
jest now, just now	*a few moments ago*
first go off	*first of all*
last go off	*last of all*
last lap	*last of all, at the eleventh hour*

EXERCISE 39: Numbers and Time

Translate into Wenglish:

1. It is 1.35pm.
2. It is half past seven.
3. The tower was built in the 11th century.
4. I haven't seen you for some time.
5. They will be here very shortly.
6. She will arrive presently.
7. The bus departs at 3.45.
8. The train was at least 20 minutes late and so we did not arrive until half

past three.

9. I haven't seen her for many years.

10. We hadn't seen each other for a whole year.

4.9 ADJECTIVES AND ADVERBS

4.9.1 Adjectives

Wenglish adjectives are used much as their Standard English counterparts but note the following differences:

1. An adjective may be intensified by repetition, as in Welsh.

The wedding dress was lovely lovely.

Occasionally, the adjective is repeated twice for extra emphasis, though this is much less common.

2. The adjective **old** (generally pronounced **ol'**) is often used to express distaste or disapproval. For example:

A lot of old work

Them knives are nasty old things

3. A number of adverbs are commonly used to intensify adjectives. For example:

beyond, thus **cheeky beyond.** This is a literal translation of the Welsh *tu hwnt,* and always follows the adjective it qualifies.

awful, thus **awful sad.** Note the adjective awful being used as an adverb.

very, used much as in Standard English, though possibly a little less common.

Pretty and **quite** provide a certain amount of emphasis, though not as much as the above.

There are a number of adjectives in Wenglish which do not exist in Standard English or have a different meaning from their Standard English counterparts. Some examples:

half soak(ed)	dopey, not wide awake, complacent
tidy	good, decent, well-done
chopsy	mouthy, talkative, argumentative
grand	well, wonderful
baad	ill, sick

rough	unwell, bad
salty	expensive
idle	unemployed, not working
apt to	liable to, likely to
hikey	stuck-up, arrogant
wit wat	flighty, unreliable
fit	cheeky, over-assertive, overbearing
sexy	having sexual content (e.g. film) lecherous

POSSESSIVE ADJECTIVES

The **possessive adjectives** are as in Standard English:

my	our
your	your
his	their
her	
its	

Your is pronounced **youer, ewer** or **yor, our** is pronounced **ouer** and **their** is pronounced **theyer**. These spellings may also be used.

When describing ownership, the **possessive pronouns** are used as in Standard English and are identical in form, though their pronunciation differs.

mine	ours
yours	yours
his, her, it's	theirs

Yours is pronounced **youers, ours** is pronounced **ouers** and **theirs** is pronounced **theyers**. These spellings may also be used. These spellings are not normally used but may be used for the sake of clarity.

4.9.2 Adverbs

In general, Wenglish adjectives double up as adverbs. They do not generally add –*ly* as in Standard English. This is another feature similar to Welsh. For example:

My feet are hurting me terrible

I was sitting there peaceful

Good is usually preferred to the Standard English *well*. Thus:

How are you feeling? Very good.

He done very good. (*He did very well.*)

We have already met the intensifiers **beyond, awful** and **very**. In addition the adverb **right** is quite often used in directions and to denote position. Thus the rather confusing:

We need to go right left. (*We need to go right over to the left.*)

Right is not used to intensify adverbs as it is in Northern English and in the English of North Wales.

Some very common adverbs do end in **–ly**, such as:

nearly (pronounced neely)

really (pronounced reely)

The **–ly** is also retained in set expressions such as:

There's something radically wrong

He was seriously hurt

A heavily fruited cake

A number of adverbs are characteristic to Wenglish or are used in a characteristic way. For example:

He have passed high. (*He has done well in his examinations.*)

I've seen him about. (*I've seen him out and about.*)

I seen him on the road. (*I saw him outside, outdoors.*)

Adverbs of place

Wenglish has very characteristic adverbs of place:

by here (*here*)

by there (*there*)

These can be combined with prepositions to denote position more exactly. Thus:

over by here, up by there, down by there

Note: The **y** of **by** is sometimes shortened in pronunciation, and in **by there**, the **y** can be dropped altogether, thus:

b' here

b'there

4.9.3 Comparison

Comparison of Adjectives

This is broadly similar to Standard English.

Comparison is achieved by using **as** or **so**, thus:

as big as or so big as

as high as or so high as

The next grade of comparison uses **–er,** as in Standard English, thus:

bigger than, dearer than, higher than

For longer adjectives, more is normally used.

more expensive than, more reliable than

Sometimes **more** and **–er** are used together, thus:

more nicer than, more kinder than

The superlative is formed as in Standard English, by adding **–est.** Thus:

the biggest, the smallest, the heaviest, the highest

For longer adjectives, **most** is used, thus:

the most expensive, the most reliable

Occasionally, **most** and **–est** are used together, though this is far from general and not to be recommended.

The most kindest, the most naughtiest

Comparison of Adverbs

This is effected in much the same way as in Standard English. For example:

Good, better, best

Slow(ly), slower or more slow(ly), slowest or most slow(ly)

The one-word forms **slower** and **slowest** are more commonly used:

The bus went slower than the car.

My butty done it better than me. (*My friend did it better than I did.*)

EXERCISE 40: Adjectives and Adverbs

Translate into Standard English:

1. Tha' new shop down the presink is too pricey for me. Salty beyond it is b'there.
2. The new dress was lovely lovely.
3. The team done grand – oany lost in the final they did.
4. I neely lost my temper with her.
5. Over by here it is, a course.
6. It's dearer than mine, yours is.
7. The bus went more slower than the motorbike.
8. She's cheeky beyond. I'm shuer she must be the most naughtiest girl in the hool class.
9. I've seen her on the road.
10. Iss better if you get a more darker one.

4.10 PRONOUNS

The **subject pronouns** are as in Standard English:

I	we
you	you
he, she, it	they

Note 1: You is sometimes pronounced **ew.**

Note 2: Where Standard English uses the impersonal form *one,* Wenglish uses **you** or sometimes **they.** For example:

You'd think they'd have done that by now.

They do say that Gladys is baad.

Note 3: These pronouns contract when used with common verbal auxiliaries, as in Standard English, for example:

I'd	we'll
you'll	you'd
he'll, she'd, it'd	they'll

Note 4: The initial **i** of **it** is sometimes lost coming at the head of a sentence or phrase, especially if the verb is stressed. For example:

't will be/'tisn't/'tint

The **object pronouns** are as in Standard English:

me	us
you	you
him, her, it	them

Note 1: The **s** in **us** is never voiced as is the tendency in Northern English and in the English of North Wales. It is always pronounced **uss**.

Note 2: Them often loses the **th**, and is thus pronounced **'em.**

Note 3: You is sometimes pronounced **ew.**

The object pronouns are used in sentences such as:

> **It's him that's doing it.**

> **Who is it? It's me!**

Standard English would strictly speaking require the subject pronouns *he* and *I* respectively.

After prepositions, the object pronouns are used. For example:

to me	with us
against you	over by you
from him	in them
off her	by it

However, in phrases such as **to Dad and I**, where Standard English would require *to Dad and me*, as the preposition **to** refers to both *Dad* and to *me*, the subject case, **I**, may be used.

The **reflexive pronouns** are as in Standard English:

myself	ourselves
yourself	yourselves
himself, herself, itself	themselves

Alternative forms **hisself, ouerselves/ouselves** and **theyselves** exist for **himself, ourself** and **themselves** respectively but they are less common.

EXERCISE 41: Pronouns

Translate into Standard English:

1. I can't see 'em nowhere.
2. It's me 'at should be doin it.
3. He can do it for hisself – he's old enough now.
4. I 'ad it off my Nan for a birthday present.

5. Iss over by there, behind you, on the floor.
6. Thar ol' photo come from them.
7. I got the house tidy against them comin 'ome.
8. I bought that one for Dad and I.
9. It's me 'oo should be goin, not him.
10. A bottle of wine she bought for us.

4.11 PREPOSITIONS

There are several differences between Wenglish and Standard English usage:

off This is used to denote 'receiving from'. Standard English would use *from*. For example:

I got that book off Mam as/for a birthday present.

by We have already encountered the characteristic combination of **by** with **here** and **there** to form adverbial phrases of place. It can also mean *according to*, e.g.:

What's the time by you?

You can set your clock by her (*i.e. her habits are so regular*)

It also means *from its appearance*, e.g:

You could tell by him there was something wrong.

A further meaning is *away*, as in:

Put them things by before the visitors come.

against As well as its usual meanings in Standard English, this can also mean *by the time that,* or *in readiness for*. This is a loan
translation of the Welsh *erbyn*. It is less common these days. For example:

I got the food ready against him coming home.

(*I got the food ready by the time he came home.*)

in **in** is used to denote being in a geographical location
(place, town or country). The Standard English *at* is never used in this context (except for the names of racecourses and other sporting venues). For example:

in Swansea

in the theatre

in France

in his sister's

in the butcher's

but:

I had a flutter on the 3.15 at Kempton Park.

It is also used where Standard English would have *at*, in the following examples:

He's no good in cricket but he's good in rugby.

She's good in maths but not much good in English.

down   This can mean **down in**, denoting position. For example:

I seen him down Swansea (*I saw him [down] in Swansea*)

It can also mean **down to**, in the sense of direction to, For example:

I'm going down Swansea this afternoon.

(*I'm going down to Swansea this afternoon.*)

up   In a similar way, this can mean up in, denoting position:

He's up his sister's.

It can also mean **up to**, in the sense of direction to:

He's going up his sister's tonight.

at   This is far less common than in Standard English. It is almost only used in the sense of target. For example:

He threw it at me.

It can be used as in Standard English in the case of racecourses and other sporting venues. For example:

I had a bet in the 3.30 at Newmarket.

of   Its use is much as in Standard English. It is often pronounced **a,** especially in unstressed positions. For example, **a cup a tea.**

There is also the loan construction from Welsh, **of + gerund**, meaning *if you are -ing*. For example:

Of buying one, you might as well get a good one.

Other prepositions such as **on, onto, into, behind, in front of, above, over, towards, between, because of, along, outside of, inside of, this side of, the other side of, under, with, without, apart from, opposite, facing**, are used much as in Standard English.

Opposite is sometimes pronounced **opposight.**

EXERCISE 42: Prepositions

Translate into Standard English:
1. I seen her in the butcher.
2. We seen her down Swansea las' week.
3. Put them toys by before the vicar do come.
4. I got the dinner ready against them comin 'ome.
5. Of getting one, get a good one.
6. The church is opposight the Town 'all.
7. We're goin down Ponty now jest.
8. He's playing up his Gran's back.
9. I took it from 'em without askin no questions.
10. They live up England somewhere.

4.12 QUESTION WORDS

what?	Used as in Standard English. Note that some speakers do not pronounce the final **t**. The **h** is never aspirated. Note also that the Standard English forms *with what?* and *from what?* are expressed with the preposition coming at the end of the sentence. For example: **What did he do that with?**
what kind of?	Usage is similar to Standard English but pronunciation sometime approximates to **wha' kin' a?** Alternatives are **what sort of?** and **what type of?**
how?	Used as in Standard English. Pronounced **'ow**.
who?	Pronounced **'oo**. Also covers *whom?*, which does not exist in Wenglish. Thus Standard English questions such as *With whom did he go?* are expressed with the preposition coming last in the sentence, as follows: **Who did he go with?**
what...for?	This is commonly used where Standard English has *why?* For example: **What are you cutting them sticks for?**
	(Why are you chopping that firewood?)
why?	Is sometimes used but **what...for?** is more common.
where?	Much as in Standard English.

where to?	Not a question about direction of travel rather position. This usage is not so common in the Western Wenglish area but is very typical of the Central and Eastern areas. It is synonymous with **where?** For example: **Where to is that?** *(Where is that?)* **Where's it to?** *(Where is it?)*
where... to?	This is a question of direction or travel, e.g.: **Where do you think you're going to?** The **to** could be dropped without much change of meaning.
what?	**Usage as in Standard English.**

Note on pronunciation of *am* and *are* following question words:

When a question word introduces a question in the present tense, progressive form, the verb forms **am** and are **are** often shortened. **Are** is sometimes dropped altogether. For example:

Where'm I going?

Where you going?

Where they going to?

EXERCISE 43: Question Words

Translate into Wenglish:
1. What sort of book was that?
2. Why did he do that?
3. Where are you going to?
4. With what did you paint that wall?
5. Who were you with last night?
6. Where is that?
7. Where are those trousers?
8. Why doesn't he keep still for a moment?
9. What is that?
10. Why is he making a noise continuously?

4.13 RELATIVE CONSTRUCTIONS

As in Standard English, the **relative pronoun (subject case)** is generally **who** for people, though **that** is also used. For things, **that** or sometimes **which** are used. For example:

A man who tries his best

The man that lives in Swansea

The things that are on the table

The subject case relative pronoun is never omitted in a relative clause.

However, there is a strong tendency to avoid relative constructions of this kind by expressing things differently. For example:

The man living in Swansea

The things on the table

The **relative pronoun (object case)** is **who** or **that** for people and **that,** occasionally **which**, for things. It is normally omitted completely:

The man I seen

The things he put on the table

With **prepositions**, the object case of the relative pronoun can be used, with the preposition coming at the end of the sentence. For example:

The car that I went in

However, the relative pronoun is usually omitted completely, with the preposition coming at the end of the sentence.

The car I went in

The book he wrote in

The place I come from

Whose (pronounced **ooze**) can be used much as in Standard English but is generally avoided by using other constructions to express the idea:

That man whose son I knew can be expressed as

That man I knew his son, and

The cups whose handles are broken as

The cups with the broken handles

EXERCISE 44: Relative Constructions

Translate the following into Wenglish. Use ways to avoid the relative pronoun where possible.

1. The man who lives in Pontypridd has sold his car.
2. The man whom I saw was very tall indeed.
3. The saucepans whose handles are loose should be thrown out because they are very dangerous.
4. The train on which I was travelling was late as usual.

5. That woman whom we met, whose son was at school with me, is seriously ill.
6. The play in which he acted was quite short.
7. The place from whence he came no longer exists.
8. The articles that he put on the desk all belonged to me.
9. The little boy whom we saw was extremely lively.
10. The box in which I put the crockery is in the attic now.

4.14 NOUNS

The usage of nouns is much as in Standard English. The genitive, denoting possession is in **'s.** Thus, **the man's jacket, the lady's coat.**
This also applies to nouns ending in **s,** e.g. **Thomas's pen.**
Sometimes, especially with names of shops and surnames, words not actually ending in **s** are made to do so. For example:
Howells's   (Howell's – the department store in Cardiff)
Morgans's   (Morgan's – the former department store in Cardiff)
For shops, **'s** is generally added, for example:
Tesco's, Asda's, down Sainsbury's, up Lidl's
However, in the case of unnamed shops, e.g. **the butcher's, the baker's,** the **'s** is sometimes omitted. Thus, **in the butcher, in the baker.**

Plural formation is very largely as in Standard English, that is, plurals are generally formed simply adding an **s.** Irregular plurals in Standard English are generally irregular in Wenglish too but are a few exceptions. In Wenglish the normal plural of **deer** is **deers** (rather than *deer* in Standard English). The plural of **reindeer** is **reindeers** (rather than *reindeer* as in Standard English).

Some loan words from Welsh have mixed plurals. Thus **milgi** (greyhound) has the plural **milgis** (not *milgwn* as in Welsh). The plural of **eisteddfod** is either **eisteddfods** or **eisteddfodau** as in Welsh. The plural of **crotyn / crwtyn** (lad, boy) is **crots / crwts.**

The plural of units of measurement often remain unchanged from the singular in Wenglish. Thus:

Two ton of coal, eight foot tall, six stone four, ten pound four ounces, two hundred pound in five pound notes, three hundredweight of sment.

The plural of **mile** could be **miles** or **mile,** the former being more commonly heard.

4.15 GENERAL NOTES ON WORD ORDER AND PRONUNCIATION

4.15.1 Word Order

The word order of Wenglish can differ markedly from that of Standard English. Such differences can usually be traced to the natural word order of the Welsh language.

In cases of emphasis, the element to be emphasised is generally placed first in the sentence. For example:

Miner he is, not a builder.

rather than the Standard English:

he is a miner, *not a builder.*

Blue it was, not green.

In general, there is greater flexibility in word order in Wenglish than in Standard English. For example sentences of the type below would not be possible in Standard English:

Thinking I was he wouldn't be able to do it.

Only wondrin' I was if she would come.

Another feature is the tagging on of gone (meaning 'has become') to the end of a phrase or sentence. For example:

He's ffibledd gone. (He has become fastidious.)

This follows the pattern in Welsh, where 'wedi mynd' – the equivalent of **gone** – is tagged on in the same way.

4.15.2 Pronunciation

Most of the following points have been covered in the section on pronunciation in the Introduction. They are repeated here as reminders.

1. **h** Do not pronounce the letter **h** except in the name of the letter, **haitch,** and in words which contain the name of the letter e.g. **Haitch TV, Haitch P sauce**

2. Generally, the final t's of **that**, **what**, **not** and **all negative contractions of verbs** can be dropped in pronunciation if there is nothing directly following. For example:

I won't say	becomes	I won' say
he isn't there	becomes	he isn' there
I ain't going	becomes	I ain' going
he don't know	becomes	he don' know

3. Intervocalic **t** (a **t** occurring between two vowel sounds) is pronounced as a trilled **r** by some, but by no means all, speakers. This is also a marked characteristic of Liverpool speech. It is by no means general in Wenglish and need not be emulated. For example:

I gorra lorra things a do   *(I have many things to do)*

It should be noted that the vowels between which the t occurs need not be in the same word. For example:

butter	burrer
better	berrer
not a lot of	norra lorra
get on my nerves	gerron my nerves
get off!	gerroff!

It should be noted also that by no means all speakers employ this pronunciation. Older, more traditional speakers of Wenglish generally would not. To use this type of pronunciation on all occasions would give your speech a very downmarket feel, though many speakers do use this type of pronunciation at least occasionally.

Unstressed vowels have a tendency to be dropped in pronunciation. For example:

it isn't can be pronounced as **'t isn't** and **it in't** as **'t in't**.

As previously mentioned, **Wenglish vowels are pure, simple sounds.** Diphthongisation should be avoided to ensure an authentic pronunciation.

4.16 EXERCISES AND TRANSLATIONS

Now that you've completed all the grammar sections, here are some more sentences and some continuous passages for you to translate. Good luck – and have fun!

EXERCISE 45: Nouns and Word Order

Translate into Wenglish:

1. I go shopping at Tesco every Friday night.
2. It was yellow, not red.
3. I saw her at the bakery.
4. He is a carpenter, not an electrician.
5. The man's jacket was green, not brown.

6. I purchased those shoes in Howell's sale.

7. It is very important to remember the details for reasons of safety.

8. They chopped the trees down before clearing the rest of the garden.

9. It's a very large house, not a little cottage.

10. He was thinking that he could manage it in one attempt.

EXERCISE 46: Translate to Wenglish

My name is Diane Jones. I live in Pontypridd. I work in Curtis' shoe shop in the shopping precinct. I am married and have three children – two boys and a little girl. The boys are in comprehensive school and the little girl is in primary school.

My husband works in the colliery in Maerdy. He likes watching rugby and meeting his friends at the Miners' Institute.

We are going on holiday to Spain with a pleasant group of people from Pontypridd.

My mother lives in Cilfynydd. She will be 70 in July. I see her or speak to her every day.

EXERCISE 47: Translate into Standard English

1. I don' care if he seen me or no: "E won' say nothing to nobody.

2. Of goin to Merthyr, you can call in to see Val.

3. Miner 'e was, not a builder.

4. We're goin on ouer 'olidays down Trecco on Satday.

5. What are you doin that for?

6. Dorian do live down by there an' all.

7. Tha' Mrs Jones 'ave gone esentric since she buried 'er 'usbunt.

8. Tha' colly's a reeal bewty.

9. John do love seein 'is butties down the club.

10. The 'anbury' 'ave been shut for a twelmunth burris open agen now, by all account.

EXERCISE 48: Translate to Wenglish

1. He is a butcher, not a baker.

2. Fair play, he's had a difficult time since his wife's death.

3. Leave me in peace! I haven't got time to do all those things at the moment.

4. Let me see the new outfit you have for Angela's wedding.

5. How many people are due to come here tonight?

6. Why are you digging the garden?

7. Her son Alan's been married for less than a year but it is rumoured he is having an affair with a woman at work.

8. All three of them have been to Cardiff to buy shoes in Howell's sale.

9. Let's put our tools aside for a while and take a break.

10. The river is deeper by the bridge than here.

EXERCISE 49: Translate into Standard English

1. Shwd mae'n ceibo? Iss time you 'ad a wiff.

2. The weather's lovely – less go down the bays.

3. 'E've made a big cawlach of it. There's no depends on 'im. Wit wat 'e is – a bit of a flag.

4. She's like a bear with a sore 'ead – you can't do nothin' with 'er when she's like 'at.

5. Rise youer arm up!

6. The funeral is risin' at 1 o'clock from the 'ouse.

7. Dim ots. If you 'aven't gorrit on you, you can give it to me agen.

8. The're eatin me out of 'ouse an' 'ome!

9. There's ewn that Brenda is! Fit – she's brazen!

10. Cera o 'ma! You're pullin 'is leg all the time!

EXERCISE 50: Translate into Standard English

1. It have got a speck of dust on it by there.

2. They do go for a walk evry afternoon after dinner.

3. I an't got a clue what he's on about.

4. In't you ready yet?

5. He haven't been feeling too good but he'll come now jest.

6. She been down Swansea again today.

7. Dai have solt his car and have bought a swanky new one.

8. Mam have rang. I told her you'd phone her back now just.

9. The clock's broke. Billy have bust it.

10. Was you down the club las' night?

11. Where's it to?

12 You musn't shout like (th)at for fear you do wake Dacu.

13. I din have time to rise my pension.

14. Of goin to Ponty, I'll pick one up in the market.

15. Gis an anch of (th)ar apple!

16. I don't need no more pencils, Mam.

17. John and Gail is comin to see us after tea.

18. Them planks aren't strong enough to 'old that weight.
19. They do say there's a gold coin buried in the garden.
20. You do know me: I do run a tight ship.
21. Give me orange!
22. I never seen (th)e news on (th)e box las' night.
23. He should be here by aa past.
24. I'll be there now in a minute.
25. I haven't seen her issages – iss donkey's years since she was down by here last.
26. First go off he said he hated it but later on he changed his mind and in the end he was in his oils.
27. The weddin dress was lovely lovely.
28. Them sharp knives are nasty old things.
29. Awful sad it was the film.
30. There's a boy he is: half soak – he'd forget his head if it wasn't fixed to his neck.
31. Chopsy bugger that Waldron.
32. We neely lost ouer train.
33. My feet are hurtin me terrible.
34. That brown dress is more smarter than the black one but iss more pricey an' all.
35. I got that book off Mam for a birthday present.
36. Put 'em things by before the visitors come.
37. I got the food ready against him comin home.
38. He's up his Gran's.
39. What are you doin that for?
40. That man livin in Swansea have moved to Llanelli now.
41. Cheeky beyond he is that baker: said I should have my hair done.
42. The y do say that Gladys is baad. Under the doctor she is by all account.
43. Islwyn is very low. He've been under the doctor a good twelmonth.
44. Fagged out he was after workin up (th)e forestry.
45. He've passed high. He's off to college up England in September.
46. You can set youer clock by him.
47. He've had a nasty pull. Started with a bilious attack.
48. My Mam don't go shoppin' down the Cop no more, she do rather go down Asda's.
49. You could tell by her that there was something wrong.

50. What are you cutting them sticks for again?
51. He've put in in the cwtch dan stâr.
52. I don't know nothing about it.
53. Penstiff he is: he'll only do it if he do want to.
54. Put me two pounds of youer best stewin steek.
55. He was paradin back and fore, back and fore in front of her house last night. Funny, mind. Funny beyond.
56. Ouer Billy had a bad stummuck after eatin them sausage but he was right as rain after takin a dose of elsolse.
57. Weddol he was yesterday but weaker he's getting all the time, poor dab.
58. That place of hers is all shandivang. Proper didoreth she is an' there's no graan on her washin.
59. He do stop for a wiff every aaf 'our. He won't finish that job this side of Christmas at this rate.
60. The old ticker's playin' him up again, what with that an' the dust, he'll be lucky to make it to Christmas, I reckon.

EXERCISE 51: Translate into Wenglish

Once upon a time, many years ago, a little girl called Goldilocks decided to go for a walk in the woods. She bade her mother farewell and set out down the path. Her mother was not in the least concerned about Goldilocks' safety as she often went to play in the forest near her house and she was well able to orientate herself. On this occasion, however, she decided to explore another part of the forest so she walked on further than she usually did. There was sunshine and birdsong, and the butterflies fluttered their little wings in the air around her. Goldilocks was in her element. She walked on happily under the shade of the trees for several hours. Eventually she felt rather tired so she sat down for a rest. In fact she felt so tired that she fell asleep on the ground.

When she awoke, it was already late in the afternoon. 'Oh no', she said. 'I'm not quite sure which way I should go. All these paths look alike.' She walked on a little further until she came to a pretty little house in a clearing. 'Thank goodness', she said. 'Someone might be able to help me.'

She knocked at the door but no-one answered. She tried once more, and then a third time before she lifted the latch and entered. In the kitchen there was a table set for three. On the table were three bowls of delicious porridge. One bowl was very large indeed, one was medium-sized and one was extremely small. She was by now so hungry – she had not eaten all day since leaving her house that morning – that she took a spoonful of porridge from the large bowl but it was far too hot. She then took a spoonful from the medium-sized bowl but it was not sufficiently sweet. She then took a spoonful of porridge from the tiny bowl, which was just to her taste – so much so that she ate it all up!

She decided to sit down to await the return of the residents of the house. There were three chairs in the drawing room. One was very large indeed, one was medium-sized and one was very small. She tried the large one. It was much too high. She tried the medium-sized one but it was uncomfortable. She then tried the tiny chair, which was just the right size for her, but unfortunately it broke and she fell on the floor with a crash.

As no-one had arrived back, she decided to venture upstairs to explore further. In the bedroom there were three beds. One was very large indeed. One was medium-sized. One was quite small. She decided to have a little nap so she tried the big bed: it was far too hard. She then tried the medium-sized bed: it was far too soft. Finally she tried the small bed and it was just right. It was so comfortable, in fact, that she fell fast asleep.

A little later, the residents of the house returned. They were the Bear Family: Father Bear, Mother Bear and Baby Bear. 'Who's been eating my porridge?' asked Father Bear in a big, loud booming voice. 'Who's been eating my porridge?' asked Mother Bear in a medium-sized voice. 'And who's been eating my porridge?' asked Baby Bear in a tiny high-pitched squeaky voice, 'and has eaten in all up!'.

They went to the drawing room. On examining their chairs they noticed that they were not as they left them. 'Who's been sitting in my chair?' asked Father Bear in a big, loud booming voice. 'Who's been sitting in my chair?' asked Mother Bear in a medium-sized voice. 'And who's been sitting in my chair?' asked Baby Bear in a squeaky voice, 'and has broken it to bits!'

The bears crept upstairs carefully in case the intruder was still in the house. They entered the bedroom and noticed that the beds had been disturbed. 'Who's been sleeping in my bed?, asked Father Bear in a big, loud booming voice. 'Who's been sleeping in my bed?' asked Mother Bear in a medium-sized voice. 'And who's been sleeping in my bed?' asked Baby Bear in a high-pitched squeaky voice, 'and is still lying on it!'

The noise the bears were making awoke Goldilocks. She sat up in shock when she saw the bears. She rushed downstairs and out of the house as fast as she could. Fortunately she found the right path and she ran quickly all the way home.

When her mother asked her if she had had a pleasant day, Goldilocks was unsure what to say. She did not want to reveal the full story concerning the difficulty in which she had found herself, lest her mother would not allow her to play in the forest again. She never returned to the part of the forest where the bears' cottage was situated.

4.17 ANSWERS TO EXERCISES AND TRANSLATIONS

EXERCISE 1

1. a) We run b) we do run c) we're runnin(g)
2. a) She goes b) she do go c) she's goin(g)
3. a) You walk b) you do walk c) you're walkin(g)
4. a) He drinks b) he do drink c) he's drinkin(g)
5. a) They work b) they do work c) they're workin(g)
6. a) I leave b) I do leave c) I'm leavin(g)
7. a) She plays b) she do play c) she's playin(g)
8. a) We read b) we do read c) we're readin(g)
9. a) They sing b) they do sing c) they're singin(g)
10.a) You write b) you do write c) you're writin(g)

EXERCISE 2

1. a) She have b) she do have c) she's havin(g)
2. a) They have b) they do have c) they're havin(g)
3. a) We have b) we do have c) we're havin(g)
4. a) It have b) it do have c) it's havin(g)
5. a) He have b) he do have c) he's havin(g)
6. a) I have b) I do have c) I'm havin(g)

EXERCISE 3

1. a) it do b) it do do c) it's doin(g)
2. a) you do b) you do do c) you're doin(g)
3. a) I do b) I do do c) I'm doin(g)
4. a) he do b) he do do c) he's doin(g)
5. a) she do b) she do do c) she's doin(g)
6. a) they do b) they do do c) they're doin(g)

EXERCISE 4

1. a) I don'(t) wash b) I'm not washin(g) / I ain'(t)/in'(t) washin(g)
2. a) You don'(t) walk b) you're not walkin(g) / you ain'(t)/in'(t)/an'(t) walkin(g)w
3. a) They don'(t) lissen b) they're not lissnin(g) / they ain'(t)/in'(t)/an'(t) lissnin(g)
4. a) I don'(t) work b) I'm not workin(g) / I ain'(t)/in'(t) workin(g)
5. a) She don'(t) sit b) she's not/she isn't sittin(g) / she ain'(t)/in'(t) sittin(g)
6. a) It don'(t) fly b) it's not/it isn't flyin(g) / it ain'(t)/in'(t) flyin(g)
7. a) He don'(t) read b) he's not/he isn't readin(g) / he ain'(t)/in'(t) readin(g)

8. a)   They don'(t) play b) they're not playin(g) / they ain'(t)/in'(t)/
an'(t) playin(g)
9. a)   She don'(t) write b) she's not/she isn't writin(g) / she ain'(t)/in'(t)
writin(g)
10. a)   We don'(t) cook b) we're not cookin(g) / we ain'(t)/in'(t)/an'(t)
cookin(g)

EXERCISE 5

1. a)   don'(t) you throw? b) isn't he throwin(g)? / ain'(t)/in'(t) he
throwin(g)?
2. a)   don'(t) we tie? b) aren't we tyin(g)? / ain'(t)/in(t) we tyin(g)?
3. a)   Don'(t) they water? b) aren't they waterin(g)? / ain'(t)/in'(t)/an'(t)
they waterin(g)?
4. a)   Don'(t) she polish? b) isn't she polishin(g)? / ain'(t)/in'(t) she
polishin(g)?
5. a)   Don'(t) it shut? b) isn't it shuttin(g)? / ain'(t)/in'(t) it shuttin(g)?
6. a)   Don'(t) i walk? b) aren't I walkin(g)? / ain'(t)/in'(t) I walkin(g)?
7. a)   Don'(t) you read? b) aren't you readin(g)? / ain'(t)/in'(t)/an'(t)
you readin(g)?
8. a)   Don'(t) they swim? b) aren't they swimmin(g)? / ain'(t)/in'(t)/
an'(t) they swimin(g)?
9. a)   Don'(t) we cook? b) aren't we cookin(g)? / ain'(t)/in'(t)/an'(t) we
cookin(g)?
10. a)   Don'(t) I run? b) aren't I runnin(g)? / ain'(t)/in'(t) I runnin(g)?

EXERCISE 6

1. Ain'(t)/In'(t) you well?
2. I ain'(t)/in'(t)/an'(t) done it
3. They ain'(t)/in'(t) an'(t) lissnin(g)
4. We ain'(t)/in'(t)/an'(t) runnin(g)
5. She ain'(t)/in'(t) goin(g)
6. He ain'(t)/in'(t) havin(g) it
7. They ain'(t)/in'(t)/an'(t) on 'olidays
8. You ain'(t)/in'(t)/an'(t) got it/gorrit
9. It ain'(t)/in'(t) 'appnin(g)
10. Ain'(t) /in'(t)/an'(t) you done 'at yet?

EXERCISE 7

1. I've acted
2. You've walked
3. They've warned

4. She've opened
5. We've looked
6. It have arrived
7. They've closed
8. He have paraded
9. They've operated
10. We've supported

EXERCISE 8

1. I've been
2. You've seen
3. She've boilt
4. They've trood/trod/trodden
5. We've solt
6. It have risen
7. I've written/wrote
8. He've read/red
9. They've put
10. You've understood

EXERCISE 9

1. Have you bust/busted?
2. Have she broke/broken?
3. Have they kilt?
4. Have we earnt?
5. Have he throwed/thrown?
6. Have I done?
7. Have we supported?
8. Have she operated?
9. Have they read/red?
10. Have you written/wrote?

EXERCISE 10

1. Haven'(t) we gone/been? / Ain'(t)/In'(t)/An'(t) we gone/been?
2. Haven'(t) they thrown/throwed? Ain'(t)/In'(t)/An'(t) they thrown/throwed?
3. Haven'(t) I understood? / Ain'(t) In'(t)/An'(t) I understood?
4. Haven'(t) she cooked? / Ain'(t)/In'(t)/An'(t) she cooked?
5. Haven'(t) he built? / Ain'(t)/In'(t)/An'(t) he built?
6. Haven'(t) they dug? / Ain'(t)/In'(t)/An'(t) they dug?
7. Haven'(t) you understood? / Ain'(t)/In'(t)/An'(t) you understood?

8. Haven'(t) you written/wrote? / Ain'(t)/In'(t)/An'(t) you written/wrote?
9. Haven'(t) she walked? / Ain'(t)/In'(t)/An'(t) she walked?
10. Haven'(t) they got? / Ain'(t)/In/(t)/An'(t) they got?

EXERCISE 11

1. They done/did
2. We understood
3. You sat
4. She scrammed
5. They chucked
6. We trood/trod
7. We wrote/writ
8. They read/red
9. He played
10. We congratulated

EXERCISE 12

1. I didn'(t) cross / I din cross
2. You didn'(t) know / you din know
3. He didn'(t) throw / he din throw
4. They didn'(t) rise / they din rise
5. She didn'(t) argue / she din argue
6. We didn'(t) go / we din go
7. You didn'(t) congratulate / you din congratulate
8. We didn'(t) support / we din support
9. He didn'(t) read / he din read
10. She didn'(t) write / she din write

EXERCISE 13

1. Did you know?
2. Did they cross?
3. Did he kill?
4. Did we ketch?
5. Did they ring?
6. Did she rise?
7. Did we sing?
8. Did he show?
9. Did you eat?
10. Did she drink?

EXERCISE 14

1. Didn'(t) they boil? / Din they boil?
2. Didn'(t) we earn? / Din we earn?
3. Didn'(t)she scram? / Din she scram?
4. Didn'(t) he plant? / Din he plant?
5. Didn'(t) you live? / Din you live?
6. Didn'(t) it show? / Din it show?
7. Didn'(t) you support? / Din you support?
8. Didn'(t) they do? / Din they do?
9. Didn'(t) he examine? / Din he examine?
10. Didn'(t) you shut? / Din you shut?

EXERCISE 15

1. You was/were watchin(g)
2. They was/were lookin(g)
3. She was drivin(g)
4. We was/were turnin(g)
5. She was polishin(g)
6. It was growin(g)
7. I was congratulatin(g)
8. He was playin(g)
9. She was writin(g)
10. It was openin(g)

EXERCISE 16

1. I wasn'(t) laughin(g) / I wan laughin(g)
2. You weren'(t)/wasn'(t) coughin(g) / you wan coughin(g)
3. He wasn'(t) sneezin(g) / he wan sneezin(g)
4. She wasn'(t) bitin(g) / she wan bitin(g)
5. It wasn'(t) closin(g) / it wan closin(g)
6. You wasn'(t)/weren'(t) doing it / you wan doin(g) it
7. It wasn'(t) openin(g) / it wan openin(g)
8. She wasn'(t) playin(g) / she wan playin(g)
9. We wasn'(t)/weren'(t) reading(g) / we wan readin(g)
10. I wasn'(t) talkin(g) / I wan talkin(g)

EXERCISE 17

1. Was he walkin(g)?
2. Was/Were you drivin(g)?
3. Was/Were we cheerin(g)?

4. Was it workin(g)?
5. Was /Were they lissnin(g)?
6. Was /Were we shovin(g)?
7. Was/Were you supportin(g)?
8. Was he talkin(g)?
9. Was she playin(g)?
10. Was I singin(g)?

EXERCISE 18

1. Wasn'(t)/Weren'(t) they losin(g)? / Wan they losin(g)?
2. Wasn'(t) he smokin(g)? / Wan he smokin(g)?
3. Wasn'(t) she eatin(g)? / Wan she eatin(g)?
4. Wasn'(t)/Weren'(t) you drinkin(g)? / Wan you drinkin(g)?
5. Wasn'(t)/Weren'(t) they huntin(g)? / Wan they huntin(g)?
6. Wasn'(t)/Weren'(t) we yappin(g)? / Wan we yapping?
7. Wasn'(t) I congratulatin(g)? / Wan I congratulatin(g)?
8. Wasn'(t) it goin(g)? / Wan it goin(g)?
9. Wasn'(t)/Weren'(t) they comin(g)? / Wan they comin(g)?
10. Wasn'(t) I lookin(g)? / Wan I lookin(g)?

EXERCISE 19

1. You used to want
2. You used to have a good time
3. They used to run
4. We used to march
5. It used to work
6. She used to try
7. He used to support
8. You used to read
9. She used to write
10. They used to type

EXERCISE 20

1. You didn'(t) used to run / you din used to run
2. He didn'(t) used to drink / he din used to drink
3. They didn'(t) used to lay / they din used to lay
4. We didn'(t) used to chops / we din used to chops
5. They didn'(t) used to hunt / they din used to hunt
6. He didn'(t) used to smell / he din used to smell
7. He didn'(t) used to manage / he din used to manage
8. She didn'(t) used to help / she din used to help

9. They didn'(t) used to write / they din used to write

10. We didn'(t) used to watch / we din used to watch

EXERCISE 21

1. Did he used to run?
2. Did we used to feel?
3. Did you used to love?
4. Did she used to water?
5. Did they used to cry?
6. Did I used to make?
7. Did we used to read?
8. Did they used to travel?
9. Did you used to work?
10. Did he used to cut?

EXERCISE 22

1. Didn'(t) they used to buy? / Din they used to buy?
2. Didn'(t) they used to sell? / Din they used to sell?
3. Didn'(t) he used to answer? / Din he used to answer?
4. Didn'(t) she used to shiggle? / Din she used to shiggle?
5. Didn'(t) we used to burn? / Din we used to burn?
6. Didn'(t) you used to sit? / Din you used to sit?
7. Didn'(t) I used to read? / Din I used to read?
8. Didn'(t) she used to write? / Din she used to write?
9. Didn'(t) he used to play? / Din he used to play?
10. Didn'(t) she used to boast? / Din she used to boast?

EXERCISE 23

1. They'd made / they had made
2. We'd mended / we had mended
3. She'd knitted / she had knitted
4. He'd driven / he had driven
5. You'd found / you had found
6. It'd gone / it had gone
7. They'd played / they had played
8. She'd red/read / she had red/read
9. He'd worked / he had worked
10. I'd been / I had been

EXERCISE 24

1. We hadn'(t)/han owned
2. She hadn'(t)/han rowed
3. You hadn'(t)/han bought
4. We hadn'(t)/han ketched
5. You hadn'(t)/han gone in
6. I hadn'(t)/han vanished
7. She hadn'(t)/han written/wrote
8. They hadn'(t)/han played
9. We hadn'(t)/han had
10. I hadn'(t)/han realised

EXERCISE 25

1. Had you given?
2. Had we crosst?
3. Had she cooked?
4. Had he worked?
5. Had it happened?
6. Had they fallen?
7. Had I had?
8. Had he played?
9. Had they lit?
10. Had we frozen?

EXERCISE 26

1. Hadn'(t)/Han we had?
2. Hadn'(t)/Han she turned?
3. Hadn'(t)/Han they cheated?
4. Hadn'(t)/Han we wiped?
5. Hadn'(t)/Han he gone?
6. Hadn'(t)/Han you done?
7. Hadn'(t)/Han you played? ·
8. Hadn'(t)/Han we worn?
9. Hadn'(t)/Han they written/wrote?
10. Hadn'(t)/Han he noticed?

EXERCISE 27

1. You'll see / you will see
2. They'll walk / they will walk
3. He'll lecture / he will lecture

4. We'll talk / we will talk
5. She'll realise / she will realise
6. He'll click / he will click
7. You'll do / you will do
8. They'll introduce / they will introduce
9. We'll manage / we will manage
10. You'll print / you will print

EXERCISE 28

1. He won'(t) understand / he will not understand
2. There won'(t) be / there will not be
3. She won'(t) crosho / she will not crosho
4. They won'(t) knit / they will not knit
5. We won'(t) burn / we will not burn
6. They won'(t) do / they will not do
7. We won'(t) play / we will not play
8. She won'(t) write / she will not write
9. He won'(t) hear / he will not hear
10. I won'(t) go / I will not go

EXERCISE 29

1. Will they hurry?
2. Will you run?
3. Will we see?
4. Will it shake?
5. Will she be writing?
6. Will we walk?
7. Will he understand?
8. Will he race?
9. Will she blame?
10. Will we put?

EXERCISE 30

1. Won'(t) they run?
2. Won'(t) he aggravate?
3. Won'(t) she put?
4. Won'(t) we finish?
5. Won'(t) he box?
6. Won'(t) John write?
7. Won'(t) I like?
8. Won'(t) you play?

9. Won'(t) he read?

10. Won'(t) she write?

EXERCISE 31

1. He's arrivin(g) on Thursday / He arrives on Thursday

2. John's leavin(g) on Monday / John leaves on Monday

3. The castle's open tomorrow / The castle is open tomorrow

4. I'm comin(g) again tomorrow

5. You're goin(g) / You go

6. We dock at 3 tomorrow / We're dockin(g) at 3 tomorrow

7. He arrives next week / He's arrivin(g) next week

8. They're callin(g) tonight

9. She's goin(g) in an hour / She goes in an hour

10. The ship sails at midnight / The ship is sailin(g) at midnight

EXERCISE 32

1. They won'(t) be runnin(g)

2. I won'(t) be worryin(g)

3. Will you be comin(g)?

4. They'll be diggin(g)

5. She'll be drinkin(g)

6. Will he be eatin(g)?

7. He will be playin(g) / he'll be playin(g)

8. They'll be arguin(g)

9. I'll be competin(g)

10. She'll be collectin(g)

EXERCISE 33

1. You won't have grown

2. We'll have caught/catched/ketched

3. They won'(t) have learnt

4. Will you have gone?

5. We'll have gone

6. She'll have knitted

7. We'll have shown/showed

8. They'll have tried

9. They'll have lit

10. I'll have played

EXERCISE 34

1. She wouldn'(t) go / she woun go
2. They'd arrive / they would arrive
3. We'd send / we would send
4. Annie'd eat / Annie would eat
5. Wouldn'(t) she like that? / woun she like that?
6. He'd work / he would work
7. I'd have / I would have
8. They'd congratulate / they would congratulate
9. You'd freeze / you would freeze
10. He'd lose / he would lose

EXERCISE 35

1. She'd have read/red / she would have read/red
2. It would have finished
3. Would he have eaten?
4. They'd have cooked / they would have cooked
5. They'd never have eaten / they would never have eaten
6. It would have opened
7. He'd have played / he would have played
8. We'd have written/wrote / we would have written/wrote
9. She'd have seen / she would have seen
10. They'd have closed / they would have closed

EXERCISE 36

1. I can lift the box.
2. I can go out now.
3. You should'(t)/shoun go out after washin(g) youer 'ed.
4. He might come now jest.
5. Can you talk Chinese?
6. It must come from theyer 'ouse.
7. Could you come?
8. It might work.
9. She might come.
10. I couldn'(t)/coun say that for shuer.

EXERCISE 37

1. He liked me playin(g) the piano.
2. Of goin(g) to Pontardawe, can you get some potatoes for me?
3. Of buildin(g) a wall, you might as well build an 'igh one.
4. If I was you, I'd go straight away.
5. Billy an' George is still under the doctor.
6. I don'(t) want nothin(g).
7. I couldn'(t)/coun find it nowhere.
8. They never go nowhere.
9. Gi' 's (an) anch of youer apple!
10. I don'(t) want no more gravy.

EXERCISE 38

1. Them two letters is in my 'ambaag.
2. 'At bloke was in 'e pub agen.
3. In 'er clecshun a models, the little girl 'ave gorran 'orse and two deers.
4. They can 'elp me with them little jobs.
5. 'Is man I seen went in 'e booky's.
6. She never understands 'em things.
7. 'Em knives is in 'e drawer.
8. 'E spoons is on 'at small table over by there.
9. I'll give you them papers after dinner.
10. Get them dirty shoes off 'at chair!

EXERCISE 39

1. Iss five and twenty to two.
2. Iss aa pass seven.
3. The tower was built in the leventh/lenth century.
4. I haven'(t)/ain'(t)/in'(t)/an'(t) seen you frages/iss ages/ this ages/ this long time.
5. They'll be here now in a minute.
6. She'll come now jest.
7. The bus goes at quarter to four.
8. The train was easy twenny minutes late an' so we din get there till aa pass three.
9. I haven'(t)/ain'(t)/in'(t)/an'(t) seen 'er for donkey's years.
10. We hadn'(t)/han seen each other for a hool twelmunth.

EXERCISE 40

1. That new shop down in the precinct is too expensive for me. It's really awfully expensive there.

2. The new dress was very nice indeed.

3. The team performed very well – they only lost in the final.

4. I almost lost my temper with her.

5. It's over here, of course.

6. Yours is more expensive than mine.

7. The bus went more slowly than the motorbike.

8. She is very insolent. I'm certain she must be the naughtiest girl in the entire class.

9. I've seen her out and about.

10. It is more advantageous for you to obtain a darker-coloured one.

EXERCISE 41

1. I cannot see them anywhere.

2. It is I who should be doing it.

3. He can do it for himself – he is old enough now.

4. I received it from my grandmother as a birthday present.

5. It's over there, behind you, on the floor.

6. That old photograph came from them.

7. I tidied the house by the time they returned home/ before they returned home.

8. I bought that one for Dad and me.

9. It is I who should be going, not he.

10. She bought us a bottle of wine / She bought a bottle of wine for us.

EXERCISE 42.

1. I saw her at the butcher's.

2. We saw her down in Swansea last week.

3. Put those toys away before the vicar arrives.

4. I prepared lunch by the time they arrived home / I prepared lunch in readiness for their arrival home.

5. If you are getting one, get a good one.

6. The church is opposite the Town Hall.

7. We will be going to Pontypridd (or Pontardawe) shortly.

8. He is playing in his grandmother's back garden.

9. I accepted it from them without question.

10. They live somewhere in England.

EXERCISE 43

1. Wha' kind a book was 'at?

2. What (did) he do that for?

3. Where you goin(g)?

4. Wha(t) did you paint (th)at wall with?

5. 'Oo were/was you with las' night?

6. Where's (th)at to?

7. Where's (th)at trousers? / Where are them trousers?

8. Why don'(t) he keep still a minute?

9. Wossat? / Wha(t)'s (th)at?

10. Wha(t)'s 'e keeping a noise for all the time?

EXERCISE 44

1. The man livin(g) in Pontypridd have solt 'is car.

2. The man I saw/seen was tall tall.

3. You should chuck the sospans with the loose 'andles out coz they're very dangerous.

4. The train I was on was late as usual.

5. That woman we met, her son was in school with me, is very low.

6. The play he acted in was quite short.

7. The place he come from don'(t) exist no more.

8. The things he put on the desk were all mine.

9. The little crwt we seen was full a beans.

10. The box I put the china in is up in the attic now.

EXERCISE 45

1. I go/do go shoppin(g) down Tesco's evry Friday night.

2. Yello it was, not red.

3. I seen/saw her in the baker.

4. Carpenter 'e is, not a lectrician. / Chippy 'e is, norra spark.

5. Green the man's jacket was, not brown.

6. I bought them shoes in Howells's sales.

7. Very important it is to remember the puticklers coz a safety, (like).

8. Chopped the trees down 'ey did before clearin' the rest a the garden.

9. Big 'uge 'ouse it is, not a little dwtty cottage / Big 'uge 'ouse irriz, norra little dwtty cottage.

10. Thinkin' 'e was 'e could do it (all) in one go.

EXERCISE 46

Diane Jones my name is. I (do) live in Pontypridd. I work down Curtis's shoe shop down the shoppin' presink. Married I am an' I got three kids – two boys an' a little girl. In compre'ensive school the boys are an' the little girl's in juniors.

My 'usbunt do work up Maardy down the pit. He do like watchin' rugby an' meetin' 'is frenz down the Stute. .

We're goin' on ouer 'olidays to Spain with a nice crowd from Ponty.

My mam lives up Cilfynydd. 70 she'll be in July. I do see 'er or talk to 'er evry day.

EXERCISE 47

1. I don't care if he saw me or not: he won't say anything to anybody.
2. While you're in Merthyr, you can visit Val.
3. He was a miner, not a builder.
4. We will be going on holiday to Trecco Bay on Saturday.
5. Why are you doing that?
6. Dorian also lives down there.
7. That Mrs Jones has become rather eccentric since losing her husband/ since her husband's death.
8. That cauliflower is a splendid specimen.
9. John loves seeing/socialising with his friends in the club.
10. The 'Hanbury' has been closed for a year but I hear it has now reopened.

EXERCISE 48

1. Butcher 'e is, not a baker. / Butcher 'e is, norra baker.
2. Ware teg, 'e've 'ad 'ard time since 'e buried 'is wife.
3. Leave me llonydd! I haven'(t) got time to do all them things jest now.
4. Let me see the new rigout you got for Angela's weddin'.
5. 'Ow many people is sposed to be comin' 'ere tonight?
6. What (are) you diggin the garden for?
7. 'Er son Alan's been married for less than a twelmunth but he've got a fancy woman in work, by all account.
8. The three of 'em 'ave been to Cardiff to buy shoes in 'owells's sales.
9. Tools ar y bar now for a bit and 'ave a wiff/spell!
10. The river is (more) deeper by the bridge than by here.

EXERCISE 49

1. How is the work progressing? / How are you coming on? It's time you had a break.
2. The weather's excellent. Let's go to the beach (generally on the Gower Peninsula).
3. He's made a complete mess of it. He's not dependable. He's unreliable – a bit of a joker.
4. She is very irritable/touchy – it is impossible to deal/speak rationally with her when she is in that frame of mind.
5. Lift your arm up.
6. The funeral commences at one o'clock from the residence of the deceased.

7. It doesn't matter. If you do not have it on your person, you can give it to me on another occasion.

8. They are eating very heartily indeed / They are eating so much that they are seriously depleting my food supplies.

9. That Brenda is very presumptuous. Pushy and forceful – she's quite shameless!

10. Come off it! You're continually teasing him.

EXERCISE 50

1. It has a speck of dust on it (just) there.
2. They go for a walk every afternoon after lunch.
3. I do not have any idea what he is talking about.
4. Aren't you ready yet?
5. He hasn't been feeling too well but his condition will improve presently.
6. She has been down to Swansea again today.
7. Dai has sold his car and has bought an impressive new one.
8. Mother has telephoned / rung. I informed her that you would return her call shortly.
9. The clock is broken. Billy has broken it.
10. Were you down in the club last night?
11. Where is it?
12. You mustn't shout in that way in case you wake grandfather.
13. I didn't have time to collect my pension.
14. As I'm going to Pontypridd, I'll pick one up in the market.
15. Give me a bite of that apple!
16. I don't need any more pencils, mother.
17. John and Gail are coming to visit us after tea.
18. Those planks are not sufficiently strong to support that weight.
19. It is rumoured that there is a gold coin buried in the garden.
20. You know me: I run a tight ship / I am strict in my management style.
21. Give me an orange!
22. I didn't see the news on the television last night.
23. He should be here by half past.
24. I'll be there very shortly.
25. I haven't seen her for ages – it's many years since she was last here.
26. At first he said he hated it but later on he changed his mind until finally he was in his element.
27. The wedding dress was absolutely magnificent.
28. Those sharp knives are particularly dangerous.

29. The film was terribly sad.
30. What a character he is: lackadaisical – he'd forget his head if it weren't attached to his body!
31. Waldron is an extremely talkative (possibly argumentative) person.
32. We almost missed our train.
33. My feet are hurting me terribly.
34. That brown dress is smarter than the black one but it is also more expensive.
35. I received that book from mother as a birthday present.
36. Put those things away before the visitors arrive.
37. I prepared the meal in readiness for his return home.
38. He is visiting his grandmother / He is at his grandmother's house.
39. Why are you doing that?
40. That man who lived in Swansea has moved to Llanelli now.
41. That baker is extremely impudent: he said that I should have my hair done.
42. It is rumoured that Gladys is ill. She's receiving medical treatment, apparently.
43. Islwyn is very seriously ill. He's been receiving medical care for well over a year.
44. He was exhausted after working in the wood.
45. He has done well in his exams. He is going to attend a college in England in September.
46. His habits are so regular that it is possible to set one's clock by his coming and going.
47. He's had an unpleasant bout of illness. It started with an attack of vomiting.
48. My mother does not go shopping at the Co-op any more, she prefers going to Asda.
49. It was apparent from her appearance/manner that something was amiss.
50. Why are you chopping firewood again?
51. He has put in the glory hole/cupboard under the stairs.
52. I don't know anything about it.
53. He is very stubborn: he'll only do it if he wants to.
54. Give me/I would like two pounds of your best stewing steak.
55. He was repeatedly pacing up and down in front of her house last night. It strikes me as peculiar. Extremely peculiar.
56. Billy had a stomach ache after eating those sausages but he recovered fully after taking a dose of health salts.
57. He was in a moderate state of health yesterday but he is becoming weaker continually.

58. Her home is a terrible mess. She is not a capable housewife and the quality of her washing leaves much to be desired.

59. He stops for a rest every half hour. He won't complete that job before Christmas at that rate.

60. His heart is causing him some problems once more. The combined effect of this and the silicosis is such that I think he would be fortunate to stay alive until Christmas.

EXCERCISE 51

Once upon a time, donkey's years ago, a little dwt called Goldilocks made 'er mind up to go for a walk in the woods. She said goodbye to 'er mam an' set off down the path. 'Er mam wasn't a bit worried 'bout Goldilocks bein' safe coz she was always playin' in the woods by 'er 'ouse, an she could find 'er way round grand. This time though, she made up 'er mind to explore another part of the forest, so she walked on further than she usually did. The sun was shinin' an' the birds was singin' an' the butterflies was flutterin' theyer wings in the air around 'er. Goldilocks was in 'er oils. She walked on all 'appy under the shado of the trees for a couple of hours. In the end she was feelin' a bit tired so she sat down for a spell. To tell the trewth she was feelin' so tired she went to sleep on the ground.

When she woke up it was neely teatime. 'Oh no', she said. 'I dunno which way to turn. All 'ese paths look 'e same to me.' She walked on a bit further till she came to a pretty, dwtty little 'ouse in a clearin'. 'Thank goodness,' she said. 'There might be someone by 'ere 'oo can 'elp me.'

She knocked the door but nobody answered. She tried agen and a third time before she rised the latch an' went in. In the scullery there was a table laid for three. On the table there was three bowls of delicious porridge. One was a big 'uge bowl, one was a middle-size bowl, and one was dwtty. By now she was so 'ungry – she 'adn't eaten all day since leavin' 'er 'ouse that mornin' – she took a spoonful a porridge from the big bowl, burrit was much too 'ot. Then she took a spoonful a porridge from the middle-size bowl, burrit wan sweet enough. Then she took a spoonful from the dwtty bowl – which was jest to 'er taste – an' she et it all up!

She made up 'er mind to sit down an' wait for the people 'oo lived in the 'ouse to come back. There was three chairs in the parlour. One was a big 'uge one, one was middle-size an' one was dwtty. She tried the big one. It was much too 'igh. She tried the middle-size one burrit wan comfy. Then she tried the tiny chair but, daro, it broke an' she fell flat on the floor with a crash!

Coz nobody 'ad come back she decided to venter upstairs an' explore a bit more. In the bedroom there was three beds. One was a big 'uge one.

One was a middle-size one. One was a dwtty little one. She decided to 'ave a bit of a nap so she tried the big bed: it was much too 'ard. Then she tried the middle-size bed: it was much too soft. In the end she tried the little dwtty bed and it was jest right. It was so comfy, in fact, that she fell fast asleep.

A bit later on, the people 'oo lived in the 'ouse came back. They were the Bear Famly: Father Bear, Mother Bear and Baby Bear. "Oo've been eatin' my porridge?' asked Father Bear in a big, loud, boomin' voice. "Oo've been eatin my porridge?' asked Mother Bear in a middle-size voice. 'An 'oo've been eatin my porridge?' asked Baby Bear in a tiny, 'igh-pitched squeaky voice, 'and 'ave eaten it all up!'

They went into the parlour. When they looked at the chairs, they noticed that they wasn't as they'd left 'em. "Oo've been sittin' in my chair?, asked Father Bear in a big, loud, boomin' voice. "Oo've been sittin' in my chair?' asked Mother Bear in a middle-size voice. 'And 'oo've been sittin' in my chair?' asked Baby Bear in a squeaky voice, and 'ave broke it to bits!'

The bears crept upstairs all careful for fear the intruder was still in the 'ouse. They went into the bedroom and noticed that the beds weren't tidy. 'oo've been sleepin' on my bed?' asked Father Bear in a big, loud, boomin' voice. 'oo've been sleepin' on my bed?' asked Mother Bear in a middle-size voice. 'And 'oo've been sleepin' on my bed', asked Baby Bear in an 'igh-pitched squeaky voice, 'and is still layin' on it!'

The noise the bears were keepin' woke Goldilocks up. She sat up frightened when she seen the bears. She rushed downstairs an' out of the 'ouse full pelt. 'T was a good job she found the right path, an' she ran full pelt all the way 'ome.

When 'er mam asked if she'd 'ad a nice day, Goldilocks din know worrw say. She din wannw say the hool hanes about the problem she'd 'ad for fear 'er mam woun let 'er play in the woods agen. She never went back to tha' part of the forest where the bears' cottage was to be found.